D1547624

The Theatre of War

THE FULL MEASURE OF WAR'S DESOLATION STAGED. THE AUGUSTUS JOHN SCENE IN "THE SILVER TASSIE"

"SOMEWHERE IN FRANCE": WITH WEARY SOLDIERS, A FIGURE OF DEATH, AND A CRUCIFIX—IN SEAN O'CASEY'S PLAY AT THE APOLLO.

Scene from Act II of Sean O'Casey's *The Silver Tassie* in the original (1929) production at the London Apollo Theatre. The set was designed by Augustus John, following O'Casey's stage directions. In O'Casey's words, 'Every feature of the scene seems a little distorted from its original appearance', thus capturing the essence of the War. The photo is reproduced here courtesy of the Raymond Mander & Joe Mitchenson Theatre Collection.

The Theatre of War

The First World War in British and Irish Drama

Heinz Kosok

First published 2007 by
PALGRAVE MACMILLAN
Houndmills, Basingstoke, Hampshire RG21 6XS and
175 Fifth Avenue, New York, N.Y. 10010
Companies and representatives throughout the world

PALGRAVE MACMILLAN is the global academic imprint of the Palgrave
Macmillan division of St. Martin's Press, LLC and of Palgrave Macmillan Ltd.
Macmillan® is a registered trademark in the United States, United Kingdom
and other countries. Palgrave is a registered trademark in the European
Union and other countries.

ISBN-13: 978-0-230-52558-0   hardback
ISBN-10: 0-230-52558-X   hardback

This book is printed on paper suitable for recycling and made from fully
managed and sustained forest sources. Logging, pulping and manufacturing
processes are expected to conform to the environmental regulations of the
country of origin.

A catalogue record for this book is available from the British Library.

A catalog record for this book is available from the Library of Congress.

10   9   8   7   6   5   4   3   2   1
16 15 14 13 12 11 10 09 08 07

Printed and bound in Great Britain by
Antony Rowe Ltd, Chippenham and Eastbourne

Contents

Acknowledgements

I would like to thank Linda and Malcolm Fry of Guildford, Surrey; Dr. Dieter Mettler of the Wuppertal University Library; Professor Christopher Murray (University College Dublin); Christine Kottsieper (Wuppertal); Karen Strugar (Wuppertal) and Rainer Kosok (Frankfurt), without whose help this book would have been even more imperfect than it is now.

Professor Hans Weber (Bonn) confirmed his friendship by regularly admonishing me to finish the book.

I have no words to express my gratitude to my wife, Gillian.

Acknowledgements

Introduction

At the end of his book *A War Imagined*, Samuel Hynes declared:

> In our reality, here at the century's end, the First World War remains a
> powerful imaginative force, in the shaping not only of our conceptions
> of what war is, but of the world we live in – a world in which that war,
> and all the wars that have followed it, were possible human acts. Our
> world begins with that war. If, as Virginia Woolf said, it killed romance,
> that is a part of our reality too, to be comprehended, to be imagined,
> and to be understood in the imaginings of others.[1]

Not surprisingly, the 'imaginings' that this War triggered off, the literary
works which attempted to discuss and/or recreate it, have attracted abun-
dant critical attention – with one exception. Whereas poetry and fiction
as well as memoirs, letters, diaries and autobiographies of World War I
have been frequently surveyed, analysed and evaluated, little notice has
been taken of the *drama* of the period. A book-length study by John
Onions which claims, in its title, to deal with English fiction *and drama* of
World War I, discusses drama on only five per cent of its pages and considers no more than eight plays.[2] A similarly disproportionate emphasis is
to be found in an older study by Margarete Günther.[3] Bernard Bergonzi's
survey of the *literature* of the Great War has merely brief references to two
plays,[4] and Paul Fussell, despite his unparalleled awareness of literary
sources and documents relating to the War, confines himself to one soli-
tary quotation from a play and two isolated citations of titles.[5] Even
Hynes, in *A War Imagined*, mentions less than a dozen titles and discusses
only three of them at some length, and the *Cambridge Companion to the
Literature of the First World War* of 2005 has no chapter on drama, although
the cover text claims that the *Companion* 'offers critical overviews of the

major literary genres'.[6] In the year 2000, it was still possible to maintain that 'The first dramatic representation of the First World War itself beyond the wartime propagandist allegories was R C Sherriff's *Journey's End.*'[7]

In contrast to these works, the present study is based on over 200 British and Irish plays. While the majority of them are not literary masterpieces, they are clearly classifiable as 'war plays' and reflect attitudes and preoccupations in British culture during or after the War. Yet even this list makes no claim to being complete; L.J. Collins in *Theatre at War, 1914–18* identifies some 75 'war plays' that were submitted to the Lord Chamberlain's office during the war years, and often subsequently produced either in the provinces or in certain London theatres, and claims that 'within the first twelve months of conflict nearly 120 war plays were passed by the Lord Chamberlain' [*sic*] office for subsequent production. The second twelve months saw a reduction in number to just over ninety.'[8] The majority of these (mostly popular spy-plays or ultra-patriotic recruitment plays of limited literary value, inaccessible in print or in reliable reviews) have not been covered in the present study; but the sheer numbers indicate that dramatists in Britain and Ireland, and subsequently theatre audiences in both countries, have been occupied to a much greater degree than has been recognised so far with events which were, after all, the single most important source of radical change both for the individual and for society at large in the early twentieth century.

The present study is organised in six parts. Part I serves as a general stocktaking. It surveys the plays as to their *subject matter* and categorises them into 10 groups. Needless to say, not every text will fit neatly into one of these; there will be a certain amount of overlapping and a number of borderline cases. Part II discusses the highly divergent modes of *presentation* the authors have employed to stage the war theme, ranging from attempts at near-mimetic realism to various forms of unrealistic theatricalism and abstract generalisation. Part III deals with authorial *attitude* or purpose: unconscious confirmation of long-established ideologies as well as straightforward propaganda for or against this particular war effort and against war in general. Part IV, on the aspect of *reception*, surveys the prominent stage successes and failures, points out the delayed response to some of these plays, and summarises critical as well as official reactions. Part V discusses the controversial issue of *evaluation*, controversial in particular where the literary quality of the plays is in conflict with the evaluation of the historical events. Part VI presents two lists of war plays, an alphabetical one with full bibliographical data, and a chronological one to indicate the fluctuating interest in the war theme on the stage.

The question of what constitutes a 'war play' is, of course, a complex one and can only be answered in full in the course of Part I. While there is a hard core of works about which there could be little disagreement, these are surrounded by a corona of less easily classifiable plays in which the wartime events are of varying emphasis and importance. For a preliminary delimitation, war plays can be defined as plays: (1) that present actual events of the War, either in the various theatres of war or on the home front; (2) which deal with the War's consequences, either for their central characters or for society at large; (3) that use the experience of the First World War as a starting point for a dramatic campaign against another war; and (4) that focus on theoretical issues raised by wartime events. However useful such a provisional definition may be, it clearly does not, in every case, allow for clear-cut decisions of inclusion or exclusion.

The problem can be illustrated briefly with reference to a few prominent examples that have been *omitted* from the present study. It has, for instance, been claimed that J.M. Barrie's *Mary Rose* (1920), although it does 'not directly depend on a war theme', is nevertheless related to war litera-ture because it deals with 'the problem of individual survival'.[9] If such a criterion were taken literally, few twentieth-century plays would remain outside the domain of war literature. The only link to the Great War in *Mary Rose* is in the figure of the young Australian soldier who, at the end of the War, returns to the home of his youth, but he has been employed simply to provide a realistic perspective for the frame plot, whereas Barrie's concern is with the conflict between good and evil forces and the role of the supernatural in the contemporary world, themes he has reduced to an idiosyncratic mixture of irrationality, sentimentality and whimsicality. In a similar way, Sutton Vane's play about a ship of the dead, *Outward Bound* (1923), is not directly dependent on the post-War situation, although in his introduction the editor maintains that Vane here gives 'dramatic expression to that widespread speculation about the afterlife which the insane massacres of the War so generally provoked'.[10] Another example where the war theme is peripheral to the play's central concern is John Galsworthy's *Loyalties* (1922), a serious analysis of the conflicts arising out of the misplaced loyalties of upper-class society. It is true that the central character is an ex-officer demobilised after the War, but his wartime career is not shown to have been responsible for his subsequent financial straits or for his moral downfall. A slightly different case can be seen in Bernard Shaw's *Annajanska, the Bolshevik Empress: A Revolutionary Romancelet* (1917). It was originally suggested by certain events in post-revolutionary and post-war Russia, but Shaw uses these as a starting point for a 'bravura piece', written for the actress Lillah McCarthy on the variety stage.

While these plays – among many others – have been excluded from the present study, some others, where the weight of the wartime events seems at first glance to be equally slight, have nevertheless been selected for inclusion. James Plunkett's *The Risen People* (1958) is a typical border-line case. It is essentially a play about the 1913 general strike and lockout in Dublin, and not until the end does the central character (the only fore-man to have come out on strike) decide to join the British Army when he is prevented from returning to his job. Yet this ending gives the play a his-torical perspective by establishing the principle of 'economic conscrip-tion' as a major cause for the involvement of Irishmen in the War. Christopher Fry's *A Sleep of Prisoners* (1951) is a different case. While the original idea (four prisoners of war confined in a church) goes back to an incident from the seventeenth-century civil war, some textual evidence (an aeroplane heard flying overhead, a reference to the War Office, the Commandant's broken English) suggests that the play is set in a modern war fought on foreign soil, and for a writer born in 1907 the First World War is the obvious choice, although Fry's theme is religious rather than historical. It is hoped that the inclusion of other similarly controversial war plays can be justified in the course of the present study, but it should be stressed once more that a number of cases remain open for discussion.

Plays about the First World War have been written over a period of more than 90 years. Although a numerical survey may not be totally satisfactory because the statistical basis is somewhat shaky, some conclusions can be drawn from the 'Chronological Listing' in Part VI. Even before the out-break of the War, a world conflict was foreshadowed in a few plays. More than 60 works in the list, ranging from light entertainment through patriotic propaganda and grim slice-of-life presentation to brave attempts at objective discussion and even braver demonstrations of pacifism, originated during the War. After 1918, although the numbers decreased slightly, the War remained a subject for stage presentation, and between the end of the First and the outbreak of the Second World War there was not a single year (not even 1929, the year of the Wall Street Crash and the ensuing Great Slump) without a war play of one kind or another, while 1928 with seven, 1922 with eight and 1934 with nine citations underline the importance of the war theme for the post-War generation. In the 1930s many of these plays pointed ahead to the horrors of another war which the authors hoped in vain to prevent. Not surprisingly, during and immediately after World War II (a subject of such plays as Sean O'Casey's *Oak Leaves and Lavender*, 1946, and Denis Johnston's *A Fourth for Bridge*, 1948) the earlier War disappeared almost completely from the stage, but from 1958 onwards, and subsequently boosted, no doubt, by the 1963 production of *Oh What a Lovely War*, the stage interest was renewed, and from the early 1970s to the late 1990s hardly a year elapsed without at least one play about World War I. This revived interest, more than surprising in view of the manifold convolutions of world history since

1918, is due in part to the contributions from Ireland, where the long-standing taboo of the Irish share in the war effort has finally been lifted, and it can also partly be explained by the fact that the Great War, with the death of the last eyewitnesses, is becoming a subject for *historical* literature. However, the dominant reason for the continued traumatic fascination the War exerts, lies in its being perceived as a watershed in history. Philip Larkin's 1964 statement 'Never such innocence again' at the end of his poem 'MCMXIV' encapsulates the larger significance of the Great War: the date '1914' symbolises the loss of innocence, i.e. the inextricable involvement in universal guilt, which is, of course, a second Fall of Man and the irreversible turning away from a world which was essentially *different* from the world in which we now live.

Not all the plays discussed here did actually reach the stage. While well over half of them were both performed *and* published, some 30 remained unpublished, and 60 apparently did not receive stage production. Admittedly these numbers are to be taken with a pinch of salt, because there may have been the odd production in the amateur theatre that has been left unrecorded. Nevertheless, the impression remains that a number of authors chose the dramatic form to voice theoretical concerns although these were not suitable for performance. Of the plays which actually did see the light(s) of the stage, approximately 80 were premiered by the commercial theatres of the West End (including, for the present purpose, the Old Vic, the Royal Court and the Lyric, Hammersmith), or were later transferred there. Several others originated in the early repertory theatres of the British provinces or in other non-commercial professional theatres such as the Dublin Abbey and its smaller stage, the Peacock, or the Lyric, Belfast. When the British amateur-theatre movement began in earnest after the end of the War, it soon produced (in both senses of the word) a considerable number of war plays, often motivated, no doubt, by the personal experience of the societies' members both before and behind the footlights. The plays of the 1930s in particular came largely from amateur societies where the threat of a new world conflagration seems to have stimulated authors, performers and audiences alike into creative activity, often of a pacifist nature.

Not all of these works were full-length plays. While the commercial theatre was (and is) expected to provide its patrons with a full evening's entertainment, the amateur-theatre movement, because of its obsession with competitive drama festivals, was primarily occupied with the production of *short plays*, which created a considerable market for the publication of such works in anthologies and made for yet another division between the commercial and the amateur theatre beyond the distinctions of finances, professionalism and emotional involvement.

It must be emphasised, however, that the short play (often, rather sense-lessly, called 'one-act play') is *not* a lesser type of drama; it is merely very different. In fact, the differences between the short play and the full-length play can be profitably compared to the contrast between the short story and the novel. Both the short form and the longer version have their undeniable advantages, but each makes use of distinct techniques and achieves different objectives. Since the short form requires a significant measure of concentration and condensation, it cannot develop a high degree of individuality and realistic detail in setting, plot and dramatis personae. Therefore the short play at its best tends to avoid the exceptional, the marginal and the eccentric; instead it often exhibits representative characters whose experience is of immediate concern to the audience: in other words, the best short plays achieve a remarkable level of 'universality', rendering the form particularly suitable for the presentation of such ultimate concerns as the war theme. Moreover, the short play is frequently characterised by the reduction of plot to the point where it shows only the *outcome* of a development, a single situation which then appears as a decisive crisis, a turning point or a terminal moment. The term 'crisis' is therefore particularly suitable to describe the essence of the short play – and it underlines the affinity between the short play and the war play. Such a crisis is often a catastrophe, the ultimate failure or death of one of the characters, but it can, of course, also be comic, even farcical in nature. If the short play is seen as a literary sub-genre in its own right, different from the full-length play but not inferior, it will be understood why the present study, while in no way undervaluing the qualities of many full-length plays, gives some prominence to a number of excellent short plays, too.

*

Who were the authors of the plays discussed here? Although this book is *not* a biographical study, a few generalisations concerning the dramatists may be in order. It will be noted from the list of plays that most of the established figures of the Edwardian theatre, such as Arthur Wing Pinero, Henry Arthur Jones, J.M. Barrie, John Galsworthy, Laurence Binyon, William Archer, St John Ervine, Harley Granville-Barker, Monckton Hoffe, Stephen Phillips and Israel Zangwill, turned to the war theme at one point or another. Most of them, however, seem to have done so from a sense of patriotic duty more than anything else. This led them to produce short-lived wartime propaganda from which they sometimes distanced them-selves at a later stage (Barrie in 1928 excluded his polemical 1914 play *Der Tag* from the collected edition of his dramatic works). Understandably, most of these older authors did not write from personal experience of the fighting, and their treatment is therefore sometimes unreliable as well as polemical and/or sentimental. Barrie is an exception among this group in that he took up the war theme more than once; it is central to some of his short plays which he collected under the title *Echoes of the War*,[11] and it also surfaces in several of his full-length works. Even more important as an exception is Galsworthy who devoted several plays to a searching analysis of the effects of the War on the individual and did so with a remarkable degree of understanding and objectivity, although in his personal comments even he sometimes succumbed to the mode of wartime polemics.[12] A special case is that of Shaw who discussed the War in numerous prose writings and also reflected on it in several of his plays before completing, in *Heartbreak House*, one of the great war plays of the period.

Among the younger generation, a remarkable number saw front-line service, either as an officer, like R.C. Sherriff, Joe Randolph Ackerley, the cartoonist Bruce Bairnsfather, William Aubrey Cecil Darlington, Hubert Griffith, A.A. Milne, Robert Nichols, Sutton Vane, Vernon Sylvaine, Reginald Berkeley, George Leslie Calderon and D.E. Hickey, or (which is even more remarkable) as a private, like Miles Malleson and the 'navvy novelist' Patrick MacGill. Edward Knoblauch/Knoblock even changed his nationality as well as his name to be able to serve with the British Intelligence. Several of these writers, for instance Darlington, Berkeley, Sherriff, Ackerley, Sylvaine and Calderon, were wounded at the front, St John Ervine lost a leg in France, and Calderon was reported 'wounded and missing' at Gallipoli, while Guy Louis Busson du Maurier was killed in action in France. Others – and this is equally significant – volunteered as ambulance drivers, for instance Somerset Maugham and Jerome K. Jerome, and Laurence Binyon, a Quaker by descent, served as a Red Cross orderly, while Cicely Hamilton worked in a hospital in France and Gilbert Cannan was a conscientious objector. Where such writers depict individual wartime situations, they can be credited with a high degree of authenticity, although this is not, of course, a guarantee for literary ability. The discrepancy between authenticity of experience and lack of dramatic skills is particularly clear in the case of D.E. Hickey who, under the title *Rolling into Action*, also published his memoirs as a tank corps officer,[13] which allows his front-line plays, set inside tanks, to be compared to his personal experience.

The 1920s saw a number of predominantly 'realistic' plays by authors who would not normally have considered working for the stage. Some of them, quite unexpectedly, found themselves projected into the limelight by their plays. Sherriff, whose *Journey's End* had a sensational success in Britain and elsewhere, is the outstanding example. Even before him Harry

Wall (whose play *Havoc* was so successful in 1923–4 that it was immediately turned both into a motion picture and a novel) was described as 'a young Keighley solicitor who was comparatively unknown before *Havoc* brought his name prominently before the public.'[14] At the same time a number of authors also tried to come to terms with the war theme on a more general level, abstracted from personal involvement and the singularity of individual experience. Allan Monkhouse, Sean O'Casey and Somerset Maugham, each of whom wrote more than one war play, were the outstanding representatives of this group. Maugham ended his career as a dramatist with a set of four plays in which he decided to please *himself* rather than his audiences, and two of these were war plays: 'I did not think any of them was likely to succeed and I knew how difficult it was for a dramatist to recover a popularity that he had lost. I was much surprised that *The Sacred Flame* and *The Breadwinner* had a considerable success. I expected nothing of *For Services Rendered*.'[15] Maugham's instinct was right, because his uncompromising presentation of the consequences of the War found a disastrous reception both in London and in New York. Noël Coward was more careful: his *Post Mortem* was not exposed to the ravages of theatre critics, and his less controversial treatment of the war in *Cavalcade* and *Words and Music* did nothing to damage his popular appeal.

Maugham and Coward were the most popular among the post–World War I playwrights who turned to the war theme, while W.H. Auden and Christopher Isherwood stand for the generation of intellectuals who addressed the subject of the War from their ideological basis (or bias). The 1920s and 1930s also saw a new type of playwright who wrote predominantly for amateur companies with their specific requirements (often quite separate from literary considerations) and whose work therefore is largely confined to short plays. Where such writers succeeded in overcoming the restrictions imposed by the amateur market (for instance the demand for 'plays for women only' or for simple scenery, capable of being set up in a few minutes), and successfully tackled the War as a subject, they belatedly deserve the praise that was usually withheld from them at the time. Muriel and Sydney Box, Lawrence du Gard Peach, Marion Reid-Jamieson, Hal D. Stewart, James Wallace Bell, Joe Corrie, Horace Flather, Vernon Sylvaine and Harold Brighouse should be named in this context.

After the Second World War Rattigan and Fry returned obliquely to the earlier war in *The Winslow Boy* and *A Sleep of Prisoners*, but the outstanding World War I play of the post–World War II decades has no individual author: *Oh What a Lovely War* was jointly produced by the Theatre Workshop company.[16] William Douglas Home (1912–92), after a successful career as 'king of British light comedy', was probably the last playwright to turn to a World War I event that had occurred during his own lifetime, when he wrote *A Christmas Truce* (premiered in 1989). But even of him it can be said that recent plays both in Britain and in Ireland are being written by authors for whom the Great War is a *historical* occasion, not a personal experience. It is interesting to observe that despite this, several dramatists have adopted the perspective of individual memory, of someone harking back to the wartime events, rather than the more detached approach of the historian.

The majority of the plays considered here were written by men. This is not surprising where the plays are a reflection of front-line experience, but not so understandable where occurrences on the home front or in post-War society are concerned, or where the War is subject to allegory, abstraction and intellectual debate. However, recent research has shown that the contribution by women was not as negligible as it had appeared for a long time.[17] For many years the general reluctance of the British stage to accept women dramatists encouraged writers to adopt male pseudonyms: when it is realised that, for instance, 'Clemence Dane' (Winifred Ashton), 'Gordon Daviot' (Elizabeth Mackintosh), 'Bosworth Crocker' (Mary Arnold Lewisohn) and 'Vernon Lee' (Violet Page) were women, in addition to a number of authors for the amateur stage, it will become clear that the female contribution was by no means insignificant. In more recent years, of course, it has no longer been necessary to cover up female authorship, and Katie Hims, Christina Reid, Margaretta D'Arcy and Jennifer Johnston have all made important contributions to the body of war plays.

It will be noticed that in a few cases the authors' birthplace was outside the British Isles. C.B. Fernald, Walter Hackett and Edward Knoblauch (later Knoblock) were born in the United States, Rudolph Besier in Java, Charles Haddon Chambers in New South Wales, Robins Millar in British Columbia, R.J. Minney in Calcutta and Vernon Lee (Violet Page), the daughter of a Polish refugee, in France. By the application of strict formal standards, they would have to be excluded from the circle of 'British' authors, if Britishness depended primarily on the – often accidental – facts of the authors' lives. They are, of course, examples of a general tendency among English-language writers to gravitate towards London, the centre of a world-encompassing cultural empire. For the present purpose it has seemed appropriate to consider the focus of the authors' life-long activities rather than classifying them by place of birth. Thus several authors born outside Britain have been included, while a number of American playwrights who wrote their war plays primarily for American audiences, like Channing Pollock and Percival Wild, have been omitted, and so has the Canadian Merrill Denison.

The question arose whether the authors' regional background *within* the British Isles was of consequence for their war plays. After all, several of them, for instance John Brandane, Joe Corrie, Gordon Daviot, Chris Hannan, Robins Millar (despite the accidence of his Canadian birth-place) and Hall Douglas Stewart, were decidedly Scottish in background, Keith Winter is normally seen as a Welsh playwright, Allan Monkhouse was instrumental in reviving drama at Manchester, John Drinkwater did the same at Birmingham, and Ida Gandy is usually apostrophied as a 'Wiltshire dramatist'. It will be shown, however, that, despite their occa-sional use of dialect or specific settings, their contribution to World War I drama did not differ significantly from those authors writing from, and for, the London-based theatre, whatever their regional loyalties may have been in other respects.

This is also true of a number of playwrights who were born in Ireland but settled in England to integrate into the literary scene there: Shaw Desmond, Monckton Hoffe, St John Ervine, C.K. Munro, Patrick MacGill or, indeed, Bernard Shaw would hardly justify a separate chapter on war plays from Ireland. The case is decidedly different, however, with other writers who deliberately set out to portray the specific situation *in Ireland* during the War or to analyse the consequences of the War in the light of Ireland's separate historical development both north and south of the border, often turning to wartime events (like the 1916 Rising) or to spe-cific problems (like the question of conscription for Ireland) which to British writers were of little importance. It is these Irish authors who have necessitated a separate chapter on the Irish contribution.

*

As early as 1915, Hall Caine published a book called *The Drama of Three Hundred & Sixty-five Days: Scenes in the Great War*[18] which, from its title, might be taken as a forerunner of the present study, but turns out on inspection to be a series of brief articles on the conduct of the War (most of them previously published in the *Daily Telegraph*). The book is of interest here, not because of its painful chauvinism which can be accounted for by the time of its production, but because of its theatrical title. It ties in with the 40-page-long chapter 'Theater of War' in Fussell's *The Great War and Modern Memory*[19] where the author demonstrates how the War was regularly, even persistently described in terminology and imagery borrowed from the world of the theatre, a practice that has con-tinued to the present day. While the theatre provided many of the images, emblems and metaphors required to come to terms with the experience of the War, the treatment of the War in the theatre itself, in a great variety of plays, produced or unproduced, has gone largely unno-ticed. The present study is an attempt to rectify such an imbalance.

Part I Theatres of War: Aspects of Subject Matter

1
Foreshadowing the War

English literature in general has frequently occupied itself with predicting future wars and with imagining their scale and consequences;[20] however, playwrights (and, by implication, theatre audiences) seem not to have been deeply concerned about the outbreak of a European war before 1914. The British public were, of course, accustomed to reading about military conflicts, but these had taken place in remote parts of the world, they had been confined to a limited number of participating nations and had been fought, on the British side, by relatively small contingents of a fully trained professional army. The vision of a 'world war' seems to have been shared by very few people, and the fact that it was to be fought on the European Continent rather than in the colonies or on the high seas must have been unimaginable.

The one idea that appears to have concerned the public was the centuries-old fear of invasion. Du Maurier dramatised it in his play with the suggestive title *An Englishman's Home*, which caused a sensation in Wyndham's Theatre in 1909, ran for 163 performances, was again a West End success in 1911–12 and must have significantly increased the recruiting for the newly established Territorial Army. Published pseudonymously by 'A Patriot', it was obviously intended as nationalist propaganda for greater defence efforts. The author depicts a bank-holiday situation in a typical middle-class home which is invaded by foreign troops. In a curious mixture of broad farce and deadly seriousness, the Volunteers who defend the house prove to be woefully incapable, but in the end there is some hope that the Army has rallied and will, after all, be able to protect the country. The message is, of course, that Britain ought to be better prepared for an invasion.[21] *An Englishman's Home* is one of the few plays which bear out Eby's assertion that before the War 'popular literature was so steeped in militant nationalism that the

Great War, when it finally arrived, came like an ancient prophecy at last fulfilled.'[22]

A similar attitude can be detected behind *The Man Who Stayed at Home* (1914) by Worrall and Terry, apparently written during the last phase of pre-War hysteria. It must have taken two authors to think up its incredibly silly incidents, but it was highly popular on the stage and was turned into a novel by Beamish Tinker in 1915. The play is set in a seaside hotel in East Anglia in September 1914 where are gathered several German spies who use the standard equipment of their trade, including carrier pigeons and a secret wireless apparatus. The Germans are treacherous and contemptible while the English prove to be heroic or, at least, eccentric and amusing. The title hero is suspected of shirking his duty but turns out to be employed in counter-espionage, and – of course – he uncovers the German spies as well as helps the Navy to capture a German submarine. The plot is clearly reminiscent of a cowboys-and-Indians story but shows the extent of spy-hysteria at the beginning of the War.

The most ambitious attempt to dramatise the threat of a future war was Israel Zangwill's obscurely titled *The War God*, premiered by Beerbohm Tree in 1911 in a matinee performance at Her Majesty's Theatre. The play is set in the fictitious state of Gothia, which bears some vague similarity to Germany. Having recently conquered the neighbouring Hunland, Gothia now expands into Africa and engages in an unprecedented arms race 'to expunge / Perfidious Alba from the map of Europe' (13). The state is threatened by two opposing forces, a revolutionary underground movement and the pacifist programme of Frithiof, a Christlike figure converted to non-violence who finally convinces even the most militant among the population to subscribe to peace. The most impressive character, however, is Count Torgrim, the Chancellor who is vaguely reminiscent of Bismarck and embodies power politics at its most intransigent. His simple creed is 'Once Alba's vanquished, Europe's at our feet, / And have we Europe, then – [...] / Then the world is ours' (38). Unfortunately, what might have become an intelligent debate about various ideological tendencies in Europe on the eve of the War is marred by melodramatic incidents, the banality of some of the observations and the formal correctness of Zangwill's blank verse.

In contrast to plays which concern themselves, however imperfectly, with the War as such, a few others project an individual plot into a future wartime situation. If Henry Arthur Jones's *The Knife* was actually performed in 1909 in the form in which it was published 16 years later,[23] it represents a remarkable case of foresight, because it refers repeatedly to the tendency of going out to fight in France, and the central character makes its purpose clear: 'I don't want to leave my practice, and my wife;

but now the old country's in such a terrible hole, if I can be of use to our poor chaps out there I've simply got to go!' (331). However, one suspects that these references, and even the stage direction 'TIME: *During the Great War*' (328), were introduced later to give the play an added topicality, because apart from them it is a conventional problem play about a doctor who is about to operate on his wife's lover and is torn between his desire for revenge and his professional integrity.

A similar play about an individual conflict of conscience is Monkhouse's *The Choice* (1910) which, although it utilises a situation from the Boer War, was included by the author in his volume *War Plays* published in 1916 and could easily be transferred to a World War I situation. It is about Ella, a girl whose fiancé has been killed in South Africa in unknown circumstances. She discovers that it was her present suitor who shot her fiancé when he was paralysed by fear during an enemy attack, and she is confronted with the conflict indicated in the title, finally deciding to reject her suitor. *The Choice* looks forward to various later plays which one would hesitate to classify as 'war plays' because they do not really dramatise the war but appropriate a wartime situation to intensify an individual conflict.

By contrast, a play by E. Temple Thurston called *The Cost*, which premiered on 13 October 1914, is unique among the theatrical fare of the time. Act I takes place on the day of Britain's ultimatum to Germany, while the following three acts are set at later moments in 1914, i.e. in the future for the author as well as for the audience. In a typical upper-middle-class family, the imminence of the War underscores everyone's negative characteristics: selfishness, chauvinism, stupidity, thoughtlessness, prejudices, xenophobia – with the exception of John Woodhouse, who is a rising authority in Moral Philosophy and is obviously intended by the author to be a focus of identification for the audience. Again and again he warns his family of the real dangers of the War, the rising tide of hysteria, the future tense in the quotation indicating the *author's* as well as the character's position:

> Don't you realise what a nation at war is like, Mater. Every man becomes a murderer in his heart. Lies of the enemy's atrocities will be published in every paper to inflame our passions. We shall hear of all their brutalities, but none of our own. A month or two of that would kindle the beast in anyone. [...] Every man will become a brute. You can't wage war with your hat in your hand and a clean pocket-handkerchief up your sleeve. War's barbaric and barbarians must wage it. Oh, there's no reason to suppose that I shall be immune from the hysteria of it all.
>
> (33–4)

John's prediction comes true; after a great deal of soul-searching he decides to enlist, soon to return with a head wound which will incapacitate him from any further academic work. Although his final words – 'Don't blame war, because as long as men are striving upwards, they must fight. [...] As long as there is fearlessness in the soul of a man, there will always be a war – always' (134) – are strangely at odds with his earlier pronouncements, the play comes across as an anti-war play, which, given the time of its creation, renders it a remarkable achievement despite the rather clumsy handling of plot and characters.

Compared to *The Cost*, A.J. Talbot's *Set Fair* (1935) must have been an easy matter to conceive because it is a case of foreshadowing by hindsight. The basic situation is not dissimilar from that of *The Cost*: Talbot depicts the Smith family on 24 July 1914, a week before the outbreak of hostilities. When Mr and Mrs Smith read about the Austrian ultimatum to Serbia, they are not certain where Sarajevo is, who the Archduke Francis Ferdinand was or what the ultimatum is all about, and in any case they think that 'it's sickening the fuss the papers make of such a simple incident; just to fill their columns, all over a thing that doesn't interest us and is bound to fizzle out' (129). Since all the wars of the nineteenth century are a matter of the past, the future seems assured, and the Smiths are unaware of the impending disaster. The play's poignancy derives from the simple ironic contrast between the characters' blindness and the audience's awareness of what is about to happen.

2
Front-Line Plays

The most obvious type of 'war play' is, of course, one that is set in a front-line situation and shows soldiers 'at war'. Such works, usually relying on their authors' personal experience, do not deal with the war as such but with specific events, seen from the perspective of a few dramatis personae with clearly developed character traits. These plays are almost exclusively limited to the British troops in the northern sector of the front in France and Belgium, ignoring all other battlefields. In fact, to judge from their evidence, the War seems, in the eyes of the British theatre public, to have consisted of the front in Flanders and very little else. Not only did the war in Eastern Europe remain unexplored, but so did the struggle in the Mediterranean and the Middle East. Equally, on the enemy side, it is only *German* troops that come into view.

Even the war at sea, which had been a major public concern before 1914 and which throughout its duration was essential for the survival of Britain, found little resonance in the theatre. Perhaps the inglorious end of the German Navy (whose crews scuttled their ships rather than handing them over) in some subconscious way reflected on the image of the Grand Fleet, which had failed to defeat it on the high seas, leading playwrights to keep away from the subject, although there had been a tradition of 'nautical drama' in the nineteenth-century popular theatre. In any case, the war at sea apparently became the subject of very few plays, among them Walter Hackett's *The Freedom of the Seas* (1918) and Commander Stephen King-Hall's *B.J. One* (1930). King-Hall's play, in its production at the London Globe in 1930, seems to have been overwhelmed by the realistic details of the stage design, with one scene actually set on the bridge of a cruiser during the Battle of Jutland:

> The cruiser comes at you through the darkness and foam, the seagulls scream around her masts, the impartial shells of friend or foe scream on to her decks, the boatswain is always calling out 'Aye, aye, sir' – and the upshot is that we don't believe a word of it because everybody says 'aye, aye, sir', or words to some such inarticulate effect, instead of bursting into forty lines of blank verse or some other intelligible form of speech, intelligible, that is to say, in the sense of fitting to a great occasion.[24]

In contrast to this amazing piece of stage naturalism (indebted to nineteenth-century melodrama) the rest of the play consists largely of discussions on the future of the steel industry and the British and German navies, conducted on a respectable level of intellect and objectivity. By contrast, Hackett's *The Freedom of the Seas* would, in a competition for the worst play about World War I, stand a good chance of coming out first. The war at sea (two of the three acts are set on a tramp steamer on the way to Britain) is merely an excuse for an exceptionally silly love story with some suspense thrown in for good measure (even the usually uncritical *Era* remarked on the 'long arm of coincidence' and questioned the legitimacy of the 'excitement' in this play[25]). While it would serve no useful purpose here to reconstruct the plot, it should be mentioned that it contains such 'front line' elements as a boat-load of survivors from a liner torpedoed by a German submarine, a British seaplane and a destroyer coming to the rescue and a suspicious cargo which is to be transferred to a German U-boat to break the Blockade.[26] A third 'nautical play', *Jolly Jack Tar* (1918) by Hicks and Shirley, described by the reviewer of the *Illustrated London News* as 'honest straightforward melodrama', remained unpublished, but the list of the hero's feats suffices to classify it as part of the melodramatic tradition, remote from the realities of war: 'Swimming out to the ship German spies try to prevent his being able to join, foiling the Hun who has placed a time-bomb in the captain's cabin, grappling with enemies galore on the Mole, cheering up fellow-prisoners in their place of torture, and escaping to freedom and the honour of the Victoria Cross [...]'[27]

Somewhat surprisingly, the role of the cavalry, not inconsiderable during the First World War, remained outside the dramatists' field of vision, too, and this despite the tradition of nineteenth-century 'equestrian drama' at Astley's Amphitheatre and elsewhere. The newly developing war in the air (described so graphically in Cecil Lewis's *Sagittarius Rising* of 1936) was also largely ignored by the playwrights. Given the fragility of World War I flying machines, it would of course have created problems to set a play inside a plane (as Denis Johnston did in his World War II play *A Fourth for Bridge*), but, with one exception, even an airfield location stayed outside the dramatists' compass. The exception is a short play by Edward Williams, *One Goes Alone* (1934), which is set in the officers' mess on an aerodrome before and after an attack on enemy targets. Despite the restrictions of the short form, the characters here have been clearly differentiated, the events sound authentic, the atmosphere (a combination of almost unbearable tension and pretended unconcern), is evoked convincingly and the officers' special jargon seems to be faithfully reproduced. However, *One Goes Alone* remained an exception. Probably it was not only the difficulty of presenting other scenes on stage, but also the public's fixation on trench warfare in Flanders that determined the playwrights' choice.

From 1928, the stage presentation of a 'trench-situation' remained associated in the public mind with R.C. Sherriff's immensely popular *Journey's End*, but a short play by Lawrence du Gard Peach, *Shells* (1937), might be regarded as the prototypical front-line play. It shows two Privates in a trench who are suffering not only from the dangers and physical discomforts of their position but even more from the inactivity, which sets them wondering about a possible afterlife: 'There ain't no job to think of – only sittin' 'ere waitin' for a shell or a minnie to drop an' blow Nobby an' me to 'ell. Ye can't 'elp thinkin' about wot it'll be like arter it's happened' (118). It does happen, and they find themselves exactly as before, except that they cannot be seen by the living. Despite the unsatisfactory conclusion, this is a convincing depiction of the trench situation, with boredom as the dominant experience, while the purpose of the War remains outside the soldiers' (and the author's) speculation. This is true, too, of *Journey's End*, although here the all-officer cast (except for the orderly used for comic purposes) might lead one to expect a higher level of reflection. *Journey's End*, as a full-length play, has a higher degree of individual characterisation than *Shells*, including some references to the characters' past lives, but the conflicts in the dugout are just as closely associated with the trench situation. A similar case is Wall's *Havoc* (1923), which was turned into a novel and a film after the stage success of the play.[28] In fact *Havoc* is in many ways so similar to *Journey's End* that one cannot help wondering whether Sherriff knew it when he wrote his own play. Wall presents four officers, two of whom suffer a personal catastrophe because of their love for the same woman. While the love plot is conventional, even melodramatic, the front-line scenes – the move forward into new positions, and then the confusion when the enemy attacks in a thick fog while the company commander out of personal rivalry does not pass on the order to retreat – are as credible as anything in Sherriff.

Conversely, Patrick MacGill's *Suspense* (1930) is clearly indebted to *Journey's End*, although the social sphere has here been modified to a group of Privates, the milieu that MacGill knew. The background events, the German spring offensive of 1918, are the same as in *Havoc* and *Journey's End*, which underlines the similarities between the three plays (they almost appear like a 1918 front-line triptych). However, *Suspense* is even less dependent on a conventional plot (in the sense of a sequence of events which develop logically, chronologically or psychologically from one another); the episodes surrounding Private Pettigrew, who comes from a wealthy family and is befriended by officers and comrades alike because they expect to profit later from his social standing, are so rudimentary that they cannot sustain a 'progression' of the action, and they are practically forgotten towards the conclusion. What the play primarily conveys is the enervating experience of passivity and boredom, intensified by the uncertainty whether the enforced inactivity will be suddenly interrupted, either by an enemy attack or by an incomprehensible order from some abstract command structure. MacGill has found a symbolic equivalent to this situation which one would call a 'happy invention' if the circumstances did not forbid such a phrase: the sound of German sappers digging a mine under the British trenches can be heard throughout, which causes the suspense of the play's title. When at the end the soldiers are relieved, and the explosion of the mine hits their luckless successors, the suspense is only temporarily lifted, because they are immediately ordered back into action.

Several other front-line plays, among them Atkinson's *'Glory Hole'* (1932), Hodson's *Red Night* (1930) and Schofield's earlier *Men at War* (1920), are little more than variations on the pattern described here. They present slice-of-life views of the trench situation, with no reflection on the War on the part of the characters or the authors; and what little plot there is usually culminates in the death of one or several of the dramatis personae. A recent Irish play, Murphy's *Absent Comrades* (1997), still follows the same pattern although it is superior in quality to most. It centres on a group of four Irish soldiers in a bunker behind the front line. They argue, bicker and occasionally agree, playing cards over the few possessions of the fifth of their number who has just been killed – including a sealed but unaddressed letter. These are won by the youngest in the group, a clear indication that he will be the next to die. Under the circumstances, Tom does a remarkable thing: he tears up the letter without allowing anyone to see it, thus protecting the dead soldier's privacy.

Muriel Box's *Angels of War* (1935) is set among a group of women, voluntary ambulance drivers in Queen Mary's Army Auxiliary Corps. The title is soon revealed as ironic because the girls are chiefly occupied with their private jealousies or their unheroic dreams of temporary escape into alcohol and short-lived affairs, and their common enemy is not the German army but the Commandant, *'a forbidding woman, hard-featured, tight-lipped and steely-eyed'* (23). Nevertheless the hardships they undergo and the dangers they are exposed to are portrayed quite convincingly, while the reality of their situation is painfully contrasted with the pretentious drivel of the Visitor, who confronts them with platitudes such as '[...] I am with you in spirit, the spirit which has built our glorious Empire and inspired our men to sacrifice their lives for its protection and continuance in this time of danger and stress' (24). Not until the end does the author's purpose – to question 'why we ever came out here at all' (72) – become clear.

Cicely Hamilton's *The Child in Flanders* (1919) is an unusual variant on the front-line play in that it is a traditional nativity play which is nevertheless firmly positioned in the wartime situation. Three soldiers, having lost their way in the snow, come to a small French house on Christmas Eve where they find the Frenchman's wife with a newborn baby. They are invited in and, shepherd-like, present the child with simple offerings: a mouth-organ, a muffler and a scarf. When they lie down in front of the fire, they dream the traditional nativity scene. Next morning, although one can still hear the big guns in the distance, they are somehow transformed. The play was apparently 'the work of one who saw the War at close quarters', the author having been associated with the Lena Ashwell organisation for providing drama at the base camps in France,[29] and consequently appears more authentic than one would expect from a front-line play with a nativity dream sequence. However, that an author's familiarity with the situation at the front does not guarantee a play's authenticity can be seen from *Tommy-by-the-Way* (1918) by Captain Oliphant Down. This is an incredibly simple patriotic play about a Tommy who has had enough and tries to inflict a 'blighty wound' upon himself, but is prevented by the Spirit of the Women of England, who delivers a rousing speech in praise of the women at home and shames Tommy into promising: 'Them 'Uns is just about goin' to get it in the neck, and I'm goin' to be one of those what gives 'em 'ell' (78). Equally unrealistic, but with a decided anti-war stance, is Sumner's ballad play

Jimmy Clay (1978), which uses mime, dance, music and improvisation to present the brief life of the title character until his death on the battlefield:

> And your face is growing mouldy where they kissed your cheek
> And said, 'Please die for us, Jimmy Clay.'
> And so you died a soldier's death and a hero's death.
> Congratulations, Jimmy Clay.
>
> (3)

Several other plays present the situation in the trenches in individual scenes, although the general canvas is enlarged to include the soldiers' previous lives, their departure from home and/or the conditions behind the lines. Pertinent examples are Monkhouse's *The Conquering Hero* (1923), Whelan's *The Accrington Pals* (1981), McGuinness's *Observe the Sons of Ulster Marching Towards the Somme* (1985) and Jennifer Johnston's *How Many Miles to Babylon?* (1993). In each of these, as in the previous examples, the authors have attempted to present the front-line situation realistically, without, however, specifying historical or geographic details which would have confined the scenes to one particular battlefield. The consequence is that such plays could easily be transferred from one section of the front and from one period of the War to all others.

This peculiar juxtaposition of credible detail and the arbitrariness of the surrounding circumstances, which underlines the sameness of the soldiers' experience throughout the War, is also a characteristic of some plays which are not directly set in the trenches. D.E. Hickey, following his personal experiences as described in his memoirs,[30] has situated two of his plays (*Over the Top*, 1934, and *Youth in Armour*, 1940) inside tanks which are rolling into action. Whereas the interior of the tank is presented in detail, even to the point where a sketch of the internal structure is provided in the printed version of *Over the Top*, the crew members are mere ciphers, conversing in a stilted language that conveys information for the benefit of the audience ('Can you see where you are driving, Corporal? – Yessir, through this 'ere slit', 206). But even here, where the author's limited skills reduce the attempted realistic effect, the conflict between individual concreteness and general opacity is apparent, because the temporal and geographic context remains deliberately vague. Malleson has a typical training-camp situation in his *'D' Company* (1914), but that it is supposed to take place in Malta is just as irrelevant as its autobiographical background. Malleson's chief interest lies in the soldiers' language which is apparently reproduced quite faithfully, the Cockney van-boys' rude but vivid expressions contrasting with the stilted if educated English of the student straight from Cambridge.

Another example of the conflict between a specific situation and the general vagueness is Monkhouse's hospital play *Night Watches* (1916) which, in its initial stage direction, demands '*a clock showing clearly the time – a few minutes after ten*' (221) but omits to state the day or the year and does not contain any clues as to its whereabouts. Monkhouse's object is to show the terrible consequences of shell shock as well as the first steps to overcome them. A hospital scene is also part of O'Casey's much larger canvas in *The Silver Tassie* (1928) where the conflict between the survivors and the victims is acted out with high intensity of feeling. The background of a hospital is used once again in Brandane's *The Happy War* (1928), where five people meet in a deserted monastery in France: two British medical officers who seem to be shirking their duties (but are not criticised for it), two escaped German prisoners and a convalescent French soldier who is out hunting the Germans, hoping to find his own brother (who, since both of them are from Alsace, has been pressed into the German army). The hunted men turn up, and while one of them dies of exhaustion, the other is shot accidentally after the French soldier has recognised him as his brother. This play is different in that it betrays no sympathy whatsoever for the characters; the callous behaviour is not confined to the medical officers but comes across as the author's attitude, too. It is, in this respect, the extreme opposite to Johnston's in *How Many Miles to Babylon?* which is also set behind the lines but where the author's deep compassion for her characters makes itself felt in every line.

Berkeley's *The White Château*, broadcast in a shorter version by the BBC in 1925 and staged at the London Everyman Theatre in 1927, is one of the rare examples where the realistic presentation of front-line situations is combined with the attempt to give the events some symbolic significance, the Flemish château taking on the role of the title hero. Its owners are surprised by the outbreak of the War. It is requisitioned by an occupation army when the country is invaded by foreign troops, is turned into the headquarters of the invaders, becomes the scene of a battle, is alternately occupied by both sides, is destroyed by artillery and is finally rebuilt by the survivors. The author has taken great pains to invest these scenes with realistic details and individual character portraits and has even invented a rudimentary storyline involving some of the English and Belgian characters, but he has equally turned the château and its owner into an *exemplum* of wartime conditions and of a hopeful outlook on the future of mankind, and the conflict between concrete details and general significance sometimes endangers its credibility on an individual level.

A few front-line plays, in contrast to what has been said so far, deal with specific historical situations. Reid-Jamieson's *Eleven A.M.* (1934) is set in a Belgian town on the day of the Armistice, declared at the time specified in the title. Two English soldiers have been hidden by Belgian women; one of them has given herself to a German officer to procure food for the Englishmen, one of whom she has fallen in love with. When the Armistice is announced, she is attacked by an angry mob as a traitor and, with her hair shorn, avoids seeing the soldiers once more before they depart. Here the author's compassion is extended to the alleged collaborator. Also set in Belgium, but at the beginning of the War (*'Between 8 a.m. on August 5, 1914, and 8 a.m. on the following day'*) is Archer's *War Is War or The Germans in Belgium* (1919). In what the author claims is a 'historical play' (v) he sketches the sudden transition from happy country life to a nightmare of brutalities when a village is occupied by German troops. Archer's text is overshadowed by his declared purpose to expose the German invasion of Belgium as 'one of the most colossal tragedies, as well as one of the most infamous transactions, that history records' (vii),[31] and consequently the plot and the characters suffer from simplification and manipulation to an extent that one would not have thought possible in the champion of Ibsen and the author of *The Old Drama and the New*. Much the same could be said for Crocker's *Pawns of War* (1918), which is situated in a Belgian town under German occupation and is punctuated by a series of reprisals against the civilian population, culminating in the shooting of hostages. As in Archer's play, the resentment against the invasion of a neutral country is projected into the characterisation of the German officers as brutal and the Belgian civilians as heroic. Less chauvinistic, but psychologically more credible, is Atkinson's short *The Chimney Corner* (1934), where an elderly Belgian lady and her niece work for the occupying forces in order to camouflage their activities in a secret resistance organisation. They hide a British officer escaped from a POW camp. When a younger niece returns from college with grandiose ideas of heroic resistance and blood sacrifice, she fails to recognise her aunt's true motives and criticises her and her sister as collaborators; but in an emergency she panics and has to be pushed into the chimney corner as a sick little girl, while the officer gets away.

Another concrete wartime event was the 'Christmas Truce' of 1914 when British and German soldiers (as has been established by recent studies[32]) fraternised on a large scale for the duration of the festival, exchanging gifts, singing carols and even playing football together. Home in *A Christmas Truce* (1989) has followed the events quite faithfully, showing the occurrences in chronological order: the initial contacts between two Privates, the transfer of responsibility to higher planes until even the Colonel becomes involved, the exchange of drinks and cigarettes, the burying of the dead on Christmas morning, Christmas dinner in no-man's-land, the football match with a ball made of a cap stuffed with straw, a German-English religious service and finally the soldiers' return to their respective trenches and the resumption of the barrage at curfew. While Home has reconstructed the events as realistically as possible, his play is marred by the simplistic attempt to preserve absolute symmetry between the two sides (even to the point where an English soldier used to have a girlfriend in Germany, and his counterpart on the German side had a girl in England), and also by his unfamiliarity with the situation in Germany at the time and his woefully inept use of spoken German (one character refers to a sum of money in 'Deutschmarks', 49).

Wilson's *Hamp* (1964) seems also to be authentic in its material. It is based on an episode from the novel *Return to the Wood* by James Lansdale Hodson, apparently the fictionalised autobiography of the Defending Officer in the play,[33] and was filmed in 1964 under the title *For King and Country* with Dirk Bogarde and Tom Courtenay. Private Hamp, after two years at the front the only survivor of his platoon, one day has simply started to walk away from the sound of the guns because 'I couldn't stand no more' (22). Taken before a court martial, he finds it difficult to understand what he has done, let alone what it will mean for him. Although he is provided with a sympathetic and eloquent Defending Officer, he is sentenced to death because morale has to be upheld. The play explores the relationship between the law, justice, responsibility and mercy. By the letter of the law Hamp is guilty, although he is obviously not responsible for his actions, and the only concession the court can permit is to render his execution as painfree as possible.

An interesting (although not a particularly successful) example of the attempt to combine individual experience with general significance can be seen in Griffith's *Tunnel Trench* (1924). It takes place during the allied offensive of 1918. Three of the play's seven scenes are set in the mess of a flying corps, two in the army headquarters, one in a dugout and one in a shell-hole just outside Tunnel Trench. Such a broad canvas (which requires a large cast and makes it difficult to introduce individual characters) results from an unusual approach: the attempt to observe an attack from three divergent points of view, the infantry on the ground, an observer's position in the air and the general staff at headquarters. This tendency at generalisation, however, interferes with the story of the central character, who loses his best friend, then is shot down himself and finally meets his dying brother in a shell-hole in no-man's-land. The play is predominantly realistic with, however, two exceptions: Scene I, ii, '*A fantastic scene*' (27), has a dream-like setting: a dugout where English and German soldiers side by side discuss the imminent

attack; while Scene III, i, is set in a shell-hole where, in a slightly confusing context, a Valkyrie, whose traditional role is to remove the dead
heroes to Valhalla, here encourages the dead soldiers to 'Find new gods,
and better if you can' (69). *Tunnel Trench* illuminates the difficulties of
the playwright who tries to combine the presentation of individual
experience with an analytic approach to war as a general event. It will
be argued below that O'Casey, in *The Silver Tassie*, was the only author
who found a wholly successful solution to this problem.

Tunnel Trench is also one of the few plays where a specific problem of
wartime conditions, homosexuality, is not disregarded by the dramatist.[34]
The relationship between the hero and his friend is clearly homoerotic,
although this could not, of course, be openly declared on the stage at
the time. Seventy years later, Johnston in *How Many Miles to Babylon?*
(1993) was able to be more explicit in her depiction of the moving relationship between the Irish landowner's son and Jerry Crowe from a tenant family, both of whom join the British Army, are posted to the same
company and succeed in remaining loyal to each other in the face of
army regulations, social conventions and the insuperable barriers separating the officers from 'their' men. When Jerry is sentenced to death
for an alleged act of desertion, Alexander takes it upon himself to shoot
his friend, which in turn will lead to his own execution – an act of keeping faith every bit as moving as the traditional lovers' death. Johnston
had shown before that the essence of a homoerotic relationship can be
the responsibility for one another's physical well-being, when, for
instance, Alexander warms Jerry with his body after Jerry's hopeless
search for his dead father. Johnston also touches upon another aspect of
front-line homosexuality when one of her characters refers to the admiration the men feel for some of their young officers (Alec is no more
than 18). This aspect of wartime sexuality is made more explicit in
Robert Graves's post-War play *But It Still Goes On* of 1930 (which the
author later tried to ignore). Here, David Casselis, a declared homosexual, remembers his wartime experience as a young officer when he was
worshipped by his men who 'killed Germans for me' and 'drilled like
angels' (244–5). Another side of wartime homosexuality is shown by
Ackerley in *The Prisoners of War* (1925), a play that was revived at the
New End Theatre as recently as 1993. It presents five RAF officers who,
for obscure reasons, have been interned in Mürren, Switzerland, where
they enjoy the luxuries of a privileged peace-time existence that were
denied to the ordinary officer, including tennis, bar service and beautiful scenery. Nevertheless, they constantly discuss their deplorable
'plight' with an intolerable degree of self-pity that is evidently shared by

the author, whose portrayal of Captain Conrad is said to be autobio-graphical.[35] Ackerley depicts the relationship between four of them as clearly homosexual, allowing his characters to behave like boarding-school girls whose petty jealousies form a painful contrast to the hardships to be experienced in the trenches; in this respect his play stands in marked contrast to all the front-line plays discussed here.

Wartime detention in a truer sense is touched upon in surprisingly few plays (considering the spate of popular literature about POW camps after the Second World War). Gregory's *Prisoners of War* (1934) follows the experience of a group of Privates who are taken prisoner and pass through the various stages of detention until eventually they hear the news of the end of the War. The play obviously tries to portray the suf-ferings of captured soldiers (primarily at the hands of their German guards), but this objective is internally defeated by the naivety of plot, characterisation and dialogue, the (unintended) effect of the frequent use of German being to illustrate the deplorable state of foreign-language teaching in Britain. When one German character swears 'Himmel don-nerwetter parfleuter magdeburg swinerei Englanders, fester arbeit' (38), this may satisfy some primitive need for basic humour, but it defeats any semblance of authenticity. A second POW play, Pakington's *All Camouflage* (1931) about two British Privates who make their escape after having been given important information by a wounded officer, conveys even less credibility. Fry's excellent *A Sleep of Prisoners* (1951), where four English prisoners of war in their sleep take on various biblical roles, centres more on the complex religious themes than on the captivity situation.

All the plays discussed in this chapter emphasise, in varying degrees, the seriousness of the front-line situation, with the likelihood of impris-onment and death overshadowing the stage events. Even *Black Adder Goes Forth*, the BBC series of 1995, a devastating if hilarious burlesque on the British side, ends in a deeply serious scene when the central char-acters assemble to go over the top for the 'final push', with their deaths only a few seconds away, a scene that then blends into a silent field of poppies. An exception to this all-pervading seriousness is Berkeley's popular *French Leave* (1920), a light comedy where the wartime situation is exploited for a comic sequence of events of a highly improbable nature. It is set in the headquarters of a brigade resting behind the lines where a mysterious and beautiful young woman appears, allegedly an opera singer from Paris, in reality Captain Glenister's wife, who could not endure being separated from her husband. In the course of various complications the complete staff, including the Brigadier, fall in love with her although they are convinced that she is a dangerous German spy.

When her true identity is revealed, her husband faces a court martial, but after a series of farcical situations (as the Brigadier describes it, 'to judge by the row, people began to fall downstairs in relays', 50), a number of preposterous coincidences allow all difficulties to be resolved, the Brigadier is promoted to Divisional General and Glenister is sent to Paris on leave with his young wife. The harmlessness, even the innocence, of this comic plot stands in stark contrast to the grim picture of the War that is painted in most other plays.[36]

3
The Home Front

The term 'home front' was used at the time both in a serious and in a derisive sense. On the one hand, it denotes the privations and sorrows of life under wartime conditions – food shortage, air-raid scares, factory work for women, evacuation and, more than anything else, the constant anxiety about sons, husbands, brothers and friends at the front; on the other hand, it suggests the misplaced excesses of patriotism, the ridiculous self-importance of small-town officials, the opportunities for petty corruption and moneymaking and the lies and excuses required to keep a person from being called up. Home-front plays offer examples of both these attitudes. They are predominantly concerned with individual cases either of suffering or of misdemeanour and leave little room for a discussion of general issues such as the causes of the War, its possible outcome or the moral principles underlying individual behaviour. The majority of them were written and performed or published during the War.

Obviously, *satirical* plays are bound to be contemporary, because they aim at changing certain patterns of conduct. The outstanding example, because of its author's prestige both as a dramatist and as a controversial figure in the public debate on the War, is Shaw's *Augustus Does His Bit* (1916). The subtitle, *A True-to-life Farce*, characterises the nature of the play: while the farcical plot is exaggerated to the point of absurdity, it nevertheless contains the seeds of attitudes that Shaw, and undoubtedly many others too, knew from wartime reality. Lord Augustus Highcastle, who has been sent to Little Pifflington to set up a recruiting office, is a pompous ass whose professed patriotism is only equalled by his painfully real stupidity. When a fascinating young lady attempts to cheat him out of a list of gun emplacements that might prove invaluable to the enemy, there can be no doubt that she will succeed. However, it is made abundantly clear that Shaw's plot is merely an excuse for his brilliant paradoxical dialogue, such as:

> AUGUSTUS [*rising angrily*] This town is inhabited by dastards.[...]
> They call themselves Englishmen; and they are afraid to fight.
> THE CLERK. Afraid to fight! You should see them on a Saturday night.
> AUGUSTUS. Yes: they fight one another; but they wont fight the
> Germans.
> THE CLERK. They got grudges again one another: how can they
> have grudges again the Huns that they never saw? Theyve no imag-
> ination: that's what it is. Bring the Huns here; and they'll quarrel
> with them fast enough.
>
> (840)

Shaw, who with *O'Flaherty V.C.* (1915) wrote another home-front play, albeit one set in Ireland and centred around the serious issue of experience-based pacifism, was, of course, concerned not only with improving wartime behaviour but also with a radical scrutiny of the moral positions underlying the British involvement in the War, and he concentrated his analysis in *Heartbreak House* (1919), which he began to write in March 1916. Naturally it would be too simple to reduce *Heartbreak House* to a satirical home-front play, but it also contains, in its comic elements, a degree of criticism of wartime behaviour, especially the callous egotism of an exaggerated liberal individualism, upheld by 'a cultivated intelligentsia that has lost control of its destiny and plays dangerous and foolish games of love as civilization drifts toward self-destruction'.[37]

The satirical attempt to improve home-front behaviour by ridiculing certain excesses is more evident in the modest *A War Committee* (1915) by Knoblauch, which satirises the flood of committees set up during the War. In this case, the purpose never becomes clear; the upper-class ladies who never get beyond electing a chairperson are more interested in society news and plain squabbling than in the war effort. That the author also wishes for the abolition of class distinctions is obvious in the person of the charwoman, who is persuaded to join the committee but refuses to sit down in the presence of her 'betters'. Before going on active service, Knoblauch/Knoblock apparently wrote a whole series of 'plays for charities of various sorts' which he later treated rather disparagingly: '[...] all this writing and producing of war sketches no matter for how worthy a purpose, began to appear more and more futile to me'.[38] Jennings's *Waiting for the Bus* (1919), a mild satire on people's wasteful shopping habits and their selfishness when waiting for a bus, is again indicative of wartime conditions, although, curiously, the War is never mentioned. Mrs Arthur Hankey's *A House-Warming in War-Time* (1917) is even more modest. When a tea-party is in full swing, news gets around that the Food Controller (who allows only one piece of bread and butter per person and no cake at all) is in the village, causing panic to break out among the guests. What there is of satirical intent is concentrated into the 'moral' of the play: '[...] this will teach you [...] not to 'ave no parties in war time, the pore young chaps wats over in France don't have no such, and we wats kep 'ere so happy and quiet like and ought to show our gratitude be doing our bit, and our bits to live quiet and sedate like say I and not go faluting with 'ouse warmings and such like' (8).

Not a single play written during the War, *Heartbreak House* apart, seems to have grasped the serious issues that must have overshadowed everybody's lives on the home front. Barrie approaches them from a distance in several of his works, but his bittersweet mood, all too often turning into downright sentimentality, prevents him from coming to grips with them. In *A Kiss for Cinderella*, produced at Wyndham's in 1916 and probably his worst play, he refers to wartime conditions: food-rationing, the blackout, the suspicion of spies, Zeppelin raids, the presence of wounded soldiers and the shadowy figure of Kitchener, but the basic situation (clad in the conventions of the Christmas pantomime) is that of mistaken fairy-tale harmony. The plot concerns the heartbreaking story of a young girl who dreams of the splendid ball where the prince will dance with her, but in real life has to make a living by taking in orphaned children whom she beds in boxes in her tiny room. Through her dream on the cold door-step she catches pneumonia but is rescued by the Policeman, who finally proposes to her. Three short plays by Barrie come closer to an analysis of specific psychological situations caused by the War. In *The New Word* (1915) he tackles the problem of father–son relations, never easy but exacerbated by the War. The 'new word' is 'dear father', occasioned by the son's imminent departure for the front; the new relationship is presented in credible dialogue that is amusing as well as moving. Given the time of the play, the slur on the enemy contributes to the authenticity without being sanctioned by the author:

EMMA. If you carry a sword the snipers know you are an officer, and they try to pick you off.
MRS. TORRANCE. It's no wonder they are called Huns. Fancy a British sniper doing that!

(861)

In *Barbara's Wedding* it is the Colonel who, in his wheelchair, fails to rec-
oncile his own memories of earlier campaigns with the 'real' situation as
it is described to him by his devoted wife, Ellen. Initially it is not clear
which of the characters whom he encounters are mere ghosts from the
past, but Ellen explains that, contrary to their expectations, Barbara did
not marry his grandson Billy, who was killed in the same battle where
Billy's friend Karl died on the other side. Instead, Barbara is married to the
gardener who is now a Captain in the Army. The Colonel's role, created
by Robert Loraine at the Savoy in 1927, is a great acting part, but the play
is less consistent in plot and mood than, for instance, *The New Word*.

Galsworthy in some of his plays conveys a far more uncompromising
view of the War. In his *Tiny Drama* called *Defeat* (1917) a young prostitute takes an even younger officer, on leave from the front, to her room.
It turns out that she is a German who can survive only by her present
way of life. The girl's bitterness and cynicism are reflected in her passionate outbursts against the War and, indeed, against humanity:

> I would like to work in a 'ospital; I would like to go and 'elp poor boys
> like you. Because I am a German they would throw me out a 'undred
> times, even if I was good. It is the same in Germany, in France, in
> Russia, everywhere. But do you think I will believe in Love and Christ
> and God and all that – Not I! I think we are all animals – that's all! [...]
> it is the men who think themselves great and good and make the war
> with their talk and their hate, killing us all – killing all the boys like
> you, and keeping poor people in prison, and telling us to go on hating;
> and all these dreadful cold-blood creatures who write in the papers –
> the same in my country – just the same; it is because of all of them
> that I think we are only animals.
>
> (958)

Her views are juxtaposed with the Officer's blue-eyed optimism, without
either position receiving authorial sanction. When he leaves her because
he senses that her nihilism endangers all he stands for, she sings in des-
peration 'Die Wacht am Rhein' while outside one hears men shouting
'Rule Britannia'. Considering the time of writing, this is a most unusual
attempt at impartiality.

Other plays, in sharp contrast, do not aspire to any amount of intellectual effort. While this may be acceptable in plays for schoolchildren like
Bulkeley's *The Scouts* (1917; about the capture of a German spy by some
adventurous youngsters)[39] or Mrs Horace Porter and George Bidder's
Patriotic Pence of the same year (where the appearance of a fairy makes a

family change their ways, giving up their amusements to save the pence for shells and cartridges), it is also true of certain plays for adults, for instance *The Breath of War* (1915) by Theresa I. Dryden (Mrs W. Dymond), an incredibly simple play about a family before, during and at the end of the War. While the wartime conditions put an end to various social conflicts – trade unions, suffragettes, Home Rule for Ireland, Socialism etc. –, some of the men die, others return as 'heroes', and the mythical figure of 'Peace' pronounces at the end of each act on the situation, proclaiming in turn distress, despair and triumph. Admittedly the play was published and produced in South Africa, but it is set in England and revolves around English values.

Not surprisingly, a number of plays are concerned with the question of whether to enlist. Monkhouse's *Shamed Life* (1916) is a straightforward discussion play between four characters: Claude who has so far refused to volunteer, his mother who provides him with an excuse for staying at home, Mrs. Bowes whose son is at the front and Isabel who is engaged to young Bowes. The various attitudes to the War and the reasons for or against enlisting are scrutinised, until news of the death of Mrs. Bowes's son becomes the final incentive for Claude to join up because he cannot any longer bear his 'shamed life'. The play reads like a trial run for Monkhouse's ironically titled *The Conquering Hero* (1923) where the question of voluntary service is discussed in much greater depth. The theme is again taken up in Thurston's *The Cost* (discussed above), which also contains some rather heavy-handed satire on wartime attitudes, especially the so-called sacrifices that those at home are prepared to make. Winter in *Air Raid* from the vantage point of 1937 once more resumes the theme of voluntary enlistment. A typical scene from drawing room comedy, with a violent quarrel between Julia and her husband Philip, is here interrupted when sirens sound the air raid alarm. Denis, the officer home on leave, is frightened out of his wits. When Philip sees this, he gives up his superior attitude ('Justice! Freedom! Dying for one's country! It passes my understanding how anyone can swallow such bunk', 128) and decides to volunteer, because he realises that the soldiers at the front are just as afraid as he is. This unlikely argument gives the play a surprise twist: having masqueraded as an objective discussion play for most of the way, it ends in a patriotic appeal.[40]

J. Hartley Manners uses the home-front situation in three short plays for the expression of his unmitigated hatred of the enemy that he also voices in the Foreword to the printed edition.[41] *God of My Faith* (1917) is set in London at the time when the sinking of the *Lusitania* is reported, which leads to a violent two-and-a-half-page outburst of resentment:

> Out of my depth I cry to Thee. I call on you to curse them. Curse the Prussian brutes, made in Your likeness, but with hearts as the lowest of beasts. Curse them. May their hopes wither. May everything they set their hearts on rot. Send them pestilence, disease and every foul torture they have visited on Your people. Send the Angel of Death to rid the earth of them and their spawn. May their souls burn in hell for all eternity.
>
> (66)

This is not, as one might expect, an individual character's spontaneous outcry of despair, but the author's considered opinion. *All Clear* (1918) is Manners's protest against Zeppelin raids on London. Norah, who had lost her husband at the front, in conversation with the local Vicar gives full expression to her hatred of the Germans; the Vicar's faint appeal to her to use some Christian charity has no effect. When an air raid occurs, Norah's child is killed – evidently just to prove that she was right. In *God's Outcast* (1919), two people meet at a lonely railway station. The woman has just lost her husband at the front after having been married for a few weeks, the man has had news that his son, with whom he had spent all his adult life, has been killed. Both are determined to commit suicide when the midnight express passes through, but realise that this would turn them into 'God's outcasts' and would prevent them from meeting their beloveds on the other side of the grave. In each of these plays, the home-front situation is not developed in detail and serves merely as a pretext for expressing the author's feelings.

Conversely, three full-length home-front plays are straightforward comedies (with farcical elements) without any pretence at depicting a serious situation or at discussing weighty problems. *Billeted* (1917) by F. Tennyson Jesse and her husband H.M. Harwood is set in a rural manor house where Colonel Preedy has been billeted. Betty, the present occupant, who has been separated from her husband for two years, forges a telegram to say that he has been killed to escape local criticism which considers it immoral for a married woman to live in the same house with an unmarried man. Unfortunately, the husband arrives on the same day, having been posted as adjutant to Colonel Preedy. The complications arising from this situation are exploited to the full, until Betty and her husband decide to give their marriage another try, while the Colonel proposes to Betty's friend. That there is a war on, and that the officers will have to go into battle in a few days' time, seems not to worry anyone.

In *The Saving Grace* (1917), a sentimental comedy about an elderly couple who are bankrupt but deeply in love with each other, Chambers uses the War as a welcome opportunity for providing a happy ending. Being able to join up solves all the problems, while the War is treated very much as a natural phenomenon, a minor earthquake or downpour which does not justify any discussion. Terry's *General Post* (1917) has at least a central theme, the class conflict, or, to put it into suitable terms for comedy, snobbery. In Act I (set in 1911) Sir Dennys Broughton, his wife and their son Alec show themselves to be natural snobs, if amusing and likable ones, while their daughter Betty is adversely affected by dangerous ideas of social equality. To the horror of her family, Betty thinks she has fallen in love with Mr Smith, Sir Dennys's tailor, who is also an officer in the Territorials, a new body much ridiculed by Sir Dennys. Smith rejects her because he sees the class system as too rigid for their marriage to succeed. In Act II (1915) Smith has become a Colonel in the regiment where Alec serves as a Lieutenant, while Sir Dennys has joined the new National Reserve as a Private. A great deal of harmless fun results from Colonel Smith's visit to Sir Dennys's house where the family are in agony over the question of how to behave to a superior officer who is also a tradesman. Act III is set in the future when Smith and Alec have both returned as highly decorated officers, Smith as Brigadier General. Now it is the older Broughtons who would like their daughter to marry the successful General, and Smith reveals that he has been in love with Betty all along, which leads to the happy ending. Unfortunately, the theme of snobbery versus wartime equality and personal worth is not taken to its logical conclusion, because the Broughtons only make an exception for Smith the successful officer while they retain their snobbery towards his less famous fellows in trade. The title, suggesting a general turnabout, applies only on the individual level.

Not surprisingly, during the War the home-front situation was sometimes exploited for melodramatic effects and sensational entertainment, especially at the Lyceum. Most of these plays remained unpublished and can only be reconstructed from reviews.[42] *The Times*, to cite an example, wrote of Melville's *The Female Hun*, produced shortly before Armistice Day (a play whose title character is the wife of a British General while the General's butler, most unfortunately, is also a German spy):

> There are enough villains [...] to suffice for two or three melodramas in less exciting days [...] the vast public which loves its Lyceum will flock to see *The Female Hun*, with its spies, its patriotic sentiments, its scenes of prison camp, aerodrome, and submarine. [...] There is little in the way of comic relief, except that provided by interjections from

the pit and gallery. At times last night these were quite as interesting as the events on the stage, and that is saying a good deal.⁴³

Another play of this type seems to have been Jerome's unpublished sketch *The Three Patriots* which, according to the *Times* review of a 1915 performance at the Queen's, 'strains belief in coincidences and plunges into melodrama, but is vivid, vigorous, and unconventional'.⁴⁴

Paradoxically, the best home-front plays were published and/or produced *after* the War, in some cases many years later. With the exception of *Gentle Caesar* (1942) by Minney and Sitwell, which focuses on the family circle of the last Russian Tsar, all of them are set in Britain. A play by Stewart that is actually called *The Home Front* (1937) is a pertinent example, almost archetypal in its simplicity. Set on a Scottish farm which is run by women while the men are away at the front, it portrays the shifting attitudes between the women – bickering and quarrelling as well as sympathising with each other's feelings – while all they really wait for is the son's return home on leave. When instead the telegram arrives to say that he has been killed, their heartbroken but unsentimental reactions are much more convincing than the explicit protestations of patriotism in other plays: in the words of Mrs M., 'We mustn't give way like this. It won't do. The war's not over yet. John's done his bit, ours is still to do. Go down to the hayfield while I get the dinner ready' (101).

Another all-women play (the wave of post-war amateur plays for women is in itself characteristic of a social problem when so many men had been killed) is Bell's *Symphony in Illusion: An Allegory in One Act* (1932). While one would take exception to the term 'allegory', the play goes beyond the specificity of an individual situation and is convincing in the relationship between a clear thesis and its concretisation. As a 'rehearsal-play', with thematic links between frame action and internal plot, it is much more sophisticated than *The Home Front*. In the play within the play, seven women discuss the War, most of them full of hatred for the (unspecified) enemy who is finally beaten when 'peace breaks out'. Mary, who has lived in the enemy country and has an 'enemy child', is insulted by the women; only a character called the Wanton dares to speak up for her. The play revolves around the difficulties of making peace after so much effort has been put into the War. This theme is taken up by the players in the frame action and expressed by the Woman Who Plays the Mad Girl: 'It is strange, you know. People make tremendous efforts, great sacrifices, use all their powers and all their knowledge, when making war. But when it comes to making peace, which is much more important, they fall into petty squabbles about nothing' (87). However, the players are far from optimistic about the future; as the same character expresses it: 'We never do seem to have time to clear up the stage before the next show' (90). If this is an educational play (for the cast as well as for the audience), the term 'education' here must be used without the slightest trace of condescension. That the differences in intellectual standards are particularly great where short plays for amateurs are concerned, becomes clear from a comparison with Rubinstein's pretentiously titled *Arms and the Drama* (1923), which is set in an army training centre and dramatises a potentially valid conflict but turns out to be the last word in foolishness.

Three full-length plays for all-women casts, published together in 1935,[45] concentrate on a totally different aspect of the home front, the changes the War caused to the Feminist Movement. Box's *The Woman and the Walnut Tree*, Popplewell's *This Bondage* and Rye's *The Three-fold Path* are chronicle plays, each showing a group of women who represent significant moments in the movement for emancipation. Box's work depicts (and supports) the most radical positions, advocating such changes as the abolition of marriage, free love and compulsory state education for all children from the age of nine months. The 1917 scene in this play places more emphasis on the passing of the bill that gives women the vote than on the reverberations of the front-line events, and this although the central character's husband is killed on the day when the bill is passed. The War is here seen as an opportunity for women to achieve independence. Popplewell in *This Bondage* strives for a higher degree of objectivity, presenting a variety of positions none of which is ridiculed or dismissed offhand. While the first two scenes, set in 1891 and 1911 respectively, dramatise the changes from the militant rhetoric of the Suffragists to the physical violence and subsequent suffering of the Suffragettes, the 1914 scene shows the representatives of the feminist movement turning to a fanatical nationalism: '*Every man* up to forty should go. [...] Why not fifty? We should break them sooner. [...] That's right! Kick the blarsted cowards into the front line' (126). Act III, set in 'the present day' (1935?), advocates a somewhat indecisive pacifism and places the blame for a possible new war on the ruthlessness of contemporary industrialists. Rye's play reflects more indirectly on the Feminist Movement. It shows three women, each of whom, according to a somewhat cryptic frame action set in 1000 B.C. and 2000 A.D., embodies the ideal combination of power, peace and love, 'the Trinity of Forces that sustains the Universe' (234). During the War they prove their worth in contrast to the clichés uttered by others (244). The War is depicted as a great calamity; nobody is made to blame for its outbreak, yet the author's feminist position is unmistakable, and the War serves as a catalyst to make this abundantly clear: 'Perhaps if women had more power there wouldn't be so many wars' (241).

Chetham-Strode's *Sometimes Even Now*, acted at the Embassy Theatre in 1933, is, as the title suggests, a play about the after-effects of the War and will be discussed later, but in its first act it also presents a convincing image of the home-front situation in fashionable society, where the seemingly light-hearted conversation is regularly punctuated by the news of someone having been killed or reported missing. A somewhat surprising use is made of the home-front situation in Harvey's obscurely titled *The Last Enemy* (1929). The main part is set in 1916 and 1917, at a time when elderly men have their hair dyed in order to be accepted into the Army and the young men return from the front on a short-term leave which may, in all likelihood, be their last visit. At such a time, normal standards of behaviour have lost their meaning, and it has become almost a patriotic duty for young ladies to forget about modesty, to give the soldiers on leave a good time. Cynthia, the central character, is offered marriage by two young officers within less than 24 hours. In one case the proposal threatens to turn into a rape when Cynthia refuses the officer, his line of drunken reasoning being 'There's a bloody war on, isn't there? In my branch of the business you've to live a lot in a short time if you want to go West knowing something of life' (57). A year later Cynthia nevertheless agrees to marry her would-be seducer (acted by Laurence Olivier in the original production) whom she had nursed when he returned seriously wounded, while the other young man meets his death in no-man's-land. This somewhat conventional plot, however, receives a surprise twist through the frame action which shows two explorers dying on an arctic expedition. On their way to Heaven (literally ascending an enormous stairway!) they are given the chance to return to life, one of them to meet the girl he would have loved if he had survived, the other to see the boy who might have been his son. In two ghostly scenes, one dead explorer saves Cynthia from rape, while the other comforts her dying lover during his last minutes. These frame scenes indicate that the author has chosen the wartime situation merely to illustrate his somewhat obscure metaphysical speculations. By 1929, it was becoming possible to instrumentalise the war experience for completely different purposes.

Rather unexpectedly, four post-World War II (and post-*Oh What a Lovely War!*) plays offer some of the most poignant scenes of the 1914–18 home front. Hannan's *Elizabeth Gordon Quinn* (1985) has, among its various somewhat ill-assorted subjects, an impressive slice-of-life picture of existence in the Glasgow slums under wartime conditions. Concentrating on the Quinn family, the squalor of their lives is shown as well as their futile attempts to escape from it. During the War, most of the women work in an ammunition factory. When the landlord raises the rent, they go on strike, in the end winning their case. Although they support the war effort, they also fight their own war against poverty, dirt, the landlords and the authorities. As Mrs Shaw explains: 'As I see it, there's two wars going on, that's all. And in this war, it's the landlords who are the Huns' (115). This theme is (not too skilfully) interwoven with the story of Aidan Quinn, who deserts from his regiment and returns to Glasgow where he is eventually arrested.

An aspect that in *Elizabeth Gordon Quinn* is only touched upon, the fundamental opposition to the War in small clusters of the British population, is at the centre of Rowbotham's *Friends of Alice Wheeldon* (1980). The author takes up the true case of a middle-aged shopkeeper in Derby who had been active in the suffragette movement before 1914 and whose home, as part of the No-Conscription Fellowship, became a safe haven for conscientious objectors on the run. She was framed by government spies, was taken to court on the charge of conspiring to murder Lloyd George and Arthur Henderson (Minister for Labour in the War Cabinet) and sentenced to ten years' imprisonment. Weakened by her time in prison, she died soon after her release in 1919. Rowbotham has apparently researched the context with great thoroughness, not just the case of Alice Wheeldon but also the various left-wing groupings in Britain who were opposed to the War, either for pragmatic reasons or on principle (the play was published together with a 100-page essay on 'Rebel Networks in the First World War'[46]). Unfortunately the characters' complicated political affiliations and their disagreements on strategies are difficult enough to realise on the printed page and must be next to impossible to understand on the stage, especially when the predominantly realistic presentation alternates with songs in the style of the Group Theatre. Nevertheless the author deserves high credit for dramatising an aspect of the home-front scene which is ignored by the rest of British drama.

Whelan's excellent *The Accrington Pals* (1981), a work which is clearly indebted to the wave of 'documentary plays' that began in the 1960s, was given prominence through the RSC production at The Warehouse one year after the premiere of *Friends of Alice Wheeldon*. Set in Accrington near Blackburn from 1914 to 1916, it portrays a group of men in the local volunteer battalion which becomes a part of Kitchener's New Army and is destroyed in the Somme offensive of 1916. While some of the scenes focus on the soldiers' lives (and deaths), most of them are set in a working-class district of Accrington, where the women, mill workers or market-stall owners, attempt to cope with the crises of the wartime situation, being drawn together but also reacting violently against each other. Finally, when no news comes through about their men's fate during the offensive, they organise a march to the town hall to force the mayor to produce information.[47] The most moving moment in the play is a scene where they hold a hen party and where, under the influence of drink, their sexual instincts grope blindly for some kind of outlet. The treatment of the women in their crudeness, violence and 'immoral' behaviour, but also their hidden kindness and generosity, is reminiscent of the early Dublin plays of O'Casey.

MacDonald's *Not About Heroes* (1982) is a moving account of the relationship between Siegfried Sassoon and Wilfred Owen from their first meeting at the Craiglockhart War Hospital for Nervous Disorders (where they are treated for shell shock) to the news of Owen's death in action one week before the Armistice. Seen mostly from the perspective of Sassoon who looks back on the War from the early 1930s, it is based on Sassoon's prose writings and Owen's letters, with long quotations from their poems. While there is no dramatic conflict apart from an occasional irritation on the part of Sassoon, and little plot progression, the play convincingly traces Owen's development from a shy youngster approaching Sassoon for his autograph, to a poet confident of his creative powers. This view of the 'home front', with shell-shocked officers temporarily convalescing in Britain before they are expected to go back into battle, is of course totally different from all other home-front plays.

The only drama in this context that goes beyond the presentation of individualised episodes is Shaw's *Heartbreak House*. Initially, it seems much like yet another comedy of social relationships, albeit between characters who are more eccentric than most. However, in the course of the action the dramatis personae crystallise into symbolic, if not allegorical, representations of dominant attitudes in society, and moreover they illuminate the various issues – ruthless capitalism, colonial arrogance and empire building, women's rights, impoverishment of the working classes and the revolution in morality – that had dominated the pre-War world and had contributed to its disintegration. Looked at from the end, *Heartbreak House* is a home-front play in the most basic sense of the term. The concluding Zeppelin attack was a common event in the South of England; it had its source in Shaw's personal experience, when in October 1916 a Zeppelin bound for London flew over Ayot St Lawrence and was shot down over a nearby village;[48] but the bombing in the play is also a symbolic catastrophe that signals the collapse of the pre-War world. In this perspective, Captain Shotover's ship of fools that has foundered on the sands of selfishness, exploitation and irresponsibility becomes a symbol of England. It is not only threatened by an enemy in the skies but has its internal source of destruction in the shape of Shotover's hoard of dynamite. 'Heartbreak' in such a context is not merely the consequence of personal bereavement or disappointment but the expression of the loss of hope for the future which leads to a secret death wish in society (Hector turning up the lights to make the house a target for the Zeppelin). The sense of anger, foreboding and imminent danger that pervades the play refracts Shaw's view of Britain and the world during the War. This view is expressed quite clearly in the *form* of the play, too: '[...] the sense of fitful activity and discontinuity conveyed in the dramatic narratives is germane to its portrayal of social disintegration and disorder. Fitfulness, abrupt changes of direction, and precipitous entrances and exits [...] are part of the play's essential aesthetic character'.[49]

4
The Return of the Soldier

The arrival home of soldiers from the front was an experience with which nearly every British family must have been familiar. More often than not, this led to confrontations of an unpleasant or even tragic type when the soldiers' memories of the gruesome reality at the front proved to be irreconcilable with civilian life and its petty problems. Plays that dramatise such a situation could be considered a 'sub-genre' of the home-front play; but since they revolve primarily around one central motif, as indicated in such evocative titles as *The Boy Comes Home* or *A Well-Remembered Voice,* it is appropriate to deal with them separately. Interestingly, dramatic versions of this type from the War years are mostly short plays. Probably the amateur companies or the early repertory theatres that produced such plays were in closer contact with the wide-spread experience of the general public than the West End managements that provided full-length plays for the entertainment market.

Few such plays bring about a happy ending. Hogg, in a superficial if vaguely amusing playlet called *The Story of Corporal Bell* (1915), has such a harmonious outcome. Cynthia, like many girls at the time, has been corresponding with an anonymous soldier at the front, copying letters from books to impress her correspondent. When Corporal Bell announces that he will be coming home, she panics, but fortunately Peggy turns up with Cynthia's letters. Bell had been engaged to her, but she had terminated the engagement when he enlisted. To win her back, he had sent her the letters to make her jealous. In the end, Peggy reveals why she has come: she has just got married to Corporal Bell.

Milne's *The Boy Comes Home* was written when the author served as a professional soldier, and was first performed on 9 September 1918, i.e. before the end of the War, but it is set on 'The Day after the War' (15). It is a light-hearted comedy, albeit one with a serious purpose: to remind the English public that the returned soldier cannot be treated as if nothing had changed. Young Philip has just come back to his uncle's house after serving as an officer. Uncle James, who has made a great deal of money during the War by manufacturing jam ('It was so nice for him, because it made him feel he was doing his bit, helping the poor men in the trenches', 17) decides to take Philip into his firm without even considering to ask what his plans are. But when he falls asleep, Philip enters with a revolver and frightens him out of his wits. Fortunately, this being a comedy, their encounter turns out to have been a dream, but Uncle James, as a representative of the audience, has been taught his lesson: the returned soldier is not a youngster any longer. The most significant moment occurs when Philip explains how he has learnt not to be afraid in the face of authority. In an untenable situation 'on the Somme' he had moved his company, or what was left of it, to a position of comparative safety against the express orders of the C.O.: '[*Quietly*] That was when I became twenty-five ... or thirty-five ... or forty-five' (25). Contrary to many others (and contrary to social reality during the post-War years) Milne seems to believe that Philip will find it easy enough to adjust to civilian life; it is the so-called pillars of society whom he addresses: it is they who have to make the necessary adjustments.[50]

The harmless *Story of Corporal Bell* and the equally optimistic *The Boy Comes Home* must be contrasted with John's ironically titled *Luck of War* (1917), set in a working-class household in the Northern Midlands among people who find it impossible to express their feelings. When Ann's husband George was reported missing, Ann had married again, but George returns, badly wounded, and finds his successor established in the house. This is a well-chosen short-play situation which reflects an experience that cannot have been unusual at a time when 'missing' soldiers eventually turned up, having been wounded, shell-shocked or imprisoned. In this case, Ann returns to George, while her new husband leaves the house. George sums up the spirit of the play with 'We'll 'ave no grudges and grievances in the 'ome-comin'. [...] You can't spend the 'ole of your bloody time 'atin' your enemies' (46). Such a sentiment is fairly common in plays of this type; in fact one of the major differences between the returned soldier and his friends or family is often that they still persevere in their hatred of the enemy while he has been relieved of such feelings at the front.

This confrontation is taken to extremes in a short play by Malleson, significantly titled *Black 'Ell* (1916). A typical middle-class family are informed that their son has been awarded the DSO for killing six Germans. When he comes home, everybody is excessively proud of him, while he seems stunned, being haunted by the apparitions of those he has killed (his private 'black hell'). He is obsessed with the similarity of the propaganda on both sides and the identity of the soldiers' sacrifices and decides that he is not going back. His arguments may not be startlingly novel, but they are remarkable since they have been put into the mouth of a 'national hero'. In its message, although it is totally different in other respects, *Black 'Ell* can be compared to Shaw's *O'Flaherty V.C.* where another highly decorated soldier returns to his native village to bear witness to the desolation the War can create in men's lives.

Barrie avoids such outspoken expressions of pacifism and concentrates on specific situations with a certain psychological credibility. In *The Old Lady Shows Her Medals* (1917), the return of the soldier is a most unexpected one because Mrs. Dowey has *invented* a son at the front, finding his name in a newspaper, to impress the other charladies. When he actually visits her, it is to scold her for her deception, but he is cajoled by her into spending his leave with her, finally accepting her as his 'mother'. While this situation is quite convincing, it is somewhat embarrassing to see the ending as a 'happy' one: when Private Dowey is killed in action, and Mrs Dowey is sent his few possessions, she is legitimately in a position to show off her medals, a rather nasty reflection on parents (or would-be parents) who need a dead son to satisfy their pride. On the other hand, Barrie's *A Well-Remembered Voice* (1918) is a deeply moving play about father–son relationships which Barrie had already dealt with in *The New Word*. The remembered voice is that of Dick, Mr Don's son, who was killed in action. His mother, who tries to monopolise the family's grief and marginalises her husband in this as in other respects, attempts to contact him through a séance, but Dick refuses to speak and returns to his father instead, who, he says, needs him more. In a bittersweet scene he admonishes his father to be cheerful because this is what the dead need from the living. Having died so young, he is still confused about his position among the dead but insists that the sectarian allegiance of the living does not count among the dead:

> DICK [...] We have a fine for speaking about the war. And you know, those fellows we were fighting – I forget who they were?
> MR. DON. The Germans.
> DICK. Oh yes. Some of them were on the same side of the veil with us, and they were rather decent; so we chummed up in the end [...]
> (1074)

The return of the soldier as a ghost or apparition is taken up in several post-War plays. In Joe Corrie's short play *Martha* (1937), the young soldier appears to his mother in a dream when he has been killed at the front. Martha has already lost three sons, and her existence revolves around memories of the fourth, 'Jimmy the bairn' (19), with whom in her imagination she communes every night. He 'tells' her that he is coming home at exactly the moment when he is known to have died. In a quite unsentimental scene he readjusts the balance of values, putting his mother's peacetime heroism on the same level as the soldiers' fighting exploits: 'They're getting' the V.C. oot in France the noo for doin' a damned sicht less for their country than you did when you were rearin' us' (24). Mercifully, in the end Martha is allowed to join her dead son. Although an explicit criticism of those responsible for the War is withheld, the author's attitude becomes clear enough in the pity he evokes for Martha, the true victim of the War.

Millar's *Thunder in the Air* (1928), a revised version of a play copyrighted but not published in 1923, begins with a scene of spectacular mystery. In Major Vexted's house a séance has taken place. Suddenly the lights go out, and a man appears out of the rain. It turns out that all the persons who had known Ronnie Vexted before his death in action will meet him again. Millar's play is exceptional in that it neither idealises nor sentimentalises the returned soldier: during his lifetime Ronnie had been a disagreeable character, he had made several women unhappy, had cheated the butler out of his savings, had misappropriated the mess funds and had forced his father to help him out of one scrape after another. However, his reappearance creates kindlier feelings in those who knew him; they do not so much see Ronnie as themselves, which turns the play into an analysis of truth and self-recognition. The author's idea, far from original, seems to be that the dead live as long as the living remember them. Consequently Ronnie in his meetings with the various characters is as young as they had known him, while they have aged in the meantime. The philosophical implications of such a discrepancy in age and the passing of time are not clear, but at least the author avoids the melodramatic ending that one might have expected from the beginning, and simply leaves his characters a shade kindlier if also disillusioned and perhaps unhappy.

Coward's 'ghost play' *Post Mortem* (1931) had its origin in the author's confrontation with *Journey's End*. According to Coward's recollections in *Present Indicative*,[51] during his holiday in the Far East he came across a touring company called The Quaints, who had *Journey's End* in their repertoire, and agreed to act the role of Stanhope in a number of performances in Singapore. On the voyage back, he wrote *Post Mortem* which begins with a scene that could be acted in the same stage set as *Journey's End*, and with the same personnel. The officer, who dies during this scene, is then shown 13 years later when he revisits the important people of his brief life: his mother, who still suffers heroically from his untimely death; his fiancée, who leads a vacuous life in fashionable society; his father, who influences public opinion with his false rhetoric about faith and patriotism; his officer friend, who has published a bitterly outspoken book about the War and is being ostracised as a result and his other comrades who have come to terms with a bourgeois existence and refuse to reflect on their war experience. John finally fades away without any problem being resolved; the possibility of a new war is already looming on the horizon. Coward's is an embittered, deadly serious play somewhat confused in the arguments, but leaving no doubt about the author's commitment.

In van Druten's *Flowers of the Forest* (1934), the dead soldier reappears through a medium 18 years after his untimely death. In a complicated plot which involves various conflict-laden family relationships in a 1934 setting as well as two flashback scenes to the War, a variety of attitudes are set against one another, ranging from fanatical patriotism to somewhat hysterical pacifism. The soldier had tried in vain on his deathbed to complete a poem. When in 1934 young Leonard on his deathbed has one of his fits, he becomes a medium for the dead soldier and in *his* voice completes the poem with the significant conclusion

> Our death they called our glory. They were lying.
> The glory was in living, not in dying.
>
> (564)

The dead man's belief in life rather than in dying for one's country becomes the final message; it is confirmed by the central character, who insists 'You *can* stop war, if you'll admit that it's an evil, like disease' (568). *Flowers of the Forest* is an excellent example of a commercial play, written with considerable skills in structure and characterisation, that nevertheless is explicit on a moral position which must have been far from welcome to part of the audience. In an earlier play, *The Return of the Soldier* (1928), van Druten had already dramatised the terrible consequences of the War for a group of harmless people. Captain Chris Baldry has been happily married for 15 years. But when he returns from France with severe shell shock, the last years have been erased from his memory, and he only remembers Margaret, his previous girlfriend with whom he is still in love. The play revolves around Chris's earlier life (revealed in analytical technique) and the various attempts to overcome his amnesia, but changes perspective halfway in that it centres on Margaret. When a psychiatrist explains that shell shock is a subconscious attempt to return to the past, Margaret, still in love with Chris, makes the supreme sacrifice of losing him a second time: she confronts him with his child's toys, thus shocking him into recognising the present. The emphasis here is, then, on the people who have stayed at home; their sufferings from the soldier's shell-shocked condition are just as important.

Clemence Dane (Winifred Ashton) had already dealt with the same subject in her 1921 play *A Bill of Divorcement*, a rather conventional divorce play, but complicated by the new experience of shell shock. The action takes place on Christmas Day 1933 (12 years into the future). Hilary Fairfield, after sustaining shell shock in the War, has been confined to an 'institution' because of 'incurable insanity', but is then released to return to his family, believing that at long last he has been cured. However his wife, on the basis of a new divorce bill (following the *Majority Report of the Royal Commission on Divorce v. Matrimonial Causes* that was under discussion in 1921), has already obtained her divorce and married the man she loves. This is a potentially tragic situation, portrayed convincingly in the hopeless entanglement of the three principal characters each of whom is confronted with a conflict between irreconcilable values. Unfortunately, towards the end the author confuses the issue by introducing the subject of hereditary insanity, which allows her to fabricate a false happy ending when the daughter, who believes she has inherited her father's illness decides to look after him so that Mrs Fairfield is free to live with her lover. The same predicament seems to have been at the centre of Trevelyan's *The Dark Angel* (1925).[52]

If the ending here appears forced, McEvoy, in *The Likes of Her* (1923), has a soldier's-return play where the happy outcome is never in doubt. Set in Stepney, it attempts to render a realistic portrait of East-End milieu and speech. The coster-girl Sally, the Cockney girl with the golden heart, has been waiting for George to be demobilised, fending off all advances from other men. George, it turns out, has lost one leg, one arm and one eye as well as having been made a Colonel – very good reasons for his friend Alf to persuade Sally that George is not worth waiting for. But when George does return, Sally's kind-heartedness to a young girl brings about a happy reunion, and their happy future together is not questioned in any way. *The Likes of Her* is one of the few exceptions that confirm the rule of the seriousness and realism of the attitude to the returned soldier in British drama.

Another exception is Maugham's *Home and Beauty* (1919), one of Maugham's commercially most successful works that was regularly revived during the next eight decades. Subtitled *A Farce in Three Acts*, the play centres on Victoria whose husband, William, was reported killed in action three years ago. After observing the customary one-year period for decency's sake, Victoria married Frederick, William's best friend. Now, a year after the end of the War, William returns from imprisonment in Germany, and Victoria finds herself with two legitimate husbands. Maugham milks the situation for all it is worth, then introduces a new twist when both husbands decide to opt out of this marriage, while finally – another twist – Victoria resolves to divorce them both since she has found a much wealthier lover. The play is shot through with references to the War, not a single one of which acknowledges the serious implications of Victoria's predicament. The overall impression is one of callous cynicism in the treatment of such a sensitive subject. Maugham's progress – not as a skilful writer, which he always was, but as a human being capable of compassion and understanding – is apparent in his later treatments of the same theme.

The basic situation of *Home and Beauty* is echoed (or should one say 'imitated'?) in Temple's *The Widow's Cruise* (1926) where again a lady finds herself married to two men because one of them has been reported killed. When the poet Varden reappears after the disaster of Caporetto on the Italian–Austrian front, he has lost his memory due to shell shock and is generally acclaimed for his bravery as 'Captain Ignoto'. Owing to a series of far-fetched coincidences, Ignoto turns up at Capri where his wife leads a contented life with her second husband, and attempts to win her back, although their marriage had been a failure. She nearly succumbs to the charm and mystery of the poet-turned national hero but in the end realises that he is incurably selfish and decides to stay with her second husband once the legal business of her apparent bigamy has been sorted out. The War is merely utilised as a convenient device to ensure the plausibility of Varden's loss of memory, and the real front-line situation at Caporetto (probably the greatest disaster in Italian military history, with one million men retreating in panic, and hundreds of thousands deserting) figures only in one isolated speech that seems wholly out of place in the context:

> [...] it was such an awful mess-up, that Caporetto retreat [...]. Night attack in torrents of rain – and a very dirty bit of trickery somewhere. Then – panic! Gad, can't I see it! Hundreds thought that all was lost – flung away their arms, and made for home. [...] All the older and more experienced officers killed – those left, too young to cope with the situation. Absolute confusion! Rain, darkness, peasants flying before the enemy advance – all mixed up with retreating troops, and wounded got out of the hospitals somehow – anyhow.

(25–6)

The similarity to Maugham's play is underlined when one character raves about 'England, Home and Beauty' (63). In contrast to Temple, however, Maugham later made amends for his frivolous treatment of the returned soldier.

A first step in the direction of recognising the tragic potential in such a situation can be seen in his *The Unknown* (1920). Major Joe Wharton has come back to his wealthy English home after a long period at the front. He expects to marry his fiancée, but, to the dismay of his pious family, admits that he has lost his faith: 'I can only tell you that all that's moral in my soul revolts at the thought of a God who can permit the monstrous iniquity of war' (59). The play centres on the exchange of ideas about death, sin, faith, individual guilt and God's responsibility. The conflict is staged very effectively because of various widely differing standpoints, ranging from the family doctor's agnosticism ('The rain falls on the just and the unjust alike, but the unjust generally have a stout umbrella', 79) to the local Vicar's wife's irrational religiosity. It is complicated by the fact that Joe's father loses his faith when he learns that he will soon die of an incurable disease, and by the interesting figure of Mrs Littlewood, who has lost both her sons in the War but refuses to resort to the conventional forms of grief, wondering whether this world is some kind of hell in which we are punished for sins committed in an earlier life. Although Maugham strives hard for objectivity and an even distribution of valid arguments, he is clearly on the side of Joe and sees the returned soldier's situation – having to decide between losing his fiancée and pretending allegiance to a faith he no longer accepts – as a tragic one. The issues of the various discussions remain unresolved, and therefore the plot has to remain unresolved, too, as Maugham himself realised, arguing that 'the drama lay in the arguments on one side and the other, and not at all in the personal relations of the characters. The result was that the play came to an end with the second act; the third consequently was meaningless [...]'[53]

Galsworthy contributed to the returned-soldier subject in two of his plays. In *Windows* (1922), a respectable upper-middle class family is drawn into the conflict between idealism and pragmatism, executed in pseudo-philosophical dialogue. Against the mother's express wishes, they employ a girl who has just served a two years' sentence for smothering her baby. The son, who has returned from the front where he has contracted an incurable idealism, insists on helping the girl, although she makes unwelcome advances to him. The play is important in the present context because nearly every one of the son's sentences refers to the front-line experience which he even equals with the girl's term in prison. In sharp contrast to *Windows*, Galsworthy in *The Sun* (1922), a minute play of less than five pages, created the archetypal returned-soldier situation. Here the girl has turned to another man. When the soldier comes back, she agonises over the conflict, while the soldier refuses to be saddened by the loss of his girl. He has gone through so much that human suffering cannot touch him any more. This, however, remains incomprehensible to the girl, and she can only assume that he has been touched by the sun.

Finally, the return of the soldier in two *Irish* plays provides a perfect illustration of the sharp divide between the British and the Irish attitudes to the War. In Trevor's *Scenes from an Album* (1981), the history of a Big House in Ulster, the (then) owner of the estate returns from the front in 1919 with the insight: '[...] there are other houses and other families, there are cities and other landscapes, and other tragedies. I spent four years in a war, twice I was nearly killed. I'm glad I escaped death' (22). And yet this has absolutely no consequences for the history of the family or for the plot of the play, and it remains a minor episode in a sequence that is primarily concerned with the Irish context. In this respect *Scenes from an Album* is reminiscent of Robinson's *The Big House* (1926), a play to which as a whole it is clearly indebted (except that Robinson's is a better work). Here the ghost of Ulick Alcock, killed in France three days before the Armistice, repeatedly returns to the family seat in Co. Cork but can only be noticed by those who share his love for Ballydonal House and all it stands for (155, 174–5, 198), and it is not the War that matters to him but the destruction of the house.

5
Departure – Combat – Return: A Soldier's Career

While a large number of plays end with the central character's death at the front, others concentrate on the post-War situation, and in others again the chief characters begin at home and then set out to the front where they are killed, a few authors make the attempt to comprise all three stages in a soldier's career: his departure from home, his experience at the front and his return to an unfamiliar world of civilian activities. Not surprisingly, all of these are full-length plays, since they require at least three acts to delineate the three situations. Rather unexpectedly, they include some of the most successful and significant plays about the War.

Coward in his much-maligned revue play *Cavalcade* (1931) covers the largest canvas. It spans some 30 years and reflects the fate of the whole country in the experience of two families. The play opens on New Year's Eve 1899, the beginning of a new era and also the moment of the imminent departure of both master and butler to the Boer War. It then proceeds through such public events as the relief of Mafeking, the death of Queen Victoria, the sinking of the *Titanic*, the outbreak of the Great War and the end-of-war celebrations, and concludes with the New Year's Eve festivities on 31 December 1929. These 'historical' events are interspersed with scenes characteristic of social life, especially before the War. Although several characters are killed at the front, Coward has deliberately omitted any dialogue-based, realistic front-line scenes, leaving the presentation of the War to the stage designer and the director, because the war experience wipes out all individuality:

Above the proscenium 1914 glows in lights. It changes to 1915–1916, 1917 and 1918. Meanwhile, soldiers march uphill endlessly. Out of darkness into darkness. Sometimes they sing gay songs, sometimes they whistle, sometimes they march silently, but the sound of their tramping feet is unceasing. Below, the vision of them brightly-dressed, energetic women appear in pools of light, singing stirring recruiting songs [...]. With 1918 they fade away, as also does the vision of the soldiers, although the soldiers can still be heard very far off, marching and singing their songs.

(105)

In the course of the action, many illusions are destroyed. During the Boer War, Jane says 'Thank Heaven for one thing. The boys are too young. They won't have to fight; Peace and Happiness for them' (8). Later, one of them is killed on the *Titanic* and the other at the front. A sense of dis-quieting insecurity, brought about by the War, pervades the play. It was sometimes criticised as chauvinistic and excessively patriotic, Peter Noble calling it 'an inferior piece of work' which 'was outrageously jingo and embarrassingly nationalist, at a time when the nationalist spirit ran high.'[54] In rejecting such views, one should point out that throughout the play chauvinistic expressions are restricted to individual characters and are unfailingly juxtaposed with the opposite position. Even Jane's lengthy patriotic speech on New Year's Eve 1929 mentions 'the sorrows' of the past in the same breath with the 'glories and victories and tri-umphs' and utters the hope that 'one day [!] this country of ours [...] will find dignity and greatness and peace again' (134). The final kalei-doscopic vision of the future includes a glimpse of '*six 'incurables' in blue hospital uniform [who] are sitting making baskets*' (138).

Sixty years after Coward's panoramic view, Bryden in *The Big Picnic* (1994) attempted a similar comprehensive vision. In what has been called 'epic popular theatre',[55] Bryden uses a group of volunteers from Govan to depict the war events; in other words, as in *Cavalcade* the emphasis is not so much on individual characters as on representative figures who stand for a broader canvas. The script consists of chronological scenes, from the act of volunteering through elementary French lessons and various events at the front, to the celebrations of Armistice Day when most of the volunteers are dead and their names go up on a war memorial. Significantly, an extended scene of the Christmas Truce of 1914 is posi-tioned centrally. While the play is devoid of anti-war propaganda, it is also far from a patriotic celebration of the soldiers, who are depicted in their fear and stupidity as well as their simple sense of comradeship and mutual dependence. In some ways, Bryden's play is reminiscent of *The Accrington Pals* except that Whelan's play lacks a third act because there was no return home for any of the 'Pals'; as stated in a programme note, 'The "Accrington Pals" battalion of Kitchener's New Army was raised and destroyed as described in the play.'

McGuinness's *Observe the Sons of Ulster* (1985) is another play about a group of soldiers who are as much representatives of their local/regional community (Ulster Protestants in this case) as individual characters. Here, Kenneth Pyper is the sole survivor who, in his old age, is haunted by the ghosts of his former comrades who perished, like the Accrington Pals, during the disastrous Somme offensive. Pyper's initial prayer to be relieved of his ghostly visitors establishes a semi-religious level that makes it impossible to view the subsequent scenes, however realistic they may appear, without their symbolic significance. In the last analysis, *Observe the Sons* is not so much a play about the War as a persistent inquiry into the meaning of a mystical identity defined by the term 'Ulster', as in Pyper's final prayer: 'I love my Ulster. Ulster. Ulster. Ulster. Ulster. Ulster. Ulster. Ulster. Ulster' (80).

Three plays attempt an analysis on an individual level of what it means to have left home, survived the front experience and returned to a world that appears utterly changed. Monkhouse's ironically titled *The Conquering Hero* (1923), dedicated 'To those who hated war and went to the war' (5), sets itself a difficult task in that it concentrates on a young man who initially refuses to succumb to the prevailing war hysteria. As a novelist, Christopher Rokeby believes himself capable of taking an objective stance, agonising for two long acts over the question whether to enlist, with his family's accusations of selfishness and cowardice ringing in his ears. When even his brother Stephen, a curate with pacifist views, joins up as a Red Cross orderly, Chris succumbs to the pressure. In Act III he is shown in France as a prisoner of war, humiliated by a Prussian officer and by his fellow prisoner and degraded by hunger and fear, before he returns to his home in Act IV. There he is welcomed as a 'conquering hero' but finds the reception utterly 'indecent' (87), especially since Stephen as well as his brother-in-law and their previous butler have been killed. The outcome is strangely inconclusive, as is the whole play: it never becomes clear where the author's sympathies lie because he evades the question whether the War, and Chris's involvement in it, is absolutely necessary. Quite different from his 1916 play *Shamed Life,* where Monkhouse seemed to think that it was mandatory for a young man to enlist, he here leaves the decision in the balance. Chris, a reluctant pacifist, a reluctant soldier and finally a reluctant hero, does not come over as a representative of a whole generation, however much the author may have wished to see him in such light.

Such a role is filled much more convincingly by O'Casey's Harry Heegan in *The Silver Tassie* (1928). Harry is a young Dublin labourer who serves as a volunteer in the British Army. While on leave, he scores the decisive goal in a cup match and thus helps his soccer team to win the 'silver tassie'. After his return to the front, he is seriously injured, and although his friend Barney drags him to safety, he remains paralysed from the hips down. In the Dublin hospital where he ends up, all attempts at an operation are unsuccessful. Finally he returns to the scene of his greatest triumph: in a wheelchair he attends the celebrations of his soccer club, and in his despair, having helplessly witnessed Barney's attempt to seduce his former sweetheart, he destroys the valuable cup. Harry is an unthinking, reckless young man whose attraction lies in his physical superiority. His 'tragic fall' and the inevitability of his fate are measured in the contrast between his physical prowess at the beginning and his degrading helplessness at the end.[56]

6
A Different Kind of War: The Great War in Ireland

Although Ireland during the War years was still undivided and part of the United Kingdom, the War experience here differed sharply from that across the Irish Sea. For the Northern Protestants it was the 1916 Battle of the Somme, where thousands of young soldiers from the 36th (Ulster) Division were killed or wounded, that overshadowed all other events and became the basis for a long-lasting patriotic myth, while in the South the independence movement that began soon after the War, triggered off by the unsuccessful 1916 Easter Rising, made the role of Irish soldiers in the British Army in retrospect appear as questionable if not downright treasonable, and for many years to come the wartime allegiance was passed over in silence, except where it was belittled, denigrated or treated with outright contempt. This sharply divided attitude to the Irish share in the war effort is also reflected in Irish drama. It took Irish dramatists, for obvious political reasons, more than 60 years to come to terms with the First World War.[57] To say so is to set aside for the moment those Irish writers who viewed the War in the context of the *British* situation, as did Desmond, Munro, Ervine, Hoffe, MacGill, and also Shaw in most of his plays, whereas the specific Wartime conditions in Ireland found little recognition in the theatre as elsewhere. Those few works that did not avoid the subject of the War altogether, serve to illustrate the situation described here. In one episode of Trevor's *Scenes from an Album* (1981) the owner of the house returns from the War, and yet his experience at the front has not the slightest consequence for the plot. Even in Robinson's earlier *The Big House*, the War where the heir to the estate is killed at the front remains a minor episode compared to the subsequent convolutions in *Irish* history. And in Plunkett's *The Risen People*, centred on the 1913 General Strike and Lockout in Dublin, the outbreak of the War serves merely as a convenient conclusion when the hero joins up after failing to get a job in Ireland.

If one ignores O'Brien's *Thirst* (a mere skit for a music-hall performance[58]), there were only two World War I plays set in Ireland, with theme and subject matter essentially Irish, which could be adduced to disprove the thesis that until the early 1980s the War was a taboo subject for Irish playwrights as well as for Irish society in general – and it is significant that both these plays were prevented from being premiered in Ireland. In fact Shaw's *O'Flaherty V.C.*, written explicitly for production by the Abbey Theatre, was banned through an intervention from Dublin Castle and has never been performed by the Irish National Theatre, while O'Casey's *The Silver Tassie*, also written with the Abbey company in mind, was rejected by the directors of that theatre and came out at the London Apollo instead. Nevertheless both of them, although widely different in structure and approach, are essential for an understanding of the Irish attitude to the War.[59]

The ironic subtitle of *O'Flaherty V.C.* as well as the farcical ending which may have deterred critics from seriously discussing the play,[60] were obviously chosen by Shaw to camouflage the grave Irish issues he approached. Shaw recognises that the Irish–English confrontation is, to a large extent, a matter of the class conflict: the impoverished tenant is less than likely to feel a strong allegiance to the landowner, and poaching his salmon or stealing his geese can easily take on the aura of Irish patriotism and political resistance. The landowner on the other hand is incapable of understanding that his tenants might feel anything but the most exalted British patriotism. Neither side can see the other's point of view (except for O'Flaherty himself who has learned his lesson at the front), and while the General naïvely takes his tenants' loyalty for granted, Mrs O'Flaherty naturally assumes that her son, when he joins up to fight in the Great War, will do so on the side of England's enemies.

One specific aspect of the precarious relationship between Ireland and England was the question of compulsory military service. Throughout the War, public opinion in Britain vociferously demanded that Ireland should not be exempted from conscription, while the leading politicians realised that this would encourage latent anti-British feelings and introduced widespread *voluntary* recruiting instead. This conflict explains Shaw's subtitle – except that no Irishman would have been motivated to enlist after witnessing Shaw's play. As early as 1915 Shaw identified the underlying reasons for the readiness of Irishmen to join the British Army: unemployment and the desperate living conditions of Irish tenants on the one hand, material security not only for the enlisted men but also for their dependants on the other. In this as in other respects, Shaw aims at debunking high-flown rhetoric, replacing the insincerity of such ideological pseudo-values as patriotism and honour with the real motivations of ordinary people. However, O'Flaherty (put forward by Shaw as a focus of identification for the audience) also questions the justification of the War as such. A sentence like 'Youll never have a quiet world til you knock the patriotism out of the human race' (823) goes against everything that was sacrosanct at the time, and is still as relevant as ever.

If *O'Flaherty V.C.* is seen as an appeal against war from a specific Irish perspective, one will recognise its similarities to that other passionate anti-war play to come out of Ireland, *The Silver Tassie*, a play that had profited in its genesis from O'Casey's admiration for Shaw and that resembles *O'Flaherty V.C.* in its stance against the futility of war. O'Casey reveals, like Shaw before him, the confused motives of Irishmen for joining the Army, their vague sense of future glory as well as their families' material interest in having a son at the front. The War is at the centre of the play; O'Casey 'investigates its fall-out on those in whose name it is being waged; and his theme is that its canker infects trench and home-front in equal proportions'.[61] Incidentally, even in 1935 when Yeats at last agreed to have *The Silver Tassie* produced by the Abbey, it met with violent opposition from a combination of religious and nationalist groups and had to be taken off, despite full houses, after only one week.[62]

O'Flaherty V.C. and *The Silver Tassie* are the exceptions that prove the rule of the tabooisation of the first World War by Irish dramatists before 1980. What followed appears like a last-minute rediscovery at the time when the last eyewitnesses were about to die, taking the War with them into oblivion. Several recent plays dramatise this process by utilising the memory-play perspective. At the end of Reid's *My Name, Shall I Tell You My Name*, Grandfather Andy, in his bed in the old-people's home in Belfast, remembers the day's events:

I walked in The Somme Parade the day.
Done the heroes proud. [...]
The Legion collected me and brung me back in a big car. Every year.
Regular as clockwork. They always look after their own.
An' they're gettin' my picture painted. They're goin' to hang it up in The Legion Hall. I'm the only one left, an' they want to honour me.
(118)

Andy at 93 is the last surviving eyewitness of the event that to him is still the Great War. Throughout the play he talks about it to his granddaughter, shows her his medals and teaches her a litany of names of those who died on the first day of the Battle of the Somme. As the title indicates, the play is about identity, Andy's eventually unsuccessful attempt to establish his identity by coming to terms with the experience of the War and his own role in it.

Andy has his counterpart in the Grandfather in Reid's earlier *Tea in a China Cup* who boasts 'I'd do it again gladly, if they'd have me, for my King and Country' (7) but has to be reminded that it is 'Queen and Country' now, and who believes when his grandson is posted to Germany in the 1970s, 'Another Samuel gone overseas to sort out the Germans' (25).[63] And in Brian Ervine's *Somme Day Mourning* occurs a scene at the 'Cenotaph by the City Hall':

> SPEAKER: At the going down of the sun and in the morning we shall remember them.
> *(Bugler sounds the last post)*
> BILLY: That's another remembrance service at the City Hall over, Rab.
> RAB: Most of the veterans are dying off. Not many here this year.
>
> (99)

Again, the situation of the last survivor, confused and uncomprehending to the end, is central to McGuinness's *Observe the Sons of Ulster*. Kenneth Pyper as an old man is haunted by memories of the War and in vain tries to understand them. In the opening words he addresses the ghosts of his previous comrades in arms: 'Again. As always, again. Why does this persist? What more have we to tell each other? [...] I do not understand your insistence on my remembrance' (9). Pyper's attitude reflects a petrified myth of loyalty and devotion which has led to the self-engendered isolation of today's Ulster Protestants. According to McGuinness, it results from the experience of the First World War. When the soldiers' devotion to Ulster leads them into extinction, this, combined with the incomprehension of the lonely survivor, is a bitter verdict on present-day Unionism and a compassionate analysis of Northern Protestant attitudes.[64]

An analogous attitude of harking back to the events of the War lies behind Jennifer Johnston's stage version of her novel *How Many Miles to Babylon?*, although here it is the *audience* that is placed in the role of eyewitness and survivor, because the two central characters are killed for the offence of struggling to preserve an independent identity based on a value system of their own choice. Both of them feel 'no absurd loyalty to the Crown of England' (4). While Alexander volunteers because his mother has told him that he is not his father's son, Jerry rejects all constitutional solutions to the Irish problem ('I'm no Home Ruler. Home Rulers are people who trust the English', 31) and foresees an armed conflict once the War is over when 'Trained men will come in handy. Hard men. Men who don't take fright easy' (7). The trenches as a training ground for a future rebellion against Britain – this is indeed an Irish perspective on the War. It links up with Barry's *Steward of Christendom* and Mac Mathúna's bilingual *The Winter Thief* which establish, in different ways, a direct relationship between the events of World War I and the subsequent Irish independence movement. Barry's play is remarkable here, not only because it adds complexity to the memory perspective by pre-dating it to 1932, but also because it links the events of the World War and the Easter Rising. In the iridescent memories of the former Chief Superintendent of the Dublin Metropolitan Police, the War in France, where he lost his only son, is set against 'that rebellion at Easter time, that they make so much of now' (77). In the words of one critic, the play dramatises the 'painful fissuring in Irish ideological consciousness by which the belief and actions of a whole body of Ireland's people [...] are denied or demonised by their fellow citizens'.[65]

Another, even more 'remote' perspective on the Irish attitude(s) towards the First World War can be found in McCartney's *Heritage* of 1998, set among Irish farmers in Saskatchewan. It presents a complex analysis of Irish as well as international conflicts: Irish Catholicism versus Irish Protestantism, Southern republicanism versus Ulster unionism, loyalty towards the old country versus loyalty towards the new home, and Canadian republicanism versus British imperialism. These four conflicts are projected onto a plot structured along the lines of two major myths: the international Romeo-and-Juliet myth and the Irish myth of Deirdre of the Sorrows. This plot is then acted out against the background of World War I; even the expatriate Irishmen in distant Canada cannot evade the conflicts created by the War at home, making *Heritage* a specifically Irish play about the War.

Over the last two decades, then, a number of playwrights have attempted to explore, and do justice to, the (often highly confused) motives of the Irish participants in the Great War and their sacrifices. Their plays counteract the impression that in Ireland the Easter Rising was the only event of the First World War worthy of attention on the stage. Nevertheless the Rising, when Irish insurgents confronted British troops and forced them into a week's battle for the possession of the Irish capital, was more frequently dramatised by Irish dramatists than any other Wartime event. When the War is seen as a *world* conflict, it would be unjust to ignore the Easter Rising and, subsequently, the plays that deal with it, although this is usually the case in discussions of the literature of World War I. When, on Easter Monday 1916 (only a few months before the Somme offensive), groups of insurgents occupied strategic points in Dublin and proclaimed an Irish Republic, few people could have foreseen the consequences that the subsequent six days' fighting would have. The plays that were written about the Rising during the past 90 years (no fewer than 14 have been identified for the present study) clearly reflect the changing attitudes in Ireland, and, taken together, they are a remarkable document of the role the Rising has played in the collective consciousness of the Irish population.

The first 1916 plays were produced or published as early as 1918, when the outcome of the rebellion was still in the balance. They are situated outside Dublin where a group of ordinary citizens receive uncertain news from the Capital, and where some members of the family decide to join the insurgents while others decry or deride their objectives. Dalton's *Sable and Gold*, produced by the amateur Munster Players in 1918, today reads not unlike a home-front play written under Irish conditions. Throughout the plot, news of the Rising reach the family in Cork, and it must have been fear of retribution either from the military authorities or the nationalists that led the author to claim in his Preface that this 'is not a play about the Rising of 1916' but 'about half-a-dozen people who lived in Cork, and whose lives were affected by the events of Easter Week'. The basic conflict, as expressed in the title, is that between fear and courage (the Villon poem quoted in the text [36] reads in part 'Fear goes in sable, / Courage in gold'[66]). While Michael, the son of a wealthy bank manager is killed in the Rising, his brother deserts from the ranks of the rebels and will in future have to live with the insight into his own cowardice. By contrast, Corkery's *Resurrection* is an unequivocal expression of the author's nationalism characteristic of most of his writings; not surprisingly its planned publication was prevented by Dublin Castle. The family constellation resembles that of *Sable and Gold*, with the father wishing to hold on to his recently acquired wealth, his oldest son (also called Michael) being killed during the Rising, and his second son deciding to take Michael's place in Dublin. However, the ending is much less ambiguous; when '*The dawn begins to break*' on Easter Tuesday, the father remembers his own days with the Fenians and gives his son directions on how to behave when facing a firing squad (36). Corkery's fanatical patriotism, sanctioned by religion as indicated in the title, exemplifies the glorification of the participants in the Rising that was to persist far into the second half of the century.

Chronologically the next among these plays is Yeats's *The Dreaming of the Bones* (1919), although to the present-day reader its relevance in this context may not be immediately apparent, since both its setting (a hillside on the west coast of Ireland) and its form (Yeats's individual variety of verse drama, adapted, in part, from the Japanese Noh play) seem equally unsuited to capture house-to-house fighting in a modern city. However, in 1919 Yeats could be certain that for his audiences two lines near the beginning – 'I was in the Post Office, and if taken / I shall be put against a wall and shot' (435) – would suffice to conjure up the Rising. For an understanding of Yeats's attitude it is essential to realise that the nameless Young Man has just escaped from a scene of bitter hostilities where the independence of Ireland has been at stake and has once again been forfeited. Only such an extreme crisis can justify his decision (evidently endorsed by the author) to withhold forgiveness from the ghosts of Diarmuid and Dervorgilla who, according to Irish mythology, are responsible for the loss of Irish freedom and have suffered from their historical guilt ever since. Yeats, then, has chosen the moment of the Easter Rising to span the whole of Ireland's semi-colonial history and has taken the first step towards placing a participant in the long line of the fighters for Irish independence whose public images were simplified beyond recognition in the process of nationalist glorification. Incidentally, with his choice of subject Yeats also confirmed his negative attitude to the greater War which, as early as 1915, he had derided in a letter to Henry James as a 'bloody frivolity'.[67] For the rest of his life, he persisted in turning his back on the wartime events on the Continent, for instance when he refused to publish any of the English 'war poets' in *The Oxford Book of Modern Verse*.[68]

The process of glorifying the 1916 insurgents has gone several steps further in Carroll's *The Conspirators* of 1934 (also published under the obscure title *The Coggerers*[69]), an excellent short play which captures the mood of the 1930s in relation to the Rising. It confronts the statues of John Mitchel, Lord Edward Fitzgerald, Wolfe Tone, Robert Emmet and Charles Stewart Parnell, icons of the various Irish independence movements who come to life when they sense that another Rising is taking place, with Brigid Anne Galgoogley, the prototypical charwoman who loses her son, her only treasure in life, through the Rising. In the end she places his body on the stone plinth from which Daniel O'Connell's statue has been removed, thus enrolling the anonymous Volunteer in the ranks of the martyrs for Irish freedom. Brigid is the personification of reality as opposed to the statues' idealism. She is also the embodiment of the city of Dublin and its people who found it so hard to come to terms with the Rising, and, by extension, she becomes Cathleen ni Houlihan, the sorrowing mother who loses her sons to the nationalist cause. The conflict between the statues' abstract patriotism and her very real suffering is resolved at the end when she resigns herself to a form of acceptance that is, however, far removed from any patriotic sentimentality.

Brigid's attitude had already been dramatised at much greater length by O'Casey in *The Plough and the Stars*, one of the great plays of the century. It was premiered by the Abbey only ten years after the Rising, which explains the degree of hostility it met with at the time.[70] O'Casey presents the Rising as reflected in a group of slum dwellers who in various ways become involved in the rebellion; while some of them go out to fight with the insurgents (albeit for personal reasons), others hide behind the high-flown rhetoric of solidarity with the proletariat, or loot shops and pubs once the City centre has been set on fire. O'Casey's great *technical* achievement lies in his ability to combine his attention to realistic detail and individualised character portrayal with a generalised symbolic recreation of the Rising as a political event involving thousands of people. Although his dramatis personae are highly differentiated characters each of whom harbours a life-sustaining illusion, they also reflect *as a group* the course of the Rising so that the play presents a sophisticated correspondence between the individual stage events and the wider political background action which allows O'Casey to do two things at the same time: to create credible individuals who survive under adverse circumstances *and* to depict the course of the Rising as a whole. If O'Casey's technical achievement lies in this dual effect, his thematic accomplishment has to be seen in the objectivity which allows him to do justice both to the insurgents and to the uncomprehending tenement dwellers, and even to the British soldiers. He does not intend to prove that one of them is right but rather to analyse how different people react to a situation of extreme crisis. If objectivity is a standard for evaluating dramatic literature, *The Plough and the Stars* deserves the highest praise, and it betrays limited critical insight when O'Casey has occasionally been applauded – or blamed – for his alleged pacifism in this play.[71]

In 1926, he was attacked for his daring decision to equip his characters with motives other than the purest patriotism, and the riots which followed on the first production reverberated down the history of Irish drama for several decades to come. They can still be sensed in Johnston's *The Scythe and the Sunset*, premiered more than 30 years later, although Johnston cannot be charged with an unqualified support for the rebels.

His title is, of course, a parodic reference to O'Casey's play, and it is clear that Johnston (who throughout his life maintained a critical distance from O'Casey) set out to correct certain errors that in his eyes O'Casey had committed. His attitude to the Rising could be defined as 'sceptical admiration' for an event which he described as 'a humane and well-intentioned piece of gallantry'.[72] *The Scythe and the Sunset* is the one play that is completely confined to the actual occurrences of Easter Week; it opens shortly before noon on Easter Monday and ends with the insurgents' unconditional surrender. It uses a specific focal point from where the Rising can be observed: a small café opposite the rebels' headquarters, which allows the author to employ *teichoskopia* as a technical device to present the military events as well as discussions between representative figures which juxtapose various ideological positions.

Whereas in O'Casey's play the emphasis is on action, and Johnston preserves a perfect balance between physical action and discussion, Gallivan's *Decision at Easter*, produced only a year after *The Scythe and the Sunset*, is first and foremost a discussion play. Its author took the daring step of bringing all the leaders of the Rising onto the stage. Only in the last scene, when they reluctantly decide to surrender to prevent the destruction of the City, do the military events invade the stage. In this play, the Rising therefore is recreated almost exclusively by dialogue in the form of a sequence of confrontational debates. How courageous Gallivan was in presenting controversial discussions between the martyred leaders, can be seen from the apologetic foreword to the printed edition of 1960 where Ignatius Johns emphasises that the 'problems confronting the author were of a peculiar delicacy and difficulty', because 'the mental pictures of the executed leaders are sacrosanct.'[73]

Dowling's *The Bird in the Net* of 1961 harks back to the earlier plays by Dalton and Corkery in that it uses a family situation for an outside perspective on the Rising. It is set in a Big House in Co. Galway that is taken over by a group of Volunteers. Here the confrontation between the uncomprehending landowner and the rebels from his own domain results in skilfully constructed discussions; as in *O'Flaherty V.C.* and *How Many Miles to Babylon?* the play foregrounds the class conflict rather than the political antagonism. The situation is complicated by a brilliant invention when Dowling introduces an Irish officer in the British Army home on leave from France who falls between the millstones of class, nationality and race. Tyrrell's presence allows the Irish Rising to be seen in the wider context of the World War; no other play shows so clearly the extent to which the events in Ireland were bound up with the fighting on the Continent. Tyrrell is cast in the role of tragic hero who cannot decide between the various meanings of 'freedom' that underlie the struggle in Flanders and the conflict in Ireland, but escapes from it by deliberately taking sides with the insurgents at the moment when their defeat is inevitable. Tyrrell's death at the front in France, reported in a concluding scene, is a somewhat meaningless coda to his tragic conflict, but his ideological function is clear: he is to take the audience with him in his movement from the unionist to the nationalist position, and his death in a War which is shown to be meaningless for Ireland, increases the sympathy the audience is intended to feel for his decision.

On its fiftieth anniversary the Rising was commemorated in several stage productions, but the evidence as to its changing role in the public consciousness (after all, by then the majority of the Irish population had not been born at the time of the Rising) is contradictory. On the one hand, Bryan MacMahon was commissioned to write a pageant on the signatories of the 1916 Republican Constitution, *Seven Men: Seven Days* which was produced by the nationalist Gaelic Athletic Association in Dublin's largest stadium. Despite some concessions to modernism in the presentation, this is a thoroughly conservative celebration of the Rising as the beginning of the new Irish nation. It pays lip service to the first language of the country in a number of passages in Irish (short enough so that the audience's attention would not flag); it celebrates the executed leaders as martyrs to the Irish cause; and it ends with the representatives of the young generation promising 'To build a joyous land close to the dream / And honour those who honoured us – by death' (33). In print, it comes uncomfortably close to the celebration of revolutionary events in dictatorship regimes. In sharp contrast to such ideological usurpations of a past event, the new Abbey, the National Theatre of Ireland and in 1966 at last housed in a building suitable for such a role, was opened with a revival of *The Plough and the Stars*. Even if the production was not an unqualified success, this performance in such a prominent position must have done much to contribute to a more detached view of the Rising, insisting as it did that the participants had their private motives for taking part, in addition to or in place of the ideological simplifications that were still being handed out by MacMahon and others.

The psychological approach was carried one step further by McCabe when, in his *Pull Down a Horseman* (premiered at the Eblana on the day of the fiftieth anniversary), he portrayed the leaders in a controversial debate about the plans for the Rising as seen against the background of the fighting in Flanders. Pearse and Connolly here stand for diametrically opposed attitudes, not merely different views on the practicability of a rebellion but fundamental differences between Nationalism and

Socialism which lead to acerbic exchanges not always complimentary to either of them. The outcome was known to the audiences at the time: the Rising *did* take place (as indicated in the title: the first casualty was an English cavalryman), and Pearse and Connolly ended up facing a firing squad, because the commanding British general refused to recognise them as combatants and treated them as 'terrorists', as the prescribed phraseology would have been at a later time.

The biographical approach introduced here was to predominate in subsequent works. McCabe himself, in his later play *Gale Day* (commissioned by the Abbey and RTE for the Pearse Centenary in 1979) perfected the technique of the biographical play about the leaders of the Rising. On 'Gale Day', Irish tenants were expected to pay their rent, an often traumatic occasion; metaphorically, it is the day of reckoning, a kind of doomsday. McCabe shows Pearse at the time when he was sentenced to death. Technically, this is a more sophisticated play than *Pull Down a Horseman*, with a large cast, flashbacks to various episodes of Pearse's youth, and scenes in a 'dream court', but once again Pearse's character is explored in a series of confrontations. The links between the events in Dublin and the larger canvas of the Western front are clearly established when Pearse's jailer, with heavy-handed irony, accuses him: '"The Western Field of War". You don't want to know about that piddling affair, millions dead, half the world involved ... not your Irish cup of tea' (40).

McCabe opened a new phase of dealing with the Rising, portraying the leaders as flesh-and-blood characters, freed from the tinsel of hero worship. Paradoxically, their 'reality' becomes more tangible where the presentation is attempted by 'unrealistic' techniques. This is particularly evident in Rudkin's *Cries from Casement as His Bones are Brought to Dublin* (1973) which, in a semi-expressionist review of Casement's life, eschews all approaches to facile realism. Casement, a former British diplomat who negotiated in Germany for the formation of an 'Irish Brigade' among the prisoners of war and for the shipping of German guns to Ireland, decided to dissuade the Irish leaders from a rebellion when he realised how little German support was forthcoming. He was landed by a German submarine on the Kerry coast but was immediately captured and later sentenced to death, certain homosexual passages in his controversial diaries serving the British government to quell public appeals for a reprieve. In Rudkin's play, the Rising is a subject for discussion, not an actual event, but it is shown as the focus of Casement's life, his final tragedy being that his bones could not return to his family home in Co. Antrim because of the partitioning of Ireland. As in *The Dreaming of the Bones*, the assumption is that the audience knows enough about the

Rising to fill in the actual occurrences. Rudkin's searching analysis reveals not only the external confrontations in Casement's life but also his inner conflicts; these can, in turn, be transferred to the Rising so that indirectly Rudkin contributes to a complex image of the Rising with all its confusions and contradictions which comes closer to reality than the hagiographic approach by others.

In this, it stands in marked contrast to *The Non-Stop Connolly Show* by D'Arcy and Arden which, despite the flippant title, is a belated attempt to glorify the life of the Irish trade-union leader who brought the workers' Citizen Army into the ranks of the underground movement. It is a mammoth work, consisting of six full-length plays; its first performance at Liberty Hall at Easter 1975 (directed by Jim Sheridan) took 24 hours. The final scene of Part VI is set in the Post Office where, not unlike Gallivan's *Decision at Easter*, the various leaders of the rebellion are portrayed, first in action and then deciding on unconditional surrender. Their situation is juxtaposed, in true documentary fashion, with episodes picturing a race meeting, the British Cabinet, the German political scene, the British military command etc., with comments by Lenin thrown in for good measure. The authors also enliven the scenes with songs, while long *verse* passages serve to ensure that nobody mistakes the stage presentation for the real events. Yet despite many entertaining features, their objective (coming close to straightforward propaganda) is clear: to install Connolly as a working-class hero.

The latest full-length dramatisation of the Rising is Murphy's *The Patriot Game* (1991), a panoramic view of the events leading up to the Rising and of the Rising itself, introducing many of the leading figures. Murphy renders the stages of the insurrection with a decidedly patriotic colouring which, given the year of the performance and the sophisticated plays preceding it, appears somewhat naïve; yet his work suggests that even in the 1990s there was an audience in Ireland ready to underwrite the type of hero worship that O'Casey, more than 60 years before, had set out to debunk. Although Murphy does not reserve his occasional sarcastic treatment for the British but applies it also to the people of Dublin and even to the rebels themselves, the dominant impression is that he has set out to create respect, even admiration for the insurgents' sacrifice, and this at a time when the glory shed over them by official propaganda seemed to pale. His somewhat anachronistic approach may be accounted for by the play's genesis: it originated from a television script commissioned by the BBC to commemorate their fiftieth anniversary which was not produced because of the high costs. At the time it seems to have been a rather daring enterprise, presenting the Rising as 'a bizarre ritual', being 'tinged with the cynicism induced by the knowledge

of what kind of Ireland it helped to create', and in 1966 it would perhaps have 'helped to undermine illusions about the glory and brilliance
of the Rising.' Twenty-five years later when it at last reached the stage,
Murphy must have felt that 'the danger in the Irish Republic was as
much one of "repressing" the Rising from national memory as of glorifying it into a national illusion' – which may explain his sympathetic
view of the insurgents.[74]

It will have become apparent that the Easter Rising fascinated a wide
range of dramatists over a period of nearly 90 years. They presented it
in all its facets, using a variety of techniques, and in the process they
showed widely divergent ideological standpoints. Taken together, these
plays support the thesis that the Irish attitude to World War I was decidedly different from the British one, with the Irish involvement in the
fighting on the Continental battlefields a near-taboo subject until
recently, while the Easter Rising, a turning point in the history of Ireland,
looms much larger than any other War event.

Towards the end of the century, however, the Rising appears to have
lost its unique position in Irish consciousness. On the one hand, as
described above, there were at least eight plays since 1981, in the North
as well as in the Republic, that deal with other occasions of World War I,
and do so with a measure of understanding for those Irishmen who,
after 1914, went out to fight for Britain on foreign soil. On the other
hand, there is Barry's great play *White Woman Street* (1992) where the
Rising is placed in the new perspective of worldwide events in which it
appears as a minor brawl, hardly registered outside Ireland. The action
in *White Woman Street* is dated to Easter 1916, but it occurs around a
small town in Ohio, and from this telescopic distance the upheaval in
Dublin is hardly discernible. The only direct reference to it comes in a
newspaper paragraph, misquoted by an uncomprehending bar-keeper:
'We get plenty Irish here. Place there burning like Richmond, I hear.
Some big mail depot or someplace. Fire and ruin in Dublin. Fellas put in
jail and likely to be shot. Fighting the English' (175). And before this,
the Irishman in the play had already placed the events in Dublin in a
wider *moral* perspective when he asks: 'Ever see an Indian town – the
tent towns? [...] Put me in mind of certain Sligo hills, and certain men
in certain Sligo hills. The English had done for us, I was thinking, and
now we're doing for the Indians' (158). Here the post-colonial approach
characteristic of all the dramatisations of the Easter Rising is extended
to encompass the share that Irishmen had in other colonialist measures
and to counteract the vision of Ireland as the one-sided victim of colo-
nialism; '[...] the "globalisation" of national history [...] takes the form
of a fundamental critique of the national narrative.'[75]

7
The Aftermath of the War

The experience of O'Casey's Harry Heegan forms the basis of a number of plays that deal with the situation of the survivor who returns to a world which everybody assumes is 'his' world but which, to him, has become confusing or even unrecognisable. It is the purpose of such plays not only to convey to the reader/spectator some understanding for the returned soldier's plight but also to encourage him to see his own world with the survivor's eyes, to problematise and possibly criticise what hitherto he has accepted as 'normal'. Most of these works are critical of post-War conditions in Britain.

One of Galsworthy's lesser known dramas, *The Foundations*, is situated at an unspecified time *after* the War although it was premiered, at the Royalty Theatre, more than a year before the Armistice. It is obviously intended to project into the future the author's warning of what might happen when the country returns to 'normality.' Galsworthy foresees that Britain will resume the class conflict as soon as the camaraderie of the trenches is over. Lord William Dromondy and his footman James, having returned from the front, suffer from chronic nostalgia for the equality of danger in the trenches. While the unemployed are starving and the people in the street are clamouring for revolution, Lord William holds an Anti-Sweating Meeting in his mansion in Park Lane, naïvely assuming that he can alleviate the conditions of the poor without relinquishing his own position in society. In the course of a preposterous plot, a bomb is discovered in the Lord's cellars, symbolically endangering the mansion's foundations, but the family are saved from destruction through the services of Lemmy the gas-fitter who knows how to defuse not only the 'bomb' but also the explosive mood of the crowd. Galsworthy derives a great deal of harmless fun from this situation; his satirical attack on the irrepressible nature of the class system (reminiscent of Barrie's *The*

Admirable Crichton of 1902) is largely lost through the uneasy combination of farcical incidents with an over-explicit significance. Naturally, he has no solution for the economic crisis that he predicts correctly for the post-War years, but he also seems uncertain as to what, if anything, he wishes to substitute for the class-structure that he envisages as resurging once the external threat has been removed.

A few comic presentations of the post-War situation, such as Milne's *The Boy Comes Home* and Maugham's *Home and Beauty*, have already been discussed. A much more serious reflection on the reaction of British society to the consequences of the War, not dissimilar from the last act of *The Silver Tassie*, can be found in two later plays by Maugham. *The Sacred Flame*, premiered in 1928, revolves around one Maurice Tabret, a former pilot who is paralysed from the waist down due to a wartime injury. His situation is nearly identical with that of O'Casey's anti-hero: 'They ask you how you are, but they don't really care a damn. Why should they? Life is for the living and I'm dead' (244). His wife has turned to his brother where she finds what Maurice can no longer offer her. However, unlike O'Casey's play, the *causes* of Maurice's injury – the War as the ultimate villain – are not under discussion here. Instead, Maugham analyses the consequences of his plight for the people around him. Maurice is dead after Act I, and the play centres on the question who has murdered him. Towards the end this whodunnit element is dissolved into sentimentality when it turns out that his mother has killed him to prevent him from realising that his wife is expecting his brother's child, and the family, full of admiration for her unselfishness, agree on covering up her deed. The audience is left with the uneasy feeling that the real issues, formulated in Act I, have been evaded.

This is quite different in *For Services Rendered* (1932), Maugham's bitterly uncompromising contribution to the discussion of the consequences of the War. In the introduction to the final volume of his collected plays Maugham declared his intention to leave the stage with four plays in which he would make no concessions to the public:

> I expected nothing for *For Services Rendered*. During the rehearsals of this piece I amused myself by devising the way in which it might have been written to achieve popularity. Any dramatist will see how easily the changes could have been made. The characters had only to be sentimentalised a little to affect their behaviour at the crucial moments of the play and everything might have ended happily. The audience could have walked out of the theatre feeling that war was a very unfortunate business, but that notwithstanding God was in his

heaven and all was right with the world; there was nothing to fash oneself about and haddock *à la crème* would finish the evening very nicely. But it would not have been the play I wished to write.[76]

It is to his continued credit that Maugham resisted the temptation outlined here, and instead wrote one of the great anti-war plays of the century. *For Services Rendered* dramatises, 15 years after the Armistice, the effect the War has had on a family. Sydney Ardsley, returned blind from the front, has become a cynic. His sister Ethel, married to a small farmer who had once impressed her in his officer's uniform, is now a mere victim to his alcoholism and vulgarity. Eva has been forced into the role of ageing spinster and yearns hopelessly for a family of her own; the only man she might have married, a demobilised officer, commits suicide when he is threatened with a prison sentence for forging a cheque. Lois, the youngest sister, equally unsuccessful in her search for a husband, allows herself to be drawn into an adventure with a married man twice her age for whom she feels nothing but contempt. All this is due to the War as a whole, not, it should be stressed, to one side, and it is an experience common to millions of people, as Sydney explains: 'Don't you know that all over England there are families like ours, all over Germany and all over France? We were quite content to go our peaceful way, jogging along obscurely, and happy enough. All we asked was to be left alone' (165–6). Maugham's indictment of the War is so complete because here the living are not any better off than the dying or the dead.[77]

Yet another post-War play with a demobilised soldier at its centre is Mackenzie's *Musical Chairs* (1931). Although set in Galicia, where the Schindler family operate an oil-drilling plant, it reflects as clearly as Maugham's plays do, the deep feeling of disillusionment that followed the initial optimism after having won the War. Its symbolic significance becomes clear when the family firm is bought out by a big American concern, and the Schindlers go back to an England swamped by unemployment and hopelessness. On an individual level, too, this play is deeply pessimistic, centring as it does on various sexual relationships in a family circle which lacks a single character with whom the audience could feel sympathy. Joseph Schindler especially, the wartime pilot who was involved in an air-raid on Düsseldorf in the course of which his fiancée was killed, has become a cynic: '[...] arranging for me to drop bombs on my own best girl was one of Providence's brightest jokes' (892). The War has left him with damaged lungs and a ruined psyche; he refuses to work, seduces his step-brother's fiancée and upsets everyone with his sarcasm. Only when one realises that it is the War that has turned him into a human wreck, can one feel some sympathy for him:

> [...] I realised that it didn't really matter a damn whether you killed Germans or Englishmen. Then it all seemed quite pointless and rather funny, especially from the air; one felt so detached. It all seemed such a fuss about nothing from 10,000 feet up. You'd load up with bombs and go rushing east into Germany, and far off you'd see a whole lot of German planes rushing west into France, in just the same terribly important way as though it all really mattered. That's my trouble; I never can convince myself that anything really matters.
>
> (867)

When he is finally drowned in a futile attempt to save another girl from suicide, this appears as the author's rather unsuccessful attempt to enlist the audience's compassion for him. It is perhaps the greatest indictment of the War that it is responsible for turning young men such as Joseph Schindler, Harry Heegan or Sydney Ardsley into the distinctly dislikeable characters they have become.

Another maimed soldier can be found in Granville-Barker's *The Secret Life* (1923), a highly intellectual analysis of a group of people during the post-War period. Whereas the author scrutinises the intersection of their private and public lives, the war experience remains only a minor issue. It could of course be argued that the pessimistic atmosphere pervading the play is due to post-war disillusionment, but this is not expressed in so many words. Only Oliver Gauntlett, who has lost an arm during the War and is now inclined towards revolutionary politics, is directly affected by his wartime experience, yet even for him the War is receding into the past: 'I meant to live with the dead. I felt I must never forget them. But they're dead to me now. I used to find courage by mustering in the dark that regiment of fellows.... I've marched miles with them night after night' (122).

Hims in her *The Breakfast Soldiers* (1996) returned more than 60 years later to a post–World War I situation that is clearly reminiscent of *For Services Rendered*. The play's two parts are set in 1919 and 1936, and the point seems to be that nothing changes, because the characters are unable to cope with the effect the War has had on their private lives. Margarita's husband was killed at the front just one month after their wedding; she is told by her sister, 'You have been dying ever since Charles was killed' (62). Emily yearns for her 'true and passionate love' (1), a soldier she has kissed only once in the general exuberance of the

Armistice Day. And their brother Freddy on his return from France is deeply unsettled and collects maps of foreign countries in the irrational hope that he will eventually visit them. Their family home, far too big for them, slowly decays, but they cannot make up their minds to sell it. Their lodger Alfredo, secretly in love with Emily, is the only one capable of a decision: he goes back to his native Spain to fight in the Civil War. All this has symbolic overtones; there are numerous references to World War I, and eventually the characters realise that they are drifting towards another catastrophe because 'everyone knows' that the Versailles Treaty 'was too severe and that that's the real reason we're facing another bloody war' (62). This is a deeply moving play precisely because it is devoid of sensational incidents, and its low-keyed despair is often conveyed through its quiet humour.

Another kind of bitterness, expressed much more idiosyncratically, can be sensed in Graves's *But It Still Goes On* (1930), called by one critic a 'sour confusion',[78] a play that reads like a postscript to *Goodbye to All That* (published a year before) and appears to be equally autobiographical. The play was later ignored by the author; it is not included in the list of his works prefixed to his *Collected Poems* of 1955 and has been disregarded by most critics.[79] On the surface it concerns the destructive relationships between six people: the elderly and pompous period poet Cecil Tompion, his son Dick, his naïve daughter Dorothy, the architect David Casselis and the two sisters Charlotte and Jane Arden. There are (mostly one-sided) love affairs right across this group, all of them doomed to failure, not only because David is a homosexual and Charlotte a lesbian, but also because Cecil is incapable of any emotion except for himself and Dick is a cynic who enjoys destroying what is left of human relations. Finally, Dorothy murders David and Cecil kills himself. On a second level, this is also a play about poetry, emphasising the contrast between three poets whom one suspects to be burlesques on living persons. On a third level, it is a play about the state of the world in the 1920s, the title being Dick's devastating judgement although, as he insists repeatedly, 'The bottom has fallen out of it' (217, 227, 241, 245, 293). It is denied that the War was the direct cause for the general loss of meaning and values. Graves suspects a more fundamental revolution in world affairs and sees the War as one of its consequences rather than its cause. Yet the play, not surprising in a writer whose personal life was so radically derailed by the War, is clearly an analysis of post-War conditions to which it refers on nearly every page.

Also critical of society, albeit in a more circumscribed sense, is Thomson's *War Memorial* (1929). It is a satire on village bickering over the plans for erecting some kind of war memorial – should one have a proper monument or rather a stained glass window, or isn't the community more in need of a village institute, a parcel shed or a district nurse? These alternatives are contrasted with the sufferings of those who have sustained personal losses during the War and do not need a memorial to remember their dead. Another short play, Flather's *Jonathan's Day* (1938), is more direct in attributing the responsibility for the deprivation suffered by the survivors. It focuses on a family who have always observed 'Jonathan's Day', the day when the son, believed to be a war hero, was killed at the front. But 15 years after his death, a visitor reveals that Jonathan was court-martialled and shot for cowardice, and that the daughter's fiancé gave the decisive evidence. Everybody is shocked at the behaviour of the 'traitor', even more so than at Jonathan's role, until the mother explains that she had known this all along, and that it was not the boys' fault: it was the families who were sending their sons out to be killed, or who at least did not prevent them from enlisting. This pacifist twist comes as a surprise, but at least it is not obtrusively propagandist in effect.

A totally different view of the post-War years, where the War appears in nostalgic retrospect as a unique experience, can be found in Chetham-Strode's *Sometimes Even Now* (1933). Progressing through six stages from 1915 to 1933, its plot centres on Sheila Grey who, during the War years, works in the War Ministry and during her free time looks after officers on leave. When one Noel Brandon is suddenly recalled, she allows him to stay with her for his last night. Soon after, he is reported missing. Eighteen years later it is revealed that the boy she had allegedly adopted, is the result of that night. This happens when she meets two other wartime friends again: Dick Gable who in 1915 had believed himself desperately in love with her but is now happily married and Charles Hartigan, a brilliantly comic character study. The play is a convincing recreation of wartime conditions; even if the plot appears somewhat contrived, the author writes brilliantly appropriate dialogue and succeeds in creating a bittersweet atmosphere. Also, he is successful in dramatising post-War situations where the memories of wartime events suddenly intervene in present-day life and black out all other problems. The present situation of the country may be 'an England slowly emerging from a morass of emotion – on to the dry land of sanity. It's much duller – but it's safer' (431), yet the War period was dominated by 'intense emotion that can never come back into our lives again. But it was wonderful while it lasted [...]' (432). And the contrast to the young generation of 1933 is described by Charles: 'These children realise that

we've had some experience of life they'll never have.... (*With emphasis*)
We've lived!' (452).

In contrast to such generalised images of society, some other works
are concerned with a deeply private view of the inability to forget the
War, often coupled with a real or imagined encounter with the ghosts
of the past (as in McGuinness's *Observe the Sons of Ulster*). Sylvaine's *The
Road of Poplars* (1930) is set in Belgium in 1922 where a previous British
soldier, calling himself 'Charley', has created for himself a new existence
as a publican. He encounters a 'Tourist' who turns out to have been his
commanding officer during the battle for the very farm where Charley
now lives. They are the only ones to have survived while 48 men died
because the 'Tourist', with Charley's knowledge, took the wrong decision.
Charley regularly sees the dead marching past his farm. In an eerie scene,
the 'Tourist' hears, and then sees, them too, even talks to them but is
rejected when he tries to join their ranks. Charley then shoots him (or
perhaps imagines shooting him?) to give him the chance to march with
the dead because he cannot cope with life. Interestingly, the dead of
both sides are now members of one great army, as one of them confirms
when he describes the scene of his own death: 'The fellow who did it was
called Hermann. A good fellow. A friend of mine' (341). The play would
be even more convincing if the two survivors did not wish to atone for
a personal error of judgement; such a psychological dimension conflicts
with the author's general anti-war stance and sets the reader/spectator
wondering whether their vision of the dead would have been different
if they had not taken the wrong decision.

The Laughing Woman (1934) by Gordon Daviot (Elizabeth Mackintosh)
is an uneven attempt to weigh up the artist's commitment to his art versus his patriotism. The frame scenes are set in the early 1930s in an art
gallery where the bust of a smiling lady has attracted an elderly woman,
apparently a down-and-out who stays near it all day. The plot proper
concerns a young French artist who in 1912 makes friends with a
Swedish lady almost twice his age and takes her to London as his 'sister'.
Together they live through the squalor of an artist's existence until, by
the summer of 1914, they have reached the first stages of affluence
when René is becoming known to art dealers, and there is even hope
that Ingrid will finish her book on philosophy. René, however, hears by
chance about the outbreak of the War, and although he had always proclaimed himself an artist and nothing else, and had even evaded
national service, he decides to return home and volunteer for the army.
One learns from the concluding scene that he was killed in action in 1915.
The author appears to support him in his decision; for her, patriotism

seems to be the supreme value, even superior to one's devotion to art, and although the characters are drawn quite convincingly, the play ends on a painfully sentimental note.

By contrast to such works, all of which make a significant contribution to an analysis of the consequences of the War (either for society *in toto* or for individual lives), one can also find pieces where the post-War situation is simply exploited for humorous, sentimental or melodramatic purposes. In Brighouse's *Once a Hero* (1922), a factory canteen is to be opened in Sir William Rumbold's works as an unusual but fitting war memorial. It is to be named after the local hero who, however, had been a ruffian and blackguard before the War. Tim, now a tramp, himself turns up before decamping to America. The play was obviously written for the fun of it; it merely conveys the ironic insight that appearances can be deceptive: neither the war hero nor the pre-War scoundrel is quite what he was supposed to be.

Hoffe's *The Faithful Heart* (1921) is an ordinary sentimental play about a man getting on in life (one Waverley Ango) who has to decide between his young bride and his daughter who has appeared out of the blue, after he had forgotten her for 20 years. His decision gains in dramatic intensity because the plot is set against the period of demobilising the Army when Ango, a Lieutenant Colonel during the War, and his previous subordinates have to find new positions in life. In the end Ango rejects the carefree life that his bride offers him, and sails away with his daughter as the captain of a tramp steamer.

Pinero's *The Enchanted Cottage* (1922), subtitled *A Fable*, utilises the situation of the wartime invalid for a fairy tale that shows little understanding for the suffering of the central character. Oliver Bashforth, a young gentleman who was wounded during the War and reduced to a state of dejection and emaciation, marries Laura who is exceedingly plain though kind. After the wedding, they begin to notice a marked change in themselves, in fact they become so beautiful, healthy and optimistic that they hide their changed appearance from the outside world. Only when Oliver's relations arrive, do they present themselves, and appear as emaciated and even ugly as they had been before. Their housekeeper unravels the situation: being in love has transformed them, and as long as their love lasts, they will appear beautiful to each other. This is the somewhat banal explanation for a situation which had been presented before with a great deal of mystification. Another wartime veteran, Major Hillgrove, tries to explain the case to the audience, but since he is conveniently blind, he can only see what others tell him, and therefore Oliver and Laura are beautiful to him (as they are to the audience), which seems to suggest that the audience are as blind as the Major. Oliver's and Hillgrove's war injuries, of which much is made at the beginning, are here simply vehicles for a mystery element which is finally resolved on the basis of downright sentimentality. Even Pinero's biographer, who sees *The Enchanted Cottage* as the most substantial of the dramatist's later work, criticises 'the peculiar mixture of cynicism and sentiment' which 'distorts the point of the play: a disenchanted cottage hardly preserves the happiness of its dwellers.'[80]

An even worse example of exploiting the post–World War I situation is Trevelyan's *The Dark Angel*. A sickeningly sentimental play, abounding in coincidences and cases of awkward plotting, it is also saturated with heroic self-sacrifice and moreover displays a type of Victorian morality that one would not believe to have survived the War. The 'Prologue' is set in 1918. Captain Hilary Trent has spent his last night at home with Kitty Fahnestock who at barely 18 is full of admiration for his heroism, while he loves her to distraction. Unfortunately they did not find anyone to marry them at short notice when his leave was cancelled. Five years later, in the main body of the play, Trent has been reported dead, but Kitty still feels bound by the promise she gave him, and also by the loss of her virginity, although she is now in love with Gerald Shannon. It is discovered that Trent is not dead but has returned blind and lives a secluded life as the pseudonymous author of adventure stories. When Kitty eventually finds him he pretends he is not blind but merely (!) suffering from shell shock, and lightly releases her from her promise. However, she discovers his real condition and is prepared to give up her life to him, and Gerald, too, is ready to make the supreme sacrifice – but Trent convinces them that he has found his peace and that it would be wrong for Kitty to renounce her love for Gerald.

Finally, Zangwill's *We Moderns* (1924) is a farcical satire on the relationship between the generations in post-War London, concluding with a sentimental happy ending. The older generation believe that social conventions must not change at any price, while the young people flout all standards of behaviour, although in certain situations they are glad enough to fall back on them. There are various references to the War, as in the young people's accusation that 'Your generation has reduced Europe to a shambles – and what touches you more nearly – to a bankrupt estate. So before you come the accusing angel, kindly remember you're in the dock' (26), but the author seems unconvinced that the War is directly responsible for the various changes in society.

8
Foreshadowing Another War

Nothing in the post-War years, not even the economic crisis or the break-up of traditional values and moral conventions, could have been as disheartening to the British public as the sickening feeling that the 'the war to end all wars' might after all not have been the last and that the country, for the same or for different reasons, might have to prepare for another conflict. Several of the plays that have been discussed as analyses of the post-War period already gave an indication that the sacrifices of the War might have been in vain and that in future the term 'the Great War' might have to be exchanged for the pessimistic numbering of 'World War I'. The following survey concentrates on plays where the emphasis is clearly on the likelihood of another conflagration *as seen against the background of the First World War;* it is not a comprehensive listing of anti-war plays before 1939. Nearly all of them fall into the category that, by analogy with 'speculative fiction', might be called 'speculative drama', because they are set in some indefinite future that the author either expects or fears to come true.

The earliest among them, Caine's *The Prime Minister* (1918), is untypical in several respects. Where plot construction, character psychology and credibility of dialogue are concerned, it is one of the worst war plays ever written; even *The Era* described it as 'melodrama pure and simple, with some of the common weaknesses of this particular brand of stage production.'[81] That it is also confusing in its authorial attitude, may be due to its genesis. According to an 'Author's Note' its origins go back as far as 1911, it was written during the First World War and produced in March 1918 at the Royalty, but it is set in the *future* when an ultimatum is issued to Germany and another war is declared. It concerns a German family settled in England who had suffered much during World War I and are now to be rounded up again as undesirable aliens. The plot revolves around various (unsuccessful) attempts to spy on the Prime Minister and finally to murder him, changing from an initial sympathy for the expatriates to a vicious hatred of anything German, pronounced by the PM who, because of his impartiality and generosity, serves as the author's mouthpiece.

During the early years after the War it seems still to have been possible to treat the prospect of another world conflict in a comic context. In Calderon's *Peace* (1922), the farcically named Sir Blennerhassett Postlethwaite is preparing a speech for the Society of Universal Peace when he is interrupted by a Burglar. They both draw their guns, and the Burglar blackmails the peace-politician into giving him a cheque for the Navy League, because otherwise he would expose Sir B. for being in possession of a gun, and when the police arrive, Sir B. even has to help the Burglar to get away. Apparently the author is on the side of the Burglar who claims that Britain has again to prepare for war, but the discussion is conducted on a level of great silliness.

The superficiality of *Peace* is confirmed when it is compared to Ervine's ironically titled *Progress* of the same year. *Progress* is a prototypical short play where a conflict of values is taken to its radical conclusion, leaving the reader/spectator no option but to take sides. The conflict here is between Professor Corrie, who has just made a revolutionary invention, and Mrs Meldon, his sister who still grieves for her son killed at the front. Corrie's invention will make it possible to create an enormous bomb which he describes with an uncanny prescience of nuclear warfare:

> When this bomb falls, the explosion will devastate a wide tract of the district in which it falls, and at the same time will release a powerful, spreading gas, without colour or smell, which will spread over a wide area and poison every person who inhales it. They won't know that they've inhaled it until they see their bodies rotting. And nothing will save them! With a single bomb we could wipe out the population of a city as big as Manchester. Single bomb, Charlotte!
>
> (44)

Corrie expects another war in 20 or 30 years and sees his bomb as 'a most humanitarian invention' because 'the only thing to do then is to make war so horrible that no nation will engage in one unless absolutely driven to it' (43). Mrs Meldon on the other hand, envisaging the amount of suffering that the bomb would cause, tries to persuade her brother to suppress his invention. When he flatly refuses, she smashes his retorts, and when he laughingly explains that he has got the formula by heart, she stabs him, taking murder upon herself to prevent a greater evil, a decision whose moral reverberations are presented with great seriousness. The objectivity of Ervine's approach was confirmed when, in teaching the play, it was found that the students in class were sharply divided as to the moral justification for Mrs Meldon's act.

The conflict over new destructive inventions is taken up in several other plays, always combining the realistic experience of World War I with the speculative foreshadowing of another disaster. The ominously titled *Eleventh Hour* by Armstrong (1933) takes place on Armistice Day a few years after the War. Sir John Mackley, a British weapons designer and industrialist, has developed a powerful machine gun which he plans to sell to the British government, although his own son was killed as a machine gunner during the War. He is visited by a delegate of the World Peace Party who wants to buy the machine gun in order to destroy it so that it will never be used. Sir John refuses to sell but learns to their mutual surprise that it must have been his visitor who killed his son, and (the ultimate irony) killed him with hand grenades designed by Sir John. The ending is left in the balance – there is no last-minute conversion to the author's point of view, which increases the dramatic quality, a convincing anti-war statement despite the play's glaring coincidences. In Evans's *Antic Disposition* (1935) it is a distinguished bacteriologist who has received a commission from the War Office to develop a new procedure 'of transporting bacteria in case of war – in hand-grenades and ice-cubes and food and on paper – whatever we can devise' (152). His son Rupert has contracted an incurable cynicism over this project; he says that 'if we destroy ourselves this time we prove that civilization and corruption are one' (153). However, the issue is somewhat blurred because the author sees Rupert (who finally shoots himself) as a foil to Hamlet, and part of the play is devoted to Rupert's Hamlet-like mutterings about the state of the world, predicting 'bodies rotting in the streets; death clamouring hideously in shuttered houses; life prostituted by the terror-stricken men and women that survive' (175) – a horribly adequate description of a coming war. In Box's *Fantastic Flight* (1934) the Oxford Union has just passed the motion 'that this University refuses in any circumstances to fight for King and country' (57) when the Union's President, one Noah Boomer, learns that he has inherited the largest chemical works in the world. Belatedly he realises that his factories produce poison gas and decides to relinquish his ownership, but is persuaded into continuing in order to reserve the monopoly on gas production, while giving peace talks in his spare time. When nevertheless in 1950 another war begins, he sends up a helicopter with 100 hand-picked people who are to make a new start for the world (hence the name 'Noah'), before mankind destroys itself with Boomer's gas. Gas, it should be noted, is here as elsewhere seen as the ultimate danger to mankind, a direct consequence of the experience of the Great War.

Yet another work with a science fiction invention at its centre is Hamilton's *The Old Adam* (1924), a clever play with a novel idea as its central motif and a sobering moral to be derived from it. The imaginary state of Paphlagonia (Britain) is threatened by an invasion from neighbouring Ruritania (which may be Germany or France or any other convenient enemy). The Cabinet is in despair because the country, having supported disarmament, is woefully unprepared for war. However, in the nick of time an inventor offers the 'negative properties of the Hertzian ray' (27) which will immobilise all mechanical equipment, from cars and trains to power stations, ensuring, or so it seems, a 'bloodless victory' (33). This device is set off at the moment when the Ruritanian ultimatum expires. Unfortunately the other side possesses the same invention, and in a total stalemate both countries are immobilised. What follows is a war along ancient lines; the soldiers fight with swords collected from the museums, while horses and mules are at a premium, and the leadership have even 'requisitioned the seaside donkeys and mobilized the circus elephants' (70). A great deal of seemingly harmless fun is derived from the situation, as when a fisherman promoted to Admiral of the new navy composed of sailing dinghies, fishing yawls and coal-barges, complains of the useless naval technicians the Admiralty sends him, specialists who cannot even sail a boat. But the basic idea, a desperately sobering one, is that the people will fight whatever the conditions, marching into war simply because the 'Old Adam' will fight. Naturally to them their own cause is righteous, because 'Would any man die in a cause that was not righteous? When the sword is unsheathed, it is always the sword of the Lord ... if you want peace on earth, you must abolish the righteous causes' (97). That the new war is designated 'The War to End War – at last!' (50) emphasises the links with World War I.

The basic plot motif – the discovery or production of a new means of destruction in a speculative future – is repeated in Dane's *Shivering Shocks* (1935). The central character here is Captain Dallas V.C., D.S.O. who has lost the use of his legs through a German grenade. His next-door neighbour discovers a new explosive: 'The country that owns my formula can crumple up the armies of the earth like a gardener spraying green fly. And simple – simple as making toffee' (124). In this case, however, the moral side is not touched upon at all. Instead two shady foreign agents (probably Russians) try to obtain the formula by force and deceit, until the clever police inspector outwits them and makes sure that the *British* government gets the formula. This is a blatant example of what can happen to the serious issues raised by World War I when they are cheapened into popular theatricals. The fact that *Shivering Shocks* is described as *A Play for Boys* makes it even worse.

However, Dane's play is an exception, because most authors are seriously committed to the cause of 'peace in our time', even if they are hoping against hope to avert another war. A pertinent example is a volume called *Ten Peace Plays* published in 1938, where most of the contributors are highly sceptical (and rightly so) about the chance of averting a second world war.[82] Corrie in his *And So to War* (1936), republished here, takes a satirical approach to the likelihood of another conflict. The harmless Pepysian title, and the overtly comic plot, cannot hide the seriousness of the play's satiric norm. Corrie shows how representatives of the Church, the Press, the Trade Unions and the Women's Movement as well as the Dictator Fanacci decide whether Disneyana shall again attack Lilliput. Although they are all for peace, the representative of Amalgamated Industries sways them into agreeing to another war, the Dictator winning the masses by decreeing that only the over-fifties shall this time go out to fight. The satire is not only directed at Germany and Italy, but also at Britain, especially in the character of 'Honest Ben', the trade-union leader who prides himself on his working-class background and his incorruptibility but is persuaded to agree to another war by the promise of a peerage. In its highly sceptical attitude, *And So to War* is not dissimilar to *Peace in Our Time* (1934) by Muriel and Sydney Box. At a meeting of the League of Nations four ladies – British, Russian, Japanese and American – proclaim their allegiance to the tenets of the League: peace in our time. Yet when a Lady in Black appears and announces that Russia is at war with Britain, and America with Japan, the ladies are immediately at each others' throats, confidently predicting that their own side will triumph. Then it is discovered that the Lady in Black has fooled them with an old newspaper of 1914, but it is also revealed who she was: a skeleton, Death. As one of the participants states: 'All your talk about peace, all the world's little ineffective plans and treaties, and bargains for peace – they're unsuccessful, because none of us has really got peace in her heart' (29).

Another play for women, Popplewell's *The Pacifist*, also published in 1934, approaches the question of resistance to a new war on a less abstract level. At a meeting of the Meresdale Women's Institute it is proposed that the members stage a protest against a pacifist meeting that is to take place on the same night. Only Mavis, whose father was gassed during the last War and who herself plans to speak at the meeting, is against the protest but is overruled. When it transpires that Mavis's fiancé is behind the protest, she returns her engagement ring, and when she hears that the organiser has cancelled the meeting because he is afraid of the opposition, Mavis decides to conduct it herself – with the help of her mother who supports her daughter although she holds no strong views on unilateral disarmament. While the emphasis here is on the relationship between daughter (idealistic) and mother (down-to-earth), the play takes a stance for pacifism after the experience of World War I.

Easily the best among this group of short plays for women only is Box's *'Bring Me My Bow'* (1937), a highly imaginative rendering of a pacifist position. The action takes place on the annual speech day at a grammar school for girls. The prize-giving ends with a disappointment because 'the very considerable expenditure on national rearmament' (204) has caused a reduction in the number of university grants, and none of the sixth-form girls will be given the chance to go to Oxford. At this point, Lady Champion-Cholmondeley, the wife of the Minister for War and guest of honour at the ceremony, offers a way out. In a rousing speech in which she defends 'the great new rearmament plan', criticises the other countries for rearming and even proposes that 'we would follow the precept of the Bible and build two guns for a gun, two planes for a plane, two ships for a ship' (206), she announces that her husband has endowed the school with a scholarship, to be awarded to the girl who writes the best essay on 'A Britain armed means a world at peace' (208). The speech day ends with the school hymn, Blake's 'Jerusalem' from which, of course, the play's title is taken. Mary Blake, the head girl who is most likely to win the prize (and whose father was killed in the War) refuses to tackle the subject and in a heated discussion marshals the arguments against rearmament. When she falls asleep, she dreams of another competition, the writing of the best nursery-rhyme about war. Every girl presents a distorted version of a traditional rhyme, such as:

> Little Boy Blue come blow the alarm!
> There's gas in the meadow and guns in the farm.
> And where are the boys who went marching to battle?
> They're falling like corn to the Lewis guns' rattle.
>
> (217)

Through this dream, Mary is strengthened in her resolve, although she will be deprived of the chance to study and will have to work in her mother's laundry instead; 'But at least [...] it'll be a clean job!' (225). The play was apparently frowned upon by the authorities in the pre-war climate of 1937, and the Lord Chamberlain ordered the following words to be omitted from any performance: 'And if you're a soldier and you're very lucky, you might be elected the Unknown Warrior. That's a great honour – and somebody has to get the job, you know, so there's no reason why it shouldn't be you'.[83]

This survey of dramas foreshadowing another war can be concluded with reference to two unusual full-length plays. Berkeley's *The White Château* (1925–7) which has already been mentioned in the context of 'front-line plays', was considered on its first appearance as 'probably the best play of its kind that England has so far achieved'.[84] In a sequence of scenes, the history of the château is portrayed, while each scene is introduced by a 'Chronicler' who places it in a wider context. In the final scene, the spirit of the house itself appears to recite its story since pre-history, and the workman who embodies the 'history of mankind' (856) warns of another war, because 'in all history there has been no war that did not pave the way for another' (857). The play brings out the futility of war and foreshadows the dangers of another conflict, but, given the time of its genesis, the dominant mode is hope for a better future and the belief that the Great War has ended war for all time. *On the Frontier* by Auden and Isherwood, written in 1938 before the authors emigrated to America, is less hopeful. In fact it is set during another war, a conflict between two fictional states: Westland which is capitalist and fascist, with a leader who is strongly reminiscent of Hitler, and Ostnia which is bourgeois and strongly patriotic if not chauvinistic, with an old-fashioned king. Their position among the real European states is not clear, but they are drawn into a war against each other which results in death, destruction and general misery. At the end of this future war, there are ominous warnings of yet another conflict when an allegorical newspaper reader declares: 'From War Office sources, comes the news that the outbreak of world war [*sic*] cannot possibly be delayed beyond the middle of March' (187). What is significant in the present context is that the future war is composed of elements derived directly from World War I: the dominance of the armaments industry, the mutual mistrust between the nations which turns into open hostility on the slightest provocation, the reciprocal accusations of atrocities, the appeals to patriotism and self-sacrifice, the sufferings of the civilian population, the confusion of strikes and mutinies towards the end, the Christmas Truth–like camaraderie among the troops, including the exchange of anti-war songs ('What are we fighting for?', 172), the ominous connotations of the term no-man's-land, and the ordinary soldiers' front-line experience of mud and rain, culminating in the song at the end of Act III, scene i:

> We're sick of the rain and the lice and the smell,
> We're sick of the noise of shot and shell,
> And the whole bloody war can go to hell!
>
> (174)

Even in 1938, a new war could only be imagined in the terms established by the Great War.

9
Fantastic Locations

A small number of plays, although unmistakably linked to the theme of the Great War, have been set in historically or geographically remote locations, or even in a fantasy world. This choice of setting may be due to the authors' spirit of playfulness or to their fear of censorship and/or public disapproval. It may also be part of the attempt to invest the plot with some universal significance.

The earliest among these plays go back to the period of the War itself. Wentworth's *War Brides* (1915) is situated in 'a peasant's cottage in a war-ridden country' (3), the characters' names suggesting Germany or Austria (obviously a protective measure on the part of the author). The Government has told the men, before they march off to the front, to marry a girl, even if they have known her only for one day, to prevent the country from becoming depopulated. While for most of the girls it is 'a glory to be a war bride' (30), for the central character who loses her husband in the course of the play, a war bride is nothing but 'a breeding-machine' (31). Hedwig is about to be arrested for seditious talk and kills herself, and also the child she is carrying, after sending a message to the Emperor saying 'I refuse to bear my child until you promise there shall be no more war' (69). Naturally the message is intercepted and Hedwig's hope that other women will follow suit is foiled. The play is a well-intentioned but naïve expression of pacifism, directed at the propagandistic attempts to involve the women in the war effort.

Also published in 1915 was another pacifist play, Brockway's *The Devil's Business*, in which the fantastic location has clear implications for the British political scene. It is set at a Cabinet Meeting of an unspecified government while *'Two Christian and civilised Powers are at war; it matters not which; you can make your own choice'* (11). The ministers, who have just heard the disastrous news of a naval defeat, are confronted with the manager of the Armaments Trust that has shareholders in both the conflicting nations and provides arms to both sides. He blackmails the government into buying a new 'aero-bomb' at enormous expense, only to reveal that it will be useless if the enemy acquires the new long-range gun which he is also offering to both parties. In the end the premier decides to break off all business transactions with the Armaments Trust: 'Open up negotiations with the enemy at once. Get the best terms you can, but the worst would be better than this hellish game of war. Stop the war, stop the war at whatever cost, and, by God [...] if I have my way this shall be the last of wars – except the war upon the devils who profit by war, and that I will wage till death' (42–3). That the play's final word is 'death' is an ominous indication that it will be impossible to terminate the machinations of the international armament industry.

The third play of this type, Drinkwater's *X=0* (subtitled *A Night of the Trojan War*) is one of the great anti-war plays of this period despite its brevity. That it was possible to stage it in 1917 can be seen as evidence of a basic liberal attitude in Britain; such a performance would hardly have been possible either in Germany and Austria or in France. The play *X=0* portrays an archetypal situation, the mathematical equation pinpointing the sameness of the ordinary soldier's fate on both sides. At the same time, the choice of the Trojan War is not an escape into a noncommittal past, because the reference, in 1917, to the present situation is unmistakable:

> [...] this is the third harvest that has gone
> While we have wasted on a barren plain
> To avenge some wrong done in our babyhood
> On beauty that we have not seen.
>
> (142)

Both Pronax the Greek soldier who scales the Trojan wall, and Ilus the Trojan who sneaks into the Greek camp, are out to kill in no-man's-land, and, 'terrible in obedience' (152), they kill each other's friends, obliterating both the poetic ambition of the Greek and the sculptor's skill of the Trojan, while the cause of all this has been forgotten. Unlike Drinkwater's preceding play, *The God of Quiet* (1916), where the references to the war remain vague and nebulous, the message in *X=0* could hardly have been more direct.

The play *X=0* seems to have been the opposite in every respect to *Kultur at Home* by Besier and Spottiswoode, produced at the Royal Court in 1916 and transferred to the Strand. Although unpublished, it can be reconstructed from contemporary reviews. In the play an English girl is apparently married to a German officer, but escapes to England on the declaration of war. As described in *The Times*, the setting in a German home seems to have accumulated all the clichés at the authors' disposal, so much so that it comes under the heading 'fantastic locations', with

> [...] the German men gobbling heavy suppers and swilling beer, and behaving vulgarly at an afternoon tea *à l'anglaise*, and being bullies and brutes to their wives; and [...] German wives turned into domestic slaves, excusing, almost boasting of, their husbands' infidelities as proof of German superabundant virility, and German girls unblush-ingly cadging for scraps from an English girl's beautiful *lingerie*.

With remarkable objectivity, the reviewer regrets 'the aesthetic poverty – inevitable, fatal – of a theme which has not originated in a pure aesthetic impulse, but which is merely an "occasional piece", a vehicle for national complacency, or, to put it at its best, an instrument for "keeping the flag flying."'[85] The term *Kultur* in the title had, during the War, 'swiftly entered the English vocabulary as a pejorative term for the enemy's idea of civilization'[86] and therefore signalled, to a contemporary audience, what attitude to expect.

Brighouse's ironically titled *A Bit of War* (1933), at a distance of almost 20 years, is reminiscent of the approach in Wentworth's *War Brides*. It is set in the fictitious state of Sarilla which is at war with Bastia. Three girls meet outside an ammunitions factory: Rebba is a glowing patriot, Lorna has lost her fiancé at the front and harbours pacifist views, Etta profits from the war because there is so much money about for a pretty girl. The people are kept in the dark about the war, and rumours abound: first a refugee reports that the enemy has broken through, then there is news of peace; but everything remains as it was before the outbreak of hostilities except that thousands of men are dead and the country has been devastated. Despite a clear anti-war message, the play avoids the fanatical irrationalities of other pacifist works.

Grant's *The Last War* takes the fantastic nature of the setting one step further, because it depicts a meeting of the animals of the world who celebrate the disappearance of Man from the face of the earth after the last War. Jim Microbe is given particular credit for having finished off mankind, and only Billy the Dog regrets the extermination of his former masters. But against all expectations a man appears: a soldier, weary from the last war and aware that he is the only one left of his race. The ani-mals decide to kill him, but he is saved by an angel who (in a surprising and inconsequential apotheosis) leads him 'home'. The idea of the animals' discussing the past history of mankind and man's innumerable crimes is wittily executed, but the author obviously did not know how to end his play, and it is not clear whether he wishes to give mankind another chance, or whether he concurs with the animals' verdict.

Not quite as far removed from observable reality as *The Last War*, but nevertheless situated in a world of fantasy, is Kramskoy's *Good Morning – And Welcome To The Last Day Of The Final Test At The Berlin Oval* (1978). The plot can be dated to 1917 by internal evidence, although the author also employs more recent devices such as television in his attempt to combine satirical and farcical elements. The satire is directed at the English side: questionable TV reporting, stupid politicians, the imbecilities of the Secret Service; while the farcical elements are reserved for the Germans, from the Emperor down (the implication being that the English can perhaps be improved, while the Germans are hopeless). The plot hinges on the German idea that all English successes have their root in the mystical game of cricket. Therefore teams are dispatched to Britain to steal or sabotage all cricket equipment. The countermeasure by the Secret Service consists in introducing their men, disguised as babies, into the imperial nursery, and when the Emperor visits his little darlings, he is taken hostage and threatened with a highly effective gun disguised as a baby's rattle, whereupon the Emperor orders the cricket equipment to be returned. Only occasionally does the serious side of the War shine through, as when the TV reporter from France announces that 'Our gallant lads have advanced no less than six inches in the last two weeks' (58). The spirit of Kramskoy's short play is not unlike some of the scenes in a much larger work that must have strongly influenced post-World War II thinking about the First World War, namely Theatre Workshop's *Oh What a Lovely War* (1963). Here the term 'fantastic location' is particularly appropriate, for to situate a chronicle of the War in the antics of a Pierrot troupe, a form of entertainment that had been popular in the pier-theatres of seaside towns before the War, is a type of *Verfremdung* that even Brecht would not have attempted.

10
Intellectual Debates

Finally one can identify a type of play which inclines more towards a dialogue on theoretical issues than towards a fully fledged drama. In such works the plot is reduced to a minimum, the dramatis personae are one-dimensional figures rather than personalities with conflicting desires and the ability to change, and the situations in which they find themselves are deliberately set apart from real-life circumstances. Most of these works were not intended for performance, while some did not find their way on to the stage although their authors had had hopes of a theatre career. For the purpose of the present survey, they fall into two chronological groups: those written and published during the War, with the outcome still in the balance, and those dating from the 1920s, when the War could be discussed and evaluated in retrospect; with a few isolated texts from a later period.

Barrie's *Der Tag* (1914), a short play that was later omitted from *The Plays of J. M. Barrie* (1928), was first produced, as part of a heterogeneous variety programme, at the London Coliseum on 21 December 1914.[87] It was published in *The Daily Telegraph* on the following day and also, still in 1914, in book form. In the German translation by Erwin Volckmann (who rather amusingly transposed Barrie's prose into blank verse) it appeared the following year in *Süddeutsche Monatshefte* because it was considered to be, 'als ein Charakteristikum englischer Auffassung und Anschauung, auch für uns Deutsche von Interesse'[88] – a remarkable instance of wartime journalism that one would not have expected in Imperial Germany, because the image of Germany that Barrie projects is decidedly negative. In the play, the Emperor agonises over signing the declaration of war on France and Russia. He is put under pressure by the Chancellor, while he hesitates to sacrifice his honour by attacking France through neutral Belgium. In a dream sequence, the Spirit of Culture insists that culture is international and appeals to him to respect Belgian neutrality. When his advisers return, the Emperor tears up the declaration of war, but the war has already begun, and the Spirit of Culture reappears with a wound in her breast. Apparently (the context is somewhat confused here) Barrie wishes to suggest that the war has been started over the Emperor's head. The title refers to 'the day' when Germany invades Britain, an event the Emperor has dreamt of for a long time because he considers Britain a nation of the past:

> Britain has grown dull and sluggish: a belly of a land, she lies overfed, no dreams within her such as keep Powers alive; and timid too – without red blood in her, but in its stead a thick yellowish fluid. The most she'll play for is her own safety; pretend to grant her that, and she'll seek her soft bed again. Britain's part in the world's making is done: 'I was,' her epitaph.
>
> (12–13)

The play's patriotic appeal lies in the author's call on his compatriots to prove that the Emperor was wrong; this seems to have more weight than the Emperor's internal debate over the question of peace or war. That the play is somewhat confused as well as naïve in its message was recognised as early as January 1915 when Virginia Woolf called it 'sheer balderdash of the thinnest kind'.[89]

Binyon's *Bombastes in the Shades* (1915) is not dissimilar in that it imputes a series of spurious arguments about the War to the German side. In an otherworldly setting, the spirits of Heine and Socrates discuss the state of the world, when they are interrupted by Bombastes, a German warrior who out-herods Herod in a caricature of national pride and self-righteousness. In fact, the appearance of Bombastes is the saving grace of the play: he is so distorted out of all proportion that he must have appeared comic (and therefore harmless) even to the contemporary public. In a discussion with Queen Elizabeth, Bombastes presents the view of Britain as seen by German wartime propaganda: 'The colony-snatcher, dead to every sentiment of honour, mean, calculating, covetous, cold! [...] Treacherously she seizes our commerce, inhumanly she blockades our coasts and seeks to starve our noble, our highly-educated population' (22). However, eventually even Bombastes, as described by Heine, will be reduced to self-recognition.

While Barrie's and Binyon's plays exhibit some exchange of ideas (however ludicrous), Phillips in *Armageddon* (1915), in the larger scope of a full-length play, betrays nothing but hatred and chauvinism. Armageddon (Har-Magedon) is, of course, the battlefield in the *New Testament* where the forces of good and evil will meet on Judgement Day as described in *Revelations* 16; not surprisingly the appellation was repeatedly given to the Great War by those who saw it as the final struggle for peace or destruction. In Phillips's play (described by one critic as 'an anthology of wartime clichés about heroes and enemies and the forces of good and evil, written in a mixture of bombastic verse and melodramatic prose'[90]), Satan, supported by Beelzebub, Moloch (the Lord of War), Belial (the Lord of Lies) and Rumour, calls up the spirit of Attila (the proverbial Hun) to devastate the world. The main body of the play serves to illustrate the Satanic scheme: at Rheims, the commanding German General orders the cathedral to be shelled; in an English orchard news arrives of the family's only son having been killed; in the German Press Bureau at Berlin a series of lies are fabricated, and the Director is punished when, for once, he has allowed the truth to slip out. The tide is turned when British, French and Belgian troops occupy Cologne and, despite their thirst for revenge, spare the cathedral, which leads to the concluding scene in Hell where Satan feels his power abating because the forces of truth, virtue and freedom are about to triumph. The debate about good and evil is a spurious one because the outcome is a foregone conclusion, as can be seen from the picture which Rumour, to Satan's dismay, paints of Britain:

> An island floats upon the Western wave,
> Whose people never yet have bowed to Force
> And will not now; a stubborn brood and free,
> They sway the varying oceans of the Earth,
> And that which was but island and remote
> Ne'er sees the setting sun go down on her.
> She against Force may bring into the field
> The turbaned East and her sea-sundered sons.
> Her most in our attempt we [the forces of Hell] have to fear.
>
> (18)

In contrast to the imagined heterostereotypes of Britain which Barrie and Binyon show, Phillips here sets up a complacent autostereotype: a country that is both invincible and unshakable in its virtue.

Jones's *The Pacifists* (1917) is more subtle. On the surface, this is a conventional farce with exaggerated characters and ludicrous plot elements. The ruffian Fergusson who has found his way to the ancient town of Market Pewbury, fences off part of the common to enlarge his private property, imprisons Peebody's mother in the coal cellar and plans to spend a week at the seaside with Mrs. Peebody – in other words, he defies all conventions of morality and social behaviour. Peebody and the local Mayor react to each new outrage with pusillanimous moderation camouflaged as humane and liberal tolerance: 'We must take care not to humiliate Fergusson, in case he should turn nasty in the future' (38), whereas Fergusson assumes the right to redefine justice and morality. When they remain inactive, formulating resolutions, founding Peebody Leagues committed to non-violence, and find no support by the local police force (which has been reduced to two, one of whom has absconded, while the other is down with lumbago), the fanatical Belcher takes the law into his own hands by introducing the infamous pugilist Tom Bluke, who beats up Fergusson and throws him into the canal. But Bluke turns out to be even worse: in a typical out-of-the-frying-pan-into-the-fire situation it is Bluke now who insists on taking Mrs. Peebody to the seaside. Given the date of its publication and production, the play has, of course, distinct political overtones. It is dedicated 'To the tribe of Wordsters, Pedants, Fanatics, and Impossiblists', the latter term being the name which Jones gave to Shaw in their controversy over the responsibility for the outbreak of the War.[91] Yet the play is *not* a straightforward allegory because it would be difficult to identify individual characters with real people or with nations. While the irresponsible and belligerent Fergusson comes close to the English wartime image of Germany, and Peebody's red-haired shopman who is so bent on fighting Fergusson reminds one of the Irish support for England, where would such an identification leave the far more dangerous Bluke? Instead the play allows the audience some leeway to conduct the debate which is the subtext of the farcical plot.[92] Another such debate, albeit on a smaller scale, is instituted in Monkhouse's *Shamed Life* (1916), a curiously indecisive play about enlisting. While the plot is minimal, the text centres on Claude's internal debate: is he staying at home for his mother's sake, or is he simply afraid, or is he basically unsuited to be a soldier, and what will the others think? When in the end he decides to enlist, he does so with just as little conviction as when he had previously resolved to stay aloof, and the author's position remains open, leaving the decision to the spectator – an unusual case of detachment during the war years.

This kind of objectivity – the confrontation of views, leaving the reader/spectator the option to decide for him/herself – became more common when the guns had been silenced and the gains were counted, often in a spirit of disillusionment. The ultimate example is *Satan the Waster* (1920) by Vernon Lee (Violet Page), a work that has been characterised as 'an ever changing quicksand of semantic subtlety'.[93] An unusually long drama of 110 pages, published with 50 pages of Introduction and 190 pages of Notes, it can only be described as a whale of a play which is difficult to summarise in the present context. In its genesis, it goes back to an anti-war book called *The Ballet of the Nations* that Lee published as early as 1915.[94] This is a prose text (albeit most of it in dialogue) printed on special paper, with decorative art-nouveau illustrations by Maxwell Armfield, a format altogether inappropiate for the grim contents. It describes how Ballet Master Death stages the Dance of Death of the Nations, with various abstractions such as Fear, Suspicion, Panic etc. making up the orchestra, and Satan, 'The Lessee of the World' and 'the World's immortal Impresario', supervising the performance. In the end, the Nations are exhausted, but when Death calls for the final figure named Revenge, they revive, and 'the Ballet of the Nations is still dancing' (n.p.).

In *Satan the Waster*, 'The Ballet of the Nations' has become a masque that Satan stages for the benefit of Clio (the Muse of History) and the Ages-to-Come, not so much a play-within-the-play as a metadramatic exploration of the staging of a metaphysical pageant. In the Prologue (set in Hell) Satan defines his own position as that of 'the Waster of Human Virtue' (11), a negative force like Goethe's 'Geist, der stets verneint' (*Faust I*, I), someone who 'is bored because he never feels love' (9) and is 'impotent on one point. He cannot take delight' (10). He revels in spoiling true virtues, for instance 'the sweet and ardent loyalty of noble lads, ready to die themselves and kill other noble lads, lest dear comrades should have died in vain' (12). This purpose is abundantly realised in the 'Ballet of the Nations', directed by Death and produced in '*The World; a Theatre of Varieties, Lessee and Manager, SATAN*' (31) in front of an audience composed of the Ages-to-Come, the Neutral Nations and the Sleepy Virtues, while the Human Passions (under the collective title of Patriotism) form the orchestra, with Heroism as the celebrated blind soloist. The ballet itself is described by Death as 'the vastest and most new-fashioned spectacle of Slaughter and Ruin I have so far had the honour of putting on to the World's Stage' (41). The dance follows the general course of the War events in an allegorical fashion. The Epilogue, the longest part of the play, consists of a series of sketches between influential people which Satan summons up to illustrate the 'Reality' (66) behind the dance of the Nations, a kind of dramatic subtext to the spectacle of the 'Ballet'. These scenes, projected with the help of a cinematograph and a gramophone (pre-dating the introduction of the talkies) show typical stages of the preparations for the War and of its course and reveal some of the responsibilities, as Lee saw them. The Conclusion, with the revolt of Death against Satan and the belated insight of Heroism into his false role, is moderately optimistic, or at least not as completely pessimistic as the rest of the play would have led one to expect.

The only work that comes anywhere near the structure and content of *Satan the Waster* is *The Rumour* by Munro (C.W.K. McMullan), first produced by the Stage Society at the London Globe in 1922 but not published until 1927. Like Lee's play, *The Rumour* has a stage action framed by a Prologue and an Epilogue, and as in the earlier play the author's anti-war position is evident from the start. However, Munro's work eschews Lee's metaphysical dimension and confines itself to exposing the mechanisms that, in Munro's view, lie behind the beginning of a war. Here the fictitious states of Przimia and Loria are set against one another by British 'developers' whose money is invested in exploiting the mineral resources of Przimia, while Loria has so far resisted foreign investment. In a series of parable-like scenes functioning both on an individual level and in the sphere of international negotiations, Munro shows how an 'incident' involving an English girl is created, which whips up public indignation in Britain and prepares the way for intervention, allowing Britain and France to dictate the peace conditions once Loria has been defeated. In the peace-treaty, large areas of Loria, containing valuable mines, will be given to the victorious Przimians where they can be exploited by British capital, while the 'noble and disinterested allies, Great Britain and France', allow themselves to be eulogised for their unselfish participation in a 'holy war' in the defence of 'the whole fabric of civilisation' (142). Although Przimia and Loria seem, at a first glance, to be situated in the Balkans, there are clear references to such World War I elements as the British Expeditionary Forces in Flanders, the Versailles Treaty, the ongoing German-French controversy over Alsace and Lorraine and the British share in redrawing the frontiers in Continental Europe.

The difficulty of combining a general analysis of the War and its causes with individualised scenes is even more evident in Desmond's *My Country* of 1921. This is a play of ideas with an absurd plot of preposterous coincidences and melodramatic scenes, but with some striking intellectual debates and radical juxtapositions of viewpoint. Act I takes place a few days before the outbreak of the War at the headquarters of the Workers' Party where an international meeting of opponents to the impending war is being held. The scene confronts all the different positions in the anti-war camp in a complex as well as credible fashion: constitutional pacifism (relying on democratic processes and the authority of Parliament) – ultra-pacifism of the Tolstoyan type, insisting on non-violence at all cost – radical resistance through a general strike in all the countries concerned – revolution without regard for the wishes of the majority – intellectual pacifism with all the soul-searchings of the intellectual – violent anarchism – traditional trade-unionism – and also conservative patriotism. The meeting disperses without having reached an agreement (here the play profits from the benefit of hindsight). In Act II a year later the same characters conduct a debate as to how far they would go in the pursuit of their beliefs. Would they surrender their country to an aggressor, would they, on a personal note, stand by to see their fiancée raped by a foreign soldier? Again, as was to be expected, the meeting ends inconclusively. Act III, still in 1915, takes place in Trafalgar Square where the Pacifists hold a rally, confronting a large hostile crowd. Again, they clash in their attitudes and also have to face the irrational patriotism of the crowd who try to lynch the speakers. This is another fascinating scene; the stupidity of the crowd who can be swayed by the silliest arguments is rendered most convincingly. In Act IV, some of the characters meet again, now in a front-line hospital. The author tries to wind up the confrontation of conflicting viewpoints by a harmonising statement that is evidently given authorial sanction:

> JIM. I saw that no man can say where right lies to-day – for we are blind – blind. These men over there are right after their light. We are right after ours. They go to battle with the love of country and the blind hate in their hearts, even as we go. They, like we, are but shadows of something else – the Shadow that Stands Behind.... We are shadows ... led by that other shadow which men call ... God.... There is something stronger than pacifism, even than country – that is love. But love can find itself not through ignoring country, but through finding it. The men and women of to-day, patriot and pacifist, Nationalist and Internationalist, noble hearts both, must agree to differ ... and sometimes ... to love. To love and differ, until the greater day when all the nations of the earth shall be one.
>
> (136)

Although this speech is given additional weight by the fact that it is delivered by a man who, true to his convictions, has served as an ambulance driver and has been blinded while carrying his personal rival out of the firing line, it is not, in its desperate optimism, an answer to the questions that had been posed so effectively in the bulk of the play.

Shaw, in *The Gospel of the Brothers Barnabas*, made a significant contribution to the debates discussed here. This is Part II of *Back to Methuselah* (1918–21), Shaw's monumental treatise on the future of mankind in five parts and seven acts, a drama completely overwhelmed by its theme. *The Gospel* is primarily devoted to the play's comprehensive subject, Creative Evolution, but it is also a specific analysis of the political situation during and immediately after the War (continuing Shaw's arguments from his 1914 pamphlet *Common Sense About the War*) and an ironic attack on the two politicians who were most responsible for the conduct of the War, Asquith (prime minister from 1908 to 1916) and Lloyd George (prime minister from 1916 to 1922), here disguised as Lubin and Burge, the last Liberal leaders before the 1922/1923/1924 elections swept the Liberal Party into its minority role. In two statements by Franklyn Barnabas, obviously endorsed by Shaw, they are described as being accountable for endangering European civilisation and for failing to establish a stable political order after the War:

> You will go down to posterity as one of a European group of immature statesmen and monarchs who, doing the very best for your respective countries of which you were capable, succeeded in all-but-wrecking the civilization of Europe, and did, in effect, wipe out of existence many millions of its inhabitants. [...]
> You were only flies on the wheel. The war went England's way; but the peace went its own way, and not England's way nor any of the ways you had so glibly appointed for it. Your peace treaty was a scrap of paper before the ink dried on it. The statesmen of Europe were incapable of governing Europe.
>
> (883–4)

At the end of the 1920s, *Wings Over Europe* (1928) by Nichols and Browne, although set in a post-War situation, is not so much concerned with an analysis of the past as with a possible solution for the future. Initially reminiscent of those plays which deal with the sinister figure of a scientist who threatens to destroy mankind, it turns out to be the inverse, because here Francis Lightfoot, the physicist who has invented a method to control the energy in the atom, is an idealist who desires his invention to be used for the benefit of mankind. Not only does he wish to liberate Man from his slavery to matter, but he envisages a new world order where Man, 'a Titan, a Prometheus, a Prometheus Triumphant', can spend his days in 'one long hymn of praise to Beauty and to Truth, the Beauty and Truth which from hour to hour Man discovers and Man creates!' (98). It is little wonder that the British Cabinet to whom he addresses such rhapsodies are sceptical, and it is the Ministers' discussions that make up the bulk of the play. While one of them argues that 'with this weapon the

Americans an' ourselves could be cock o' the walk an' teach all other peoples on the globe where they got off' (108), others are distrustful of a perfect humanitarianism, and they all lack the courage to put any trust in Lightfoot's idealism. Instead they try to persuade him, first by words, then by force, to abandon his scheme. Rather than destroying his secret, Lightfoot, the frustrated idealist, threatens to blow up the whole of the island, and, when his vision of a new world is not shared by the Cabinet, decides to wipe out the whole planet. Fortunately he is shot in the nick of time, but news arrives from the League of United Scientists of the World that the League also has discovered the secret of the atom and demands the prime minister's attendance, threatening Britain with atomic bombs if she does not comply; in other words, the very debate which the Cabinet members have conducted for the three acts of the play, will be rekindled. The optimistic ending, promising, 'if Man can find faith, the Beginning' (119), is hard to accept in view of what has gone before, but it is in agreement with the tenets of the New York Theatre Guild where the play was premiered and ran for 'more than a hundred performances'.[95]

Another scientific debate, but of a much more spurious nature, is instituted in Fernald's *To-Morrow* (1928), an uneasy mixture of a pseudo-philosophical discussion play and a society drama with speculations on para-scientific phenomena like telepathy. The scientist Laurie Greville has invited the four ladies (with their present husbands) whom he has loved in his life. They discuss such highfalutin subjects as death, the meaning of life and the power of love. What is significant here is that they do so in a setting linked to World War I: Greville lives two floors below street level, and the doors are airtight – a consequence of two wartime traumas, an air attack on London and the military use of gas. Both apprehensions come true in a new war, and the characters die of an improved form of gas that seeps in through the floorboards. In the Epilogue they find themselves in an otherworldly no-man's-land where they continue their bickerings until they realise that they are dead, and an angel, cryptically called One of Us, explains that the 'beyond' is what the individual makes of it: hell, paradise or annihilation.

Pilcher's *The Searcher* (1929), subtitled *A War Play*, is even closer to the subject of the War, since it is set in a front-line hospital (it is deliberately left open on which side of the front[96]). The central figure is The Searcher, a middle-aged lady who on behalf of the Red Cross searches for missing men but in the complex configurations of the play turns out to be a spiritual searcher for the meaning of this war, and any war. Although there is a vague attempt at a final catharsis, the real impression the play leaves is contained in her last long speech, an inversion of orthodox Christian views (and an example of the play's exalted style):

> I say attend, O audience of this theatre of war! Come and hear, and howl at what ye hear. For it is we – we who remain – who shall fulfill this prophecy! The sins of the sons shall be visited upon us and it is we, their country's citizens, who shall waste the world and break faith and forget, and prevent peace. We shall befoul ourselves with our own filth and make a dunghill of the earth and smell our own stink, and stagger about among the nations as a drunken man staggereth in his vomit. [...] And the grace of God, which is death, shall be far from us until we have been suffered to understand that life deals treacherously with all – with the quick and with the dead – who do not keep covenant with life.
>
> (81)

Both the expressionist mode and the sentiments expressed here make it understandable that the play did not reach the larger stages and was published in a 'Reading Version' where the stage directions have been incorporated into a running commentary on the dialogue.

While the majority of these plays belong either to the War years or to the 1920s, two authors returned later to the mode of an intellectual debate. Gandy's *In the House of Despair* (1937) has a frame plot in which Despair awaits the time when she will be crowned queen of the world. Her servants, Fear and Stupidity, have been doing their fearful and stupid work; as their crowning achievement, they have spoilt all the Peace Conferences and have instigated the construction of new battleships and fighter planes. On a less abstract level, a group of human outcasts, victims of the War and all of them on the verge of giving in to despair, take shelter in the house where they are welcomed by Despair as her 'honoured guests' (77). Yet when '*the faint sound of a horn*' is heard outside (78), they allow themselves to be led on by the messenger of the spring who promises them 'warmth and joy' (79) and decide, in the young man's final words, to give life another chance: 'I'll have another shot. You never know your luck' (82). It is, however, difficult to see under these premises what there is to justify the play's concluding optimism.

A final intellectual debate is provided, not surprisingly, by Stoppard. His *Travesties* (1974) is, of course, a sophisticated memory play, suffering structurally from an overdose of cleverness. Henry Carr, the near-fictitious character who encountered Lenin, Joyce and the Dadaist Tzara in Zürich in 1918, looks back on his adventures as a very old man. In Act

I he reminisces extensively about the War (the real Carr having been wounded in France): '[...] I was there, in the mud and blood of a foreign field, unmatched by anything in the whole history of human carnage. Ruined several pairs of trousers. Nobody who has not been in the trenches can have the faintest conception of the horror of it' (37). When he claims that 'Wars are fought to make the world safe for artists', Tzara replies: 'War is capitalism with the gloves off and many who go to war know it but they go to war because they don't want to be a hero. It takes courage to sit down and be counted' (39). And Joyce replies, when asked accusingly by Carr 'And what did you do in the Great War?' – 'I wrote *Ulysses*' (65). Much of what had been discussed extensively in the earlier plays is here compressed into witty aperçus and paradoxical aphorisms.

Part II Staging the War: Aspects of Presentation

1
Realism versus Reality

When Sherriff, 40 years after the premiere, remembered the rehearsals for the first West End production of *Journey's End*, nothing seems to have stuck in his mind as clearly as the problems with the sound effects. The noises of the War outside the famous dugout caused enormous difficulties for the stage crew:

> The sounds of war had been entirely realistic at the Apollo Theatre when the play had been given a private performance, but in the Savoy Theatre the situation was different and disastrous. The space between the stage and the back wall was narrower, and the sound effects, so realistic at the Apollo, were hardened against the bare brick wall at the Savoy. They were thrown back into the auditorium stripped of all their realism, and *without realism the play was lost.*[97]

The quotation pinpoints the problems surrounding the concept of stage realism, as Sherriff and others saw it, often confusing 'realism' with 'reality'. What Sherriff referred to was after all a kind of *fake realism*, substituting (as the stage regularly does) imitation effects for the reality of the War:

> The sharp rapping of a machine gun was produced by a man with a cane in either hand, hitting the hard leather seat of a chair as fast as he could do it. The solitary crack and whine of a sniper's bullet came from a blow on a wooden box and a thin drawn-out note on a whistle. The nearby explosion of light shells was done by detonating charges fixed in a big iron tank, and distant heavy gunfire came from a big drum hanging from a cross beam that swung when hit, to give a deep echoing rumble.[98]

What Sherriff did not understand was that the 'realism' of the sound effects was merely a minor aspect of the 'realism' of the play as a whole, encompassing dialogue and characterisation as well as setting, mood and plot:

> Dialogue came easily: I merely had to write down what people said. I didn't have to turn up the dictionary for flowery words and hunt through my book of synonyms. The other characters walked in without invitation. I had known them all so well in the trenches that the play was an open house for them.[...]
>
> A Company Headquarters dugout in the front line made a perfect natural setting for the theatre.[99]

The impression of surface 'realism' was underlined when Laurence Olivier, who created the role of Stanhope at the Apollo, wore on stage Sherriff's tunic, Sam Browne belt and revolver from his front-line service.[100]

Sherriff's tacit assumption, put into so many words at the time by nearly all the reviewers, was that his play presented (rather than *repre*-sented) the reality of the War. Most writers of 'realistic' war plays at the time would have agreed with Malleson who wrote of *'D' Company* that 'there is scarcely a sentence in it that I did not hear, or an episode I did not witness.'[101] With the benefit of hindsight it is easy to see that such a view is far from the mark. This is glaringly obvious in Sherriff's dialogue: not only does it omit all the words (four-letter, six-letter or otherwise) characteristic of front-line vocabulary; his characters also converse in grammatically correct and well-formulated sentences and, even at moments of high emotional strain, politely refrain from interrupting each other. The dialogue of course reflects the personalities, and these to a large extent were types familiar from a section of popular literature which in turn reflected the experience of British society: that of the public school. A.C. Ward was one of the first to identify the provenance of Sherriff's characters: '[...] the famous Somme dug-out was a replica of any good public-school – narrower, dirtier, and more dangerous. All the regular public-school figures appeared in it: the attitude, emotions and psychology derived wholly from public-school standards.'[102] Ward later exempts the minor figures of Hardy and Trotter from this judgement; but Stanhope and Raleigh in particular are in his view products not only of the public-school system but of public-school *literature*.

Again, the *plot* of *Journey's End* is far removed from the haphazardness of reality. In Act I the characters arrive in the dugout, entering at suitable intervals so that they can be introduced one by one, and in Act II the tension between them builds up so that the catastrophe of Act III becomes unavoidable. That Raleigh should be posted to the very company commanded by his former school-hero who is also his sister's boyfriend, is a one-in-one-thousand-and-eight-hundred coincidence (as Stanhope works out, 45), the sort of unlikely event the dramatist requires to set his plot in motion (although Sherriff provides a rather lame justification when Raleigh refers to the intervention by his general uncle [28]). Finally, the presentation of the front-line atmosphere was bound to lag far behind the situation experienced in the trenches; even the most ingenious scene designer could not replicate the sense of the ubiquitous mud, the permanent rain, the stench from overflowing latrines and the interminable irritation caused by the ever-present lice.

All this is not to say that Sherriff is not a skilful writer; in fact his dialogue is excellently suited to his purpose, his characters generate a certain amount of empathy, and the structure is well made in the sense of a 'well-made play' (which, of course, is eminently preferable to a badly made play). The play's national and international success would be difficult to understand if it did not have such qualities. The point here is that the play's claim to authenticity, in the sense of one-to-one approximation to observable reality, is limited.

Such a statement goes against what was felt almost unanimously by the contemporary reviewers. Bracco, in summarising the play's press reception, concluded, 'The leitmotif of the reviews in Britain was praise of its realism',[103] and from the examples she cites it is clear that 'realism' here was seen as synonymous with 'reality'. C.O.G. Douie, in a lengthy article written after the spate of first-night notices had subsided, still concluded that 'We are spared nothing in this play. This is war as it really was. [...] To the soldier *Journey's End* is a record, remarkable in its fidelity, of his own experience of war.'[104] There were few dissenting voices, and most of these came from authors who did not take issue with the presentation of front-line reality but objected to *Journey's End* because they claimed that the War had been fought on a higher level of morality and patriotism. Frank Fox, while generously conceding that the play 'is not to be put in the same class with the German masterpieces of muck', claimed that 'in the view of every soldier who served, whom I have questioned on the subject, it gives a false idea of that life; [...]'.[105] This was echoed in Douglas Jerrold's pamphlet *The Lie about the War* which admitted that *Journey's End*, 'that fine play', was 'to the credit of present day war literature', but criticised that it erred on the grounds of 'statistical falsity'.[106] Where such extraneous motives did *not* obtain, it was only when the gap between experienced reality and staged artificiality became excessively wide, that the reviewers commented on it, as in a *Times* review of Page's 1918 spy play *By Pigeon Post*: 'To and fro, and up and down, and in and out goes the action, never flagging, never quite so intelligible as to be taken for granted, *never even approaching the line that divides, and must divide, the real war from the war of which the stage can make entertainment.*'[107]

The one dissenting voice that went to the heart of the problem came from O'Casey who, when writing *The Silver Tassie*, had set out to capture the War in a totally new way:

> I had seen war plays where attempts at 'realism' would consist of explosions that would near lift one out of one's seat. I determined to do a play in which a shot wouldn't be heard. And, to depict the war it would have been useless to try to make it real (I've heard of a pro-duction of *Journey's End* in which real grass grew on the sandbags); so I set out to show the spirit of war, and, to judge by the howling, it seems to be a success.[108]

The crux of the matter is, of course, the dichotomy between 'realism' and 'reality', a dichotomy that cannot be bridged on the stage by real grass growing on the sandbags. As O'Casey saw it, drama cannot directly mir-ror 'life' as experienced by the spectator in the stalls. In a text designed for performance, the irrationality of human behaviour is subjected to the conventions of 'characterisation', to the demands of the actor and to the necessity to create recognisable human beings which can be 'summed up' in a limited time span. Isolated (and often haphazard) occurrences are streamlined into a coherent plot; the author's thematic concerns are foregrounded to an extent that would be impossible in 'real life'; the requirements of the stage demand a reduction in the num-ber of settings; the author imposes a structure on events that is utterly foreign to the spectator's experience; and the concept of a 'beginning' and an 'end', unavoidable in a stage play, is far removed from the world of observable reality. Life as experienced outside the theatre has no fore-knowledge of the future, every moment holding the seeds of countless possibilities, while in a play one can be certain that the future is struc-turally implicit in the stage events, because the author has already preselected a limited number of possibilities and has taken them to some kind of conclusion. The spectator therefore will tacitly accept that everything he sees on stage has been processed through a net composed of practical stage requirements, the limitations of time and space and the author's specific intentions.

In a wider sense, this is an aspect of the conflict between 'realism' and 'illusion', a theme that is developed simultaneously on several levels in Bell's little-known play *Symphony in Illusion*. On one level, the group of amateur actresses who prepare for the performance of an anti-war play, discuss the necessity of realistic scenery to achieve an impression on the audience. While one of the girls insists, 'If you want to convince people you must give them reality' (88), another counters, 'Well, if we make this scene realistic we'll have to fire shells into the audience, and then we'll have no audience' (72) and adds later: 'Realism! Are not thousands of maimed men going about to-day? They are real enough, aren't they?' (88). From this, she draws the only possible conclusion: 'What are we trying to do? To create an illusion!' (72). On a further level, the play *in its structure* demonstrates the conflict between reality and illusion. While in the frame scenes the girls practise the irrationalities and non-sequiturs of ordinary conversation, with questions that remain unanswered, arguments that lead nowhere, and personal animosities obscuring the seriousness of the issues under discussion, the play they perform presents – in measured speech, long monologues and clearly structured conflicts – the illusion of the theatre as opposed to the reality of everyday life. This play is a remarkable document of theatrical thinking in that it goes beyond the strategies underlying most other war plays.

'Realism', probably the most abused term in the history of literary criticism, has in the course of time been invested with a variety of meanings. Applied to the drama in general and to World War I drama in particular, the nearest approximation to a definition might be that 'realism' denotes a sequence of stage events that do not immediately provoke the spectator's scepticism and do not make great demands on his suspension of disbelief, events that one might accept as *not impossible* to have happened to certain people under certain circumstances at certain places and times. As such, it is opposed to a variety of plays where the author has deliberately set out to *disturb* the spectator's sense of 'reality'. It is under such restrictions that *Journey's End* can be accepted – and praised – as a realistic play. Quite clearly it is part of the crisis of representation that has always been implicit in 'realistic' literature but came to a head when the events of the War, and in particular the events of the front-line situation, were to be shown on stage. *Journey's End* has been chosen here to illustrate this crisis of representation precisely because it is one of the best examples of a 'realistic' World War I play. As such, it is representative of the majority of plays, except that it is a better work than most.

It is not surprising that most plays do not give a *comprehensive* picture of the War. Three hundred years before, Shakespeare's Chorus, in the Prologue to *Henry V,* had already asked, 'Can this cock-pit hold / The vasty fields of France?' and had humbly begged

> [...] to admit th'excuse
> Of time, of numbers, and due course of things,
> Which cannot in their huge and proper life,
> Be here presented.

What distinguishes many World War I plays from *Henry V* is that the authors have not even *attempted* to encompass the War in their metaphorical cockpits but have restricted themselves to the recreation of individual situations. It is precisely this aspect that in later years led to the widespread criticism of such plays as not 'true' or 'faithful', because each of them approaches the War from the angle of some specific, personalised occurrence that differs markedly from others and can therefore be dismissed as not 'typical'. Approximately two-thirds of the plays discussed in the present study fall into the category that can, with the reservations in mind that have been voiced above, be classified as 'realistic'.

Nearly all the texts that have been grouped together as 'front-line plays' are 'realistic' in the sense described here. This is true in particular of the three plays that almost give the impression of a front-line triptych (although they were not intended as such): *Journey's End* flanked by Wall's *Havoc* and MacGill's *Suspense*, each of them set during the German spring offensive of 1918. In the field of dialogue, *Suspense* comes closer than the others to the reality of the front-line situation, not only because the play has a remarkable character who 'can rip for five minutes and not the same swear word twice' (28), but also because it has scenes that, in the use of minimal syntax, trench vocabulary and rhyming slang, sound more authentic than anything in *Journey's End*:

VOICE. Who's out there?
SCRUFFY. Me and Lomax if there's anything on.
VOICE. Righto. Crown and Anchor.
SCRUFFY. Don't play Crown and Anchor, me. Gave it up since I've 'ad trench fever.
VOICE. You ain't 'ad trench fever, Scruffy. 'Ave you the rhino?
SCRUFFY. Splashed it last Red Lamp parade![109]
VOICE. Righto. You ain't no good if you ain't got the dough.
ANOTHER VOICE (*from left*). It's all right. There are six o' us 'ere, now.

FIRST VOICE. Put it down thick and 'eavy. The more you put down the
less you pick up. The Di, the Mud Hook, and the Ole Sergeant-Major.
Where you like and where you fancy! The old man doesn't mind.

(12)

Even some of the post-World War II plays, like Home's *A Christmas
Truce*, Johnston's *How Many Miles to Babylon?*, Wilson's *Hamp* or Murphy's
Absent Comrades, still revert to the conventions of the realistic front-line
play by concentrating on individual scenes between individualised characters, without any attempt to derive some general significance from the
characters' specific experience. The different degrees of credibility that
these plays achieve are merely a matter of the authors' varying ability to
recreate a semblance of reality, with Hickey's *Over the Top* at the bottom
of the list and Murphy's *Absent Comrades* near the top. The confusions
resulting from the application of the term 'realism' to such plays can be
illustrated from a review of Ackerley's *The Prisoners of War* at the
Cambridge Amateur Dramatic Club in 1929:

> [...] it forced itself on us, not so much from any greatness of theme,
> as rather because in the most comprehensive sense of the word [?] it
> was 'Realistic'. [...] there is in the action and dialogue something so
> very personal to all of us. And thus though the characters may be
> rather too cleverly portrayed, and viewed perhaps from only one
> angle, yet they convince us that, had we been inside their very smart
> uniforms, we too would have behaved in the same ridiculous way. And
> since the story is most improbable, this becomes a singular feat.[110]

The group of realistic war plays is not, however, restricted to works
situated in a front-line setting. A number of 'home front' and 'return-
of-the-soldier' plays are equally characterised by the limitations of the
sub-genre and the absence of a generalised authorial purpose. Sometimes,
as in Hannan's *Elizabeth Gordon Quinn*, the author's attempt at slice-of-life
presentation is blurred by a peculiarly out-of-focus perspective, occasioned perhaps by the semi-autobiographical background. Even where
(as in Rowbotham's *Friends of Alice Wheeldon*) it is the author's declared
intention to depict the stage characters as representatives of a larger
group, the emphasis is on individual experience and the (often irrelevant) details of private events. Such plays are not so much about the
War as about individuals whose misfortune it is to exist at such a time.
This is true in particular of most of the wartime and post-War *comedies*,
especially those produced in the West End, such as Berkeley's *French*

Leave and Jesse's *Billeted*. Given the type of audience they attracted, the suspension of disbelief, the acceptance of coincidences and awkward plotting and the submission to the superficialities of characterisation were here more easily achieved than elsewhere, but the authors' tendency is the same: to create an illusion of reality by avoiding all suggestions that would run counter to such an illusion.

One of the most illusion-destroying elements is the manipulation of the passing of time. Few full-length plays present a continuous action; the majority offer three or five uninterrupted scenes separated by pauses that are supposed to last from a few minutes to several years. Usually the authors relegate the gaps in the temporal continuum to the breaks between the acts, indicated by the lowering of the curtain and often additionally emphasised by an interval for the audience, while some (like *Journey's End*) provide for additional discontinuities in the time sequence by demanding the lowering of the curtain in the middle of an act. Such a hiatus necessitates either an exposition scene at the beginning of each act, informing the audience how much time has passed in the interval, or (which is even more awkward) an explanation in the printed programme. While the manipulation of the progression of time is not specific to the war play, it is of particular relevance to works that focus on the consequences of the wartime experience in future years, such as Chetham-Strode's *Sometimes Even Now*, where the passage of time is foregrounded even in the title.

The one dramatic form that as a rule avoids the lacunae in the time sequence is the *short play*. By virtue of its brevity and its concentration on one isolated situation, it dispenses with the – essentially unrealistic – splitting-up of the continuum and is closer in this respect to the direct presentation of reality than the average full-length play. Some of the short plays discussed above are therefore distinguished by an approximation to the reality of war that three- or five-act plays cannot achieve. This is true of plays by the recognised masters of the short form such as Barrie (especially in *The New Word*), Galsworthy (in *The Sun* and *Defeat*) or Brighouse (*Once a Hero*), but also in works by lesser known authors such as Flather's *Jonathan's Day*, Malleson's *Black 'Ell*, Monkhouse's *Night Watches*, Peach's *Shells* and Stewart's excellent *The Home Front*. The latter is exceptional in that it comes close to portraying an *archetypal* rather than an individualised wartime situation without however relinquishing the hold on observed reality. The advantages of the short form for depicting a real-life situation are taken to their limits in Murphy's *Absent Comrades* which could be termed a 'long short play'.

The great diversity of interpretations that underlie the seemingly innocuous concept of realism becomes clear when even one of the worst cases of polemical propaganda, Archer's *War Is War,* is claimed by the author to be 'a piece of quite terrestrial realism' or 'an almost literal transcript of fact'.[111] The polemicist is, of course, obliged to insist on the authenticity of his presentation to effect the audience reaction he wants to achieve. It is in such cases that the authors' claims about the truthfulness of their works are to be mistrusted most.

The existence of a bulk of 'realistic plays' in the most basic sense of the term renders all the more remarkable those works which deviate in some specific way from the superficial approach to reality. Nearly all the plays to be discussed in the following sections present an *alternative* to stage realism because they indicate from the start that what is being shown has been deliberately manipulated to serve a specific purpose and/or has been invested with some general significance that raises them above the level of individual experience.

2
Realistic Ghost Plays

Before discussing the various 'unrealistic' approaches to staging the War, it may be appropriate to look at a surprisingly large group of plays which present scenes as part of the course of everyday events that in their nature ought to be blatantly unrealistic. This is, of course, fully in keeping with the authors' thematic intentions. Most of these plays are of the 'returned-soldier' variety, and they centre on the reappearance of the dead soldier in a family environment. Under conditions that are as abnormal as the wartime situation, it must seem 'normal' for a soldier to return home as a ghost. The authors therefore put in considerable effort to obliterate the distinction between the living and the dead, and to do so they developed various strategies.

The most self-evident solution to this not inconsiderable problem of linking the worlds of the living and the dead is the contact established through a séance. Millar's *Thunder in the Air* begins with a mystery scene where, after a séance, a shadowy figure appears out of the dark. Later the melodramatic element is reduced when all the persons who knew Ronnie Vexted before his death are again forced to confront him – either as a ghost or as a product of their imagination. In a much lower key, in van Druten's *Flowers of the Forest* Richard Newton-Clare makes his presence felt through a medium who in one of his fits completes the poem that Richard had tried to write on his deathbed, a poem that embodies the pacifist message of the play. In Barrie's *A Well-Remembered Voice*, the ghost of young Dick appears after a séance that had apparently been a failure, addressing his self-effacing father rather than his melodramatic mother. Barrie succeeds in making the ghost 'real' precisely because he remains invisible to the audience; only Mr Don can see him while the audience merely hears his voice and has to be convinced through the actor's skill in the role of the father that the boy has returned.

Other plays do not even require the fiction of a séance to convince the audience that the ghost of the returned soldier is as 'real' as any other character. In Coward's *Post Mortem*, John confronts the important people in his life to clarify their attitudes to the sacrifice of the dead, and if it was not for the front-line scene at the beginning that dramatises John's death, it would be difficult to determine whether the John of the following acts is alive. In Robinson's *The Big House* it is the last scene that brings about the confrontation of the living with the dead, when Atkins the butler sees a vision of Ulick O'Connor five years after his death in action:

ATKINS [...] Miss Kate, Miss Kate, Miss Kate!
KATE (*coming back quickly*) What is it, Atkins? What's the matter?
ATKINS (*babbling*) I seen him there – in the summerhouse – as clear as the day – Master Ulick
KATE. Ulick? Go away, Atkins, go away [...] Ulick! Are you there?... (*Her face lights up.*) Oh, my dear, you've come to me again, after all these years.... And you're smiling, so I'm right, it's what you'd have done.... (*A pause, she seems to listen to someone talking.*) Yes .... Yes .... So – kiss me, my dear.

(198)

Ulick's appearance strengthens Kate's resolve to hold on to the family home despite the upheavals of the Irish 'Troubles'. One of the most elaborate attempts at confirming the reality of the ghostly apparitions is Sylvaine's *The Road of Poplars* which has a whole company of dead men marching past. The author here has taken special care to make them *gradually* 'real': while at first only the stage characters can hear the ghostly parade, the audience is slowly becoming aware of '*the faint sound of men marching*', although when the door is opened '*the noise ceases. The moonlight shines on the white road*' (339); but in the end, 'real' to everyone in the stalls, '*five or six shadowy figures pass along the road outside the door*' (340), and one of them even enters into dialogue with the stage characters, until finally, with the disappearance of the suicidal officer's body, the reality of the ghosts is once more called into question.

A few plays utilise the more conventional motif of the dream to suggest the presence of the dead. In Corrie's *Martha*, it is the title character's final dream which is employed to explain that the dead soldier has returned to his mother shortly before her death. Conversely, in Milne's *The Boy Comes Home* it is the living soldier who, in a dream scene, enforces on his uncle his right to share in the decision-making at home, while in Box's *Bring Me My Bow*, a play without a returned soldier, the central character through a realistic dream is encouraged in her resolution not to write the patriotic essay expected of her. Another example of an obviously unrealistic scene being presented as part of the realistic context occurs in Griffith's *Tunnel Trench* where Scene ii of Act I, described as a *'fantastic scene'*, appears exactly as any dugout scene from a front-line play, *'but inasmuch as both a group of English privates and of German privates are sleeping peaceably in it, divided only by a small methylated cooking stove, it can obviously be no dug-out that ever existed'* (27). The purpose here is to illustrate the similarities between the conditions on both sides, and moreover the similarities between the private lives of soldiers in both camps, which highlight the absurdity of such people fighting each other.

3
Symbolic Generalisation

Whereas most war plays confine themselves to the presentation of individual experience, a smaller number transcend such limitations by suggesting, in a variety of ways, that the 'realistic' scenes shown on stage have a general meaning that goes beyond a single case. The obvious choice for a writer who aims at some degree of generalisation without wishing to relinquish his hold on observable reality is the mode of symbolism. It will be remembered that a symbol (whether a symbolic object, character or plot sequence) has three basic characteristics: (1) it is rooted in observable reality and can be perceived as 'realistic', one can even (in contrast to allegory) ignore its wider associations without losing sight of its surface value; (2) it is invested with a significance that, when recognised, transcends the singularity of the individual case and assumes a degree of universality that is not possible with mere realism; (3) such meaning is not easily identifiable in so many words, and a symbol can have different meanings for different interpreters, in other words a symbol is *ambiguous*. This is not to say that a symbol can signify *anything*, but, founded on its basic reality, it possesses an 'aura' of suggestions which, when observed from different angles, offers different shades of meaning. These three characteristics contribute to the complexity of the symbol which has made it such a preferred mode of presentation throughout the nineteenth and twentieth centuries.

However, only a limited number of writers of war plays have availed themselves of the symbolic mode, and none of them has dared or been able to create a symbolic representation of the War as such. But in the process of putting the War on stage, they utilised symbolic objects or (occasionally) symbolic characters for a variety of purposes. The most popular among such symbols is the *house symbol*, as is evident from a number of titles. *The White Château, The Big House, The Foundations* and

Heartbreak House indicate the centrality of this symbol, while in other plays where this is not signalised by the title, such as O'Casey's *The Plough and the Stars* and Trevor's *Scenes from an Album*, the central position of a symbolic building is of equal importance. The majority of these plays date from the late 1920s, while *Heartbreak House* and *The Foundations* were written before the end of the War, and *Scenes from an Album* (perhaps indebted to *The Big House*) is a late addition to the list. The meaning generated by the building differs from play to play, and it is of great interest, while describing the process of establishing such a symbol, to observe also what they stand for.

In *The Foundations*, the title-building is introduced realistically when the first Act is set in the cellar of Lord William's mansion. Numerous references in the text necessitate elaborate scenery; there is therefore no mistaking the 'reality' of the building. Its symbolic overtones are equally impossible to overlook, as when Lemmy the plumber (the author's spokesperson) exclaims: 'Next time yer build an 'ouse, daon't forget – it's the foundytions as bears the wyte' (512). The 'foundations' of the title, then, symbolise the traditional structure of society as it was going to re-emerge, in Galsworthy's sceptical vision, after the end of the War. The plot, utilising farcical and satirical means, demonstrates how rotten these foundations are. Galsworthy's approach here is so simplistic that it is impossible to ignore his intended meaning, and his use of the house symbol is the least successful of all such plays.

In this, it stands in sharp contrast to the play that was practically contemporaneous with it: *Heartbreak House*. The building here is usually interpreted as a straightforward symbol: 'That house is more than simply a setting for a Shavian conversation-piece: it is a symbol of England – its traditions, its social structure, its values, its follies, and its fate.'[112] However, its symbolic quality is far from obvious at first glance and its message is open to a variety of interpretations. Beginning with the enigmatic title, the play presents conflicting evidence as to the building's position in reality and its intended meaning. The excessively detailed introductory stage direction makes for a high degree of ambiguity: the room '*has been built so as to resemble the after part of an old-fashioned high-pooped ship with a stern gallery*', while a door '*strains the illusion a little by being apparently in the ship's port side, and yet leading, not to the open sea, but to the entrance hall of the house*', and a small table '*suggests (not at all convincingly* [!]*) a woman's hand in the furnishing*' (758). Peopled by eccentric characters who occasionally utter enigmatic sentences like 'Theres something odd about this house' (767) or 'Oh, this is a crazy house' (777), the ship-like building is not easily identifiable as a symbol of the country. Not until Act III does Shaw provide two explicit clues when Hector asks, with a false alternative: 'Is this England, or is it a mad-house?' (796) and again: 'And this ship that we are all in? This soul's prison we call England?' (801), the question marks undermining any over-confident singularity of interpretation. It is only when one assembles all available *external* evidence[113] (such as the state of the country, Shaw's personal situation at the time of writing, the various literary and biographical influences, and in particular Shaw's views on post-War civilisation) that the clues in the text obtain enough weight to justify the interpretation quoted above. If *The Foundations* suffers from the over-explicitness of its message, *Heartbreak House* at the other end of the scale, has taken the possibilities of symbolic ambiguity to their very limits.

Among the 1925–6 plays, *The White Château* stands out as the most ambitious project to present a building that is equally real and unmistakably symbolic. The château in Flanders is shown from a variety of angles: in Scenes i and ii from the inside, with its dining room being described in realistic detail; in Scene iii from the outside, as seen from the trench-line; in Scene iv as a shadowy ruin; and in Scene vi during the process of rebuilding. Its varying 'social' functions are also portrayed realistically: in Scene i it is the setting for a comfortable upper-class household; in Scene ii the headquarters of the invading army; in Scene iii the target of a barrage by heavy guns, reported in *teichoskopia* by the liaison officer: 'Marvellous! The whole west wall's caved in! Go on. There won't be a stone standing to-night' (837); in Scene iv the object of an infantry attack; in Scene v, set in a hospital, the subject of discussion, with Diane insisting, 'I am going to build up my poor Château again' (849); and in the final scene the object of the plans for rebuilding. It is in this final scene, too, that the author's purpose is revealed with unnecessary explicitness in the speeches of the highly unrealistic Workman who regards himself as the spokesperson of mankind. He equates the house with the world at large as it has to be rebuilt, and in a long speech in which he explains that 'this house of yours embodies the whole history of Europe', he summarises the château's history as a symbol of the development of civilisation.

While Berkeley's château is situated at the terminal point of a long history reaching back to prehistoric times, O'Casey's tenement house in *The Plough and the Stars*, at the other end of the social scale, presents a symbol of Irish lower-class society at the time of the War. Although the early reviews of O'Casey's play correctly emphasised 'the astonishing accuracy of his photographic detail',[114] it becomes clear on closer inspection that such details are the necessary obverse of a highly symbolic situation. The building (originally the town-house for one wealthy family but now occupied room by room by the Dublin proletariat) is presented as a microcosm of Irish society, reflecting the various attitudes that formed the confusing background to the 1916 Rising. The braggart patriot Peter, the hot-tempered revolutionary Jack, the Covey who, as a confessed Socialist, rejects any national conflict, Fluther who is interested in politics and religion only as the subject of personal quarrels, the Protestant Unionist Bessie, the selfish Nora who strives for social advancement, the naïve Mrs Gogan who is untroubled by all problems, and Mollser the passive victim of social injustice, in their totality represent the conflicting attitudes immediately before, and during the course of, the Rising. Moreover, the individual scenes on stage reflect the general progress of the rebellion: when, for instance, the insurrection has been suppressed, the stage characters are huddled together in one room and are finally expelled even from there, while British troops re-enact the occupation of the city in the requisitioning of the room. This 'suggestive use of dramatic space' has been justly praised as 'one of the central symbols in the play'.[115] In contrast to Berkeley and Galsworthy, O'Casey never explicitly states the representative nature of the house, which renders it all the more convincing, albeit also open to a variety of interpretations.[116]

Robinson's *The Big House* and Trevor's *Scenes from an Album* are more examples of Irish plays where the building is the central symbolic protagonist. Both are set in country seats of the landowning class. Robinson's Ballydonal House is shown at three historical moments: at the end of World War I, during the Irish War of Independence and at the height of the Irish Civil War. These three stages characterise the individual history of the Alcock family as well as symbolise the history of the Ascendancy class: at the end of the War the heir to the house is killed; in the second stage the family is reduced to indigence in the conflict between unprincipled insurgents and the brutal auxiliaries who occupy the house; in the third stage the house is burned down by so-called diehard Republicans as a futile reprisal against the newly established Free State. However, the house stands also in a much longer tradition: the drawing room contains *the vestigia of generations* (139), and it is clear that it is not so much an individual building as the setting of a social scene (in Ireland 'Big House' being a social rather than an architectural term). The house is given a character of its own, when the local vicar explains: '[...] I'm extraordinarily interested in watching this house and the fight it's making' (143). This curious device is repeated throughout: 'Well, the big houses have had their fling, drank claret deeply in their youth, gambled and horse-raced in their middle-age. [...]' (185). It is abundantly clear, then, that Ballydonal House symbolises the history of the Ascendancy class. Not unlike *The White Château,* the ending, with Kate's determination to rebuild the house, suggests an optimistic vision of the role the Big House will still have to play in an independent Ireland.[117]

Such optimism is absent, not surprisingly after the experience of the past decades, from *Scenes from an Album,* although Trevor's play superficially resembles *The Big House.* It shows a number of stages in the history of a Big-House family in Co. Tyrone in 1610, 1795, 1907, 1919 and the 1980s. The house was built by an English officer during the Plantation of Ulster, and its realistic-cum-symbolic nature is evident from the start: '*The house Malcolmson has referred to takes form on the stage*' (7), a stage direction that can only be realised in a symbolic way. From then on, both the house and the family become entangled in a series of disasters that arise out of the catastrophes of Irish history. This historical approach is emphasised when, in Act II, a professional historian is engaged to write the history of the house. However, the building does not simply stand for the processes of history but symbolises the *guilt* arising from it, resulting from the dispossession of the original inhabitants of the land.

The house symbol is the most frequent, and the most successful, example of the symbolic mode in war plays, although the symbolic buildings are joined only obliquely to the war experience. Where other symbolic objects are employed, the relationship is equally indirect – with one exception. The 'silver tassie' in O'Casey's play provides a direct link between the two stages of the central character's war experience.[118] The football cup is introduced realistically in Act I when Harry enters triumphantly, having scored the decisive goal in the cup final. Nevertheless, even the first stage direction suggests an added significance, with Jessie '*carrying a silver cup joyously, rather than reverentially, elevated, as a priest would elevate a chalice*' (25). The religious association suggests that Harry drinks the wine that will soon be turned into his own blood. Such symbolic quality is confirmed in Harry's first speech: 'Lift it up, lift it up, Jessie, sign of youth, sign of strength, sign of victory!' (26). When, a few months later, Harry, paralysed and emasculated, returns to the club celebrations, he destroys the cup, exclaiming 'Mangled and bruised as I am bruised and mangled' (102). The tassie, then, represents Harry's vitality which he has irrevocably lost through the war experience, and is thus directly linked to the play's central theme.

At the same time, Harry is also a prime example of a symbolic *character.* That he is not just an individual (although his psychological situation is

portrayed most convincingly) but the representative of a whole generation, in Ireland as well as in England, is confirmed by a sequence of
strategically placed metaphors, by the religious symbolism of the silver
cup/chalice, and by the creation of other characters whose parallel existence underlines the fact that his fate is far from unique. Paradoxically,
Harry's role as a typical member of his generation is stressed by Act II, a
radical expressionist depiction of the front-line situation (to be discussed
below) where Harry as an individual does not figure at all, because he is
submerged by the war experience which turns every individual into a
mere cipher.

Another interesting case of a symbolic character can be found in
Carroll's *The Conspirators* where the plaster statues of various heroes of
Irish history, conversing in patriotic clichés, are contrasted with the charwoman who is down to earth, even crude and obscene and unmistakably
'real' in her use of Dublinese: 'Och, you! You imp! Divil the word I can
have with Robert, without you puttin' in your spake' (119). When her son
is killed in the Rising, she at first rejects all nationalist sentiments in a
wonderful poetic outburst: 'They've kilt him on me, the villains and
vipers! Me one little dropeen o' gold, me one little sprig with the green
leaves on it' (125). But in her final acceptance she turns into the symbolic
figure of the sorrowing mother, a Cathleen ni Houlihan of the Liffey
quays who allows her son to be accepted into the ranks of the country's
dead patriots.

The symbolic mode, however popular in other fields of literature, is
the exception with the authors of war plays. Those writers who have
tried to capture the War in a comprehensive image that went beyond
realistic representation, turned to the allegorical or – occasionally – the
expressionist mode.

4
The Allegorical War

Allegory was not a popular mode with twentieth-century writers. There is a widespread feeling that its possibilities have been exhausted by medieval religious literature, especially the morality play, and by the resurgence of religious writing at the time of *The Pilgrim's Progress*, where certain attitudes are anthropomorphised into stylised human figures. The chief objection appears to be that allegory, in its over-explicitness, is not commensurate with the complexities of contemporary life, in other words the absence of all forms of ambiguity is considered a defect that makes allegory unsuitable for present-day writing. Furthermore, allegory has (in contrast to the symbolic mode) always been criticised for the neglect of observable reality. Whereas a symbolic work can appear plausible even if its general meaning is disregarded, an allegorical one will collapse if its intended message fails to be understood. Again, allegorical works are devoid of the constant surprises and unexpected sudden turns which seem to be a prerequisite of modern literature; once the intended meaning of an allegorical work has been detected, there is little to startle the reader, which is why allegory is regarded as 'boring'.

In spite of such objections there exists a body of English war plays where the writers have turned to the allegorical mode. Most of these are polemical or propagandist works, uncompromisingly supporting or violently rejecting the war effort. In such cases, the authors seem to accept, or even welcome, the tendency in allegory to present foreshortened versions of complex issues in order to convince their readers or spectators of the 'truth' that they themselves felt was self-evident. A number of such works are short plays where the allegorical mode is easier to sustain than in full-length plays where the expectation of changes and developments (in characters as well as in plots) runs counter to the inflexibility that allegory demands. It cannot surprise anyone that the allegorical war plays have found little critical recognition. Nevertheless, some of them deserve more attention than they have received so far.

Their allegorical nature is frequently indicated in the title, either by abstractions such as *The Rumour* or by the naming of unrealistic figures such as *The War God, Satan the Waster, Bombastes in the Shades* or *The Old Adam,* or else by reference to unrealistic events like *The Devil's Business* or abstract settings such as *Armageddon* and *In the House of Despair.* Not all playwrights appear to have been certain about the nature of 'allegory'. Some of them subtitle their works with terms like *Melodrama* (Auden/ Isherwood, *On the Frontier*), *Modern Epic Drama* (Phillips, *Armageddon*), *Fantastic Comedy* (Hamilton, *The Old Adam*), *Tragedy* (Zangwill, *The War God*), *Satirical Comedy* (Corrie, *And So to War*), *Fantasy* (Grant, *The Last War*), *Parable in a Farce* (Jones, *The Pacifists*) or simply *Play*; conversely Bell gives his *Symphony in Illusion* the misleading subtitle *An Allegory in Illusion.*

Lee's *The Ballet of the Nations* of 1915 comes closest to the traditional morality play-like allegory. Although it is set out as a prose text, it consists almost completely of dialogue and prefigures Lee's much more ambitious stage version of 1920 called *Satan the Waster,* where *The Ballet of the Nations* forms part of the dialogue. The earlier work musters among its figures the full range of Deadly Sins, but adds others such as Fear, Suspicion, Panic, Famine and finally Revenge – all these as members of Ballet-Master Death's company who perform, under the supervision of Satan, the Dance of Death. The allegory is structured with remarkable precision to convey the image of a world hopelessly exposed to the machinations of Satan and Death. In the second – 1920 – play (described above in some detail[119]) the number of allegorical figures has increased almost beyond comprehension, the Orchestra of the Human Passions alone comprising some 40 players such as Self-Interest, Vanity, Pugnacity and Indignation: a veritable dictionary of negatively connoted abstractions. In keeping with the general tendency, the number of Virtues (designated *Sleepy* virtues) is shorter; it includes Truthfulness, Justice, Temperance, Equanimity, Prudence and Fairness, while the body of the dramatis personae is further increased by allegorical groups such as the chorus of the Ages-to-Come, the Neutral Nations and the Dancing Nations. A totally different set of 'characters' is then introduced in Part III (the 50-page-long Epilogue): human types such as Father, Son, Prelate or Monarch have here been substituted for the personified abstractions of Part II, with numerous unidentified 'Voices' thrown in for good measure. Thematically this large array of figures is positioned around the allegorical presentation of World War I. To illustrate Lee's approach, the beginning of the War with the German invasion of Belgium (as described by the Muse of History) will be quoted in full:

[...] among these Dancing Nations there was a Very Little One, far too small to have danced with the others and particularly unwilling to dance at all, because experience had taught it that the dances of Ballet Master Death were apt to take place across its prostrate body. This being the case, it was always informed that all it need do was to stay quite quiet for the others to dance round. And as it stood there, at the western side of the stage, two or three of the tallest and finest dancers danced up in a graceful step, smiling, wreathing their arms and blowing kisses, all of which is the Ballet language for 'Don't be afraid; we will look after you.' And danced away, wagging their finger at a particular one of their *vis-à-vis*, who was also curtseying and smiling in the most engaging manner on the other side. During this prelude, Idealism, Self-Righteousness and Routine played a few conventional variations on the well-known Diplomatic Hymn of Peace, the music being conducted, so far, not yet by Ballet Master Death, but by the Deaf Prompter Statecraft from his little hidden box. And to this music the various Nations pirouetted unconcernedly about, although Fear, with Suspicion and Panic, were beginning to whistle, and to clatter that mediæval tocsin-bell concealed in newspapers. Science and Organization were also busy putting rollers into their mechanical instruments.

And as the Smallest-of-All the Corps de Ballet stood quite alone in the middle of the western stage, that same tall and wonderfully well-trained Dancer sidled up with polite gestures of 'by your leave,' and, suddenly placing his huge horny paws on the Tiny One's shoulders, prepared for leap-frog.

(47–8)

The example indicates that Lee's equating of real-life events with their allegorical representation functions admirably and in every detail. Nevertheless, Lee transcends the natural bounds of allegory in a number of ways. The most obvious is the play's indirectness: the whole progression of the War is presented in an extended scene of *teichoskopia*, as narrated by Clio who, alone among the characters, is in a position to observe the stage where the Nations perform their deadly dance. In Part III the indirectness is taken one step further when Satan presents his recorded version of what has gone on *behind the scene* during the Dance of the Nations. Lee also goes beyond the standard practice of allegory in the sophistication of the arguments, especially in Part I (the 'Prologue in Hell') where the eloquence of Satan leads away from the subject proper and prevents the one-to-one equation normally expected of the allegorical mode. The character of Satan (described in a stage direction as *'beautiful, archangelic, without age or sex, all powerful, omniscient, sad, but with much sense of humour'* [5], to which should be added his infinite bitterness because of his inability to feel love or delight) is much more complex than is customary in allegory and appropriate for his role as Manager of the World Stage. And finally, Lee's use of irony is untypical of traditional allegory. Lee's is a threefold form of irony. There is *personal* irony in Satan's treatment of Clio whom he describes in a soliloquy as 'irreclaimably classic and never forgetting her plastic poses; indiscreet beyond all other Immortals, and, of course, an hour before her time!' (4) but whom he flatters to her face into believing that she is essential to his designs. The play also shows *structural* irony when Part III upturns everything that had been accepted as the allegorical truth in Part II. Most importantly, the play is based on *authorial* irony employed to indicate the discrepancy between the sentiments of Satan, which dominate the action, and the author's view which is diametrically opposed to them. In *Satan the Waster*, then, the possibilities of allegory have been taken beyond their traditional limits.

The singularity of Lee's approach becomes even clearer when one compares it to other war plays that apply the allegorical mode. The play nearest to Lee's technique (but not, of course, to the complexity of Lee's thought) is Gandy's short play *In the House of Despair*, which confronts human types in the tradition of *Everyman* or *Mankind* with the allegorical figures of Fear, Despair and Stupidity. The latter hold absolute sway over the world, until the Messenger of the Spring proves to be more attractive than the forces of darkness. As in late-medieval plays, the allegorical figures here characterise themselves not by their actions but by their boastful self-description. Stupidity brags: 'Who is it slips into cabinet meetings and international conferences and makes his presence felt at once? [...] Me! Who writes half the leading articles in the newspapers? Who –?' (60), and Fear claims: 'It is I who occupy the foremost place in the world to-day' (62). That they fail in their designs is demonstrated in a gesture, Despair *'stretching out impotent hands towards each departing guest'* (82), while the reason for humanity's escape from their dominion lies in the sounds of the messenger's trumpet rather than in any rational argument.

Other allegorical war plays dispense with the personifications of abstractions and concentrate on type-figures such as 'the Chancellor', 'the Manager', 'an Officer' or 'a Prisoner'. This is true, for instance, of

Brockway's *The Devil's Business*. Phillips, in *Armageddon*, has a frame action set in Hell with some Satanic figures who are infinitely inferior in their intellectual shallowness to Lee's Satan. The four scenes of the main body of the play are then conducted between type figures (the German ones amusingly remaining anonymous, while the English have been given names, without, however, attaining the complexity of stage personalities), before the Epilogue returns to Hell where Satan suffers the loss of his powers because of the force of English humanity.

In a number of plays, the stage characters are distinguished by personal names, although they remain just as one-dimensional as the type-figures mentioned above. Their allegorical nature becomes clear from the fictitious appellations which have been given to the countries that are at war with each other: Paphlagonia versus Ruritania (Hamilton, *The Old Adam*), Westland versus Ostnia (Auden and Isherwood, *On the Frontier*), Gothia versus Alba (Zangwill, *The War God*), Przimia versus Loria (Munro, *The Rumour*), Disneyana versus Lilliput (Corrie, *And So to War*), Sarilla versus Bastia (Brighouse, *A Bit of War*) or, indeed, Greece versus Troy (Drinkwater, *X=0*). On the other hand, in *The Rumour* the two states 'referred to as Britain and France [...] are intended to typify any great modern states. No special reference is intended' (6), in other words, even specific names do not always signify what they suggest. In each case, the author's allegorical intention is clear: to convey an abstract meaning (if not a 'message') rather than creating credible characters and situations, and the few features preserved from observable reality are little more than excuses for the intended short-cut to an intellectual statement.

Some short-play writers have found interesting variations on the dramatic potential of allegory. Barrie in *Der Tag* confronts the German Emperor with the allegorical Spirit of Culture (*'a noble female figure in white robes'*, 22) who tries to persuade him to desist from the plans to invade Belgium, but the Emperor has already been overruled by the 'men of action', and the War takes its course, whereupon the Spirit of Culture, in allegorical over-explicitness, *'returns, now with a wound in her breast'* (33). Binyon's *Bombastes in the Shades*, set among the Shades *'of various times and countries'* (5), introduces the allegorical personification of the worst British prejudices against Germany in the shape of a *miles gloriosus*. He meets Heine, Socrates and Queen Elizabeth I who, of course, are also typified reductions of historical personages. Down's *Tommy-by-the-Way* allows the type-figure of an English soldier to encounter the Spirit of the Women of England who sends him on his way back to the trenches. Corrie in *And So to War*, in contrast to the three preceding plays, takes a stance *against* the War when he shows how the impersonations of powerful institutions are swayed by the personification of industry into agreeing to another war. Similarly, in Box's *Peace in Our Time*, the national representatives in the League of Nations are manipulated by the figure of Death into taking up arms once more. The three central characters in Brighouse's *A Bit of War* personify typical attitudes to the war between two fictitious states. In Grant's *The Last War*, the discussion about the nature and the causes of war that the other authors wish to instigate among their audiences, has here been taken to the stage itself in a debate among the animals of the world, all of them personifications of various attitudes towards humanity.

Finally, a number of plays occupy the space (one might almost say the no-man's-land) between the presentation of observable reality and the documentation of generalised meaning. Jones's *The Pacifists* wavers between a farcical and an allegorical approach, as expressed in the subtitle, *A Parable in a Farce*. While one is uneasily aware that the ruffian Ferguson, the law-abiding Peebody and the fanatical Belcher are meant to personify general attitudes towards the illegal use of force, certain individualised elements in their characterisation and in the plot render it impossible to attribute an unequivocal significance to them. The same might be said of Desmond's *My Country* where allegorical figures who represent the whole gamut of attitudes to the War are exposed to near-realistic events which diminish their status as representative figures. And in *Wings over Europe* by Nichols and Browne, as well as in Hamilton's *The Old Adam*, Ervine's *Progress* and others, the discussion about the dangers of new destructive weapons has been foreshortened into a near-allegorical sequence, although the pretence is that this is a realistic action.

5
Parables

While traditionally the emphasis in allegory is on the dramatis personae who personify forces of good and evil or moral positions, some of the plays briefly mentioned in the last chapter rely more on *plot* to convey the intended meaning. Such plays are traditionally termed 'parables', a dramatic form that might be defined as 'plot-allegory' where the sequence of events clearly stands for an alternative action that the author does not wish, or does not dare, to present directly.

Jones's *The Pacifists* is a case in point. It is the course of the incidents in Market Pewbury rather than the characters (or for that matter the setting) that carries Jones's intended meaning. The progression from idyllic peace to a series of outrages that eventually produces counter-violence equals the current events on the international political scene. A similar emphasis on plot rather than on figures can be observed, among the plays described as allegorical or near-allegorical in the last chapter, in Zangwill's pre-War *The War God* and in Munro's post-War *The Rumour*.

In Zangwill's play, the dramatis personae are too numerous as well as contradictory in characterisation to carry the author's intended meaning, while the plot, in a combination of one-sided political analysis and sheer wishful thinking, attempts to reflect the movement towards peace that the author means to convey as his message. In *The Rumour* the sequence of 17 scenes reflects the various business transactions that, according to the author, lead to the outbreak of a war, influence its atrocities and determine its outcome. While the characterisation hardly deserves such a name, the progress of the action conveys Munro's meaning. *The Rumour*, however, differs from other plays by its original construction within a framework of Prologue and Epilogue. Whereas one would normally expect a framework of an allegorical nature that encloses an *exemplum*-like sequence of individualised scenes, this order has here

127

been reversed. The two frame scenes present recognisable human beings who are even distinguished by first names, while the main bulk of the play is a sequence of generalised occurrences which in their totality illustrate the manipulative processes behind a 'patriotic' war. Another case of a parable-like action is Box's *Fantastic Flight* where the meaning embodied in the central character is less important than the allegorical significance of the plot, leading up to the startling ending where 100 people are sent up in a helicopter in order to survive the next war and, Noah-like, recolonise the earth.

It will have become clear that no distinct line can be drawn between allegory, with the emphasis on representative figures, and what has been described here as parable with the emphasis on a representative plot. A number of further plays, especially those designed as a warning against another war, could be listed as bearing some signs of a parable-like action. However, distinguishing between clear-cut categories, invalidated by the infinite variety of literary creation, is perhaps less important than the demonstration of literary strategies which the authors have applied in their struggle with the enormous problem of presenting the War.

6
Expressionism

Expressionism was the dominant mode in German drama at the time of the First World War. Dramatists such as Fritz von Unruh, Reinhard Goering, Friedrich Wolf, Hanns Johst, even Bert Brecht and, most importantly, Ernst Toller, rejecting the limitations of naturalism, turned to the techniques of expressionism and its *Weltanschauung* when they tried to cope with their personal experience of the War (all of them having served at the front, either in the line or in the medical profession). The majority of their startlingly new works did not reach England, and expressionism left few traces in British war drama. The reasons for such neglect of a major international movement are many: the non-commercial theatres of the pre-War years that had opened themselves to international works were either closed when the War ended, or, like the Liverpool Playhouse, succumbed to the pressures for easily digestible entertainment, and the West End theatre retained its traditional aversion to foreign influences, while the amateur movement lacked the literary and technical expertise to cope with foreign works, most of which remained untranslated. Moreover, German expressionist drama is distinctly the drama of defeat, the collapse of all established values, a deep disillusionment and the search for a new beginning, an attitude that the young generation of British playwrights were spared, however much they might have suffered individually from the War. Even an occasional influence from other foreign plays, for instance from Strindberg or O'Neill, did not help to render expressionism popular on the British stage. Nevertheless, those few isolated items of expressionism that are found in British and Irish drama deserve special attention because they are among the most successful cases of transcending the limitations of individual experience and of capturing the universality of the war experience.

Expressionism, in rejecting traditional aesthetic forms, relies on a deliberate distortion of observable reality without however completely severing the links with 'real' life. In fact *the irrational linking of rational elements* is one of the constituent characteristics of expressionist literature. In drama, this is equally true of language, characters, structure and stage scenery. The dialogue is often dissociated from the personality of the speaker, discovering instead new effects in rhythm, abstraction and choral recital. The pathos of human brotherhood, so irritating to the disillusioned readers of later generations, is a particular feature of expressionist dialogue. The dramatis personae are reduced to puppet-like (and often nameless) figures which show only a few traits of recognisable human beings and function instead as representatives of larger groups or as embodiments of ideas. The structure does not follow the conventional disposition of logically or psychologically linked scenes which proceed 'naturally' from one another. Instead the scenes (or 'stations'), reduced to a few basic features without individualistic trimmings, are often arranged by the principle of contrast. Since expressionism has one of its roots in pictorial art, it is not surprising that the scenery is of exceptional importance. It often has a dream-like quality, few relics of observable reality being crudely juxtaposed with unrealistic designs of a symbolic or allegorical nature. The use of music and new technical devices like projections, film sequences and unconventional lighting effects are introduced to support the author's meaning. Such meaning can often be found in the radical tension between the individual and society and in the attempt to establish a new relationship between the person and the world, with the concomitant intention to bring about radical changes in society. Frequently, such a purpose is expressed in ecstatic rhetoric rather than being implied in the plot and characterisation, since ideas are deemed more important than dramatic technique. The authors' programmatic protest against established systems of authority, imperialism, militarism, industrialism and the values of bourgeois respectability, combined with a search for new forms of love and dignity in individual relationships, is a *raison d'être* for this type of literature.

Although nothing is known about the genesis of her play, it can be assumed that Pilcher, when writing *The Searcher*, was intimately acquainted with German expressionist drama. When she set up, with Peter Godfrey, the London Gate Theatre Studio in 1927,[120] she apparently hoped that it would be possible to write, and produce, similar plays in England. The Gate in Villiers Street (the second project under this name) was 'a formal venture [...] to set up a regular theatre which, because theoretically run as a "club", was free from interference either by the London County Council or by the Lord Chamberlain'.[121] Among its earliest productions were Toller's *Hoppla* and O'Neill's *The Hairy Ape*, while its predecessor, the first Gate (opened in 1925), had already produced Toller's *Hinkemann*, Kaiser's *From Morn to Midnight*, Rice's *The Adding Machine* and Wedekind's *Erdgeist*.[122] It is from such a background that *The Searcher* originated. One can only surmise that it was intended for the same stage but was rejected – possibly because of its uncompromising application of expressionist principles. It was, however, produced in 1930 at another newly founded 'little theatre', the Grafton Theatre in Tottenham Court Road where it seems to have been the opening production and where it lasted for the respectable number of 19 nights.[123] It was only in the context of the newly burgeoning little-theatre scene with its unorthodox tastes that such a play had the chance to reach the stage.

The Searcher is almost a model of an expressionist play, amalgamating as it does all the major characteristics to an extent to be found in few of its German predecessors. The scenery, as suggested in the printed text, makes use of a tunnel perspective repeated in each scene, whether set in a hospital ward, a cinema, a lane between the hospital huts, an ambulance train or a cemetery, in each case giving the impression of an endless series of nameless victims. Sound effects (the noise of the barrage arranged into rhythmical patterns) and visual devices (such as utilising the screen in the cinema scene for expressionist purposes, and the general colour scheme of black, white and khaki) emphasise the unrealistic nature of the action. While most of the 'characters', grotesque figures moving like string-puppets, are mere ciphers, the title-character (who literally takes her appellation from her function to search for missing men) is, in true expressionist fashion, a searcher for Truth (emphatically capitalised). The language is hymnic, far removed from everyday speech, and often merges into choral recitation or chant. An example of such rhetoric, beginning with the typical appeal to the audience and utilising the stylistic conventions of the King James Bible, has already been quoted above. From a historical perspective, it is difficult to see such language as anything but hysterical, but in an expressionist context, designed to thrust through the defence mechanisms of everyday conventions, it holds a significant position.

It is tempting to speculate whether *The Searcher*, published in 1929 although not yet produced, was influenced by O'Casey's *The Silver Tassie*, published in June 1928, 16 months before its premiere at the London Apollo Theatre. It cannot be ruled out that Pilcher, who was active in the theatrical scene, was aware of the printed version which had caused something of a stir, especially in experimental circles. Both

O'Casey and Pilcher must have had some grounding in German expressionist plays, although in a letter written in 1951 O'Casey declared: 'I don't know what Expressionism means. I never did anything to perpetrate it in any play of mine.'[124] O'Casey had had the opportunity to witness several expressionist plays in the productions of the Dublin Drama League, a theatre club that guaranteed its members a certain number of productions per year. Founded by Lennox Robinson, it flourished between 1919 and 1929, during O'Casey's formative years as a playwright, and it mainly produced works by contemporary Continental dramatists which did not fit into the predominantly Irish repertoire of the Abbey Theatre.[125] An eyewitness from this period confirms that O'Casey regularly attended the performances and 'was particularly attracted by Strindberg and the work of the German expressionists', and he continues: 'But the play in the Drama League's repertoire which had a lasting (and some say a blasting) effect on Sean O'Casey's career as a dramatist was undoubtedly Toller's *Masse Mensch* which was presented at the Abbey Theatre under the title *Masses and Man*; and it was the form even more than the content of the play that appealed to him.'[126] Here O'Casey found a language severed from the person of the speaker, relying on rhythm, pathos, abstraction and group chanting, and enacted against a dream-like background that retained few vestiges of reality, while the dramatis personae were nameless figures conceived as representatives of anonymous groups or cipher-like personifications of ideas. Such a form must have deeply impressed the self-taught O'Casey, opening his eyes to new possibilities of dramatic creation. The conclusions he drew for himself from such models can be seen in Act II of *The Silver Tassie*.

This act is set in an anonymous front-line situation, anonymous not only because the characters are nameless but also because it is immaterial to which unit they belong, on which battlefield they are fighting, what side they are on, and even what war they are fighting. The contacts with reality are restricted to those elements that are common to every war: hunger, fatigue, dampness, dirt, coldness, pain, homesickness, antagonism towards the superior officers and envy of those who have stayed at home. These, and the unanswered question as to a purpose of the war, the undefined longing for a religious justification and the very real fear of the enemy's attack, are the constituent elements of this act. The anonymous soldiers are envisaged by O'Casey, in true expressionist fashion, as 'a close mass, as if each was keeping the other from falling, utterly weary and tired out. They should appear as if they were almost locked together' (3). They betray no personal characteristics, the war having wiped out all individuality. By contrast, the intruders from the outside world (a Staff Officer and a civilian Visitor) are grotesque caricatures, moving like string puppets *'with a springing hop'* (42) and uttering meaningless sentiments or issuing nonsensical orders. There is little verbal communication between the stage figures. Instead their utterances appear as miniature soliloquies, addressed to no one and expecting no reply, even if they consist only of three or four words, such as 'Gawd, I'm sleepy' (38). They repeatedly evolve into what O'Casey calls 'chants', verse-passages either conjuring up dreams of home or extended visionary metaphors of the War:

> Squeals of hidden laughter run through
> The screaming medley of the wounded
> Christ, who bore the cross, still weary,
> Now trails a rope tied to a field gun.
>
> (53)

According to an introductory note, O'Casey wished these 'chants' to be presented in the mode of medieval plainsong (*cantus planus*), and he even provided musical notations. It is difficult to imagine a better form of staging the monotony of life at the front than the soldiers' monotonous litany-like chants.

The stage figures and their language tie in with the scenery that O'Casey envisaged, and are described in detail in a stage direction (35–6). It consists of the ruins of a monastery, the rubble of destroyed houses from which *'lean, dead hands are protruding'* and the barbed wire bordering the trenches, all of this dominated by *'the shape of a big howitzer gun, squat, heavy underpart, with a long, sinister barrel now pointing towards the front at an angle of forty-five degrees'*. At the end of the act, when the enemy is attacking, this gun is graphically described as firing, but *'Only flashes are seen; no noise is heard'* (56). These threatening embodiments of the War are contrasted with a stained-glass window depicting the Virgin, miraculously preserved and lit from the inside, and a life-size crucifix: *'A shell has released an arm from the cross, which has caused the upper part of the figure to lean forward with the released arm outstretched towards the figure of the Virgin.'* O'Casey had the good fortune to persuade his friend Augustus John to devise the scenery for this act.

It might be assumed that O'Casey here had distanced himself completely from observable reality. This, however, is not the case. The scenery contains 'real' objects which have merely been dislocated from their natural context and have been juxtaposed in a thoroughly unreal fashion. Although he never visited the battlefields, O'Casey seems to have been fully aware of what went on in Flanders. The war-damaged crucifix, leaning over and appearing to point an accusing finger, is a clear reference to the numerous calvaries in the war zone and even more to what came to be known as 'the Golden Virgin', the gilded figure on top of the ruined Basilica at Albert which, due to shell damage, leant over horizontally but refused, against all probability, to tumble down; it became one of the major myths of the War, giving rise to numerous contradictory interpretations.[127] The brief interlude of the football match behind the lines was related to certain much-publicised acts of bravado where British troops tried to kick a football towards the enemy trenches while attacking.[128] The hostility of the front-line troops towards the staff officers that evoked O'Casey's satire of the Staff Wallah (49) seems to have been widespread.[129] The figure of Barney crucified on a gunwheel for a minor breach of discipline reflects a field punishment regularly practised in the British Army.[130] And the language the soldiers speak, despite its litany-like character, is shot through with crudely remembered details from pre-War life.[131] O'Casey's presentation, then, is not unrealistic; it renders observable reality unfamiliar through a bizarre mixture of objects and experiences taken out of their familiar context.

It should be stressed that O'Casey uses expressionist techniques only in the one act set in a front-line situation, while the three Dublin acts employ the realistic-cum-symbolist mode. The sharp division between Act II on the one hand and Acts I, III and IV on the other is a sophisticated device to set the War experience apart from life at home, and to dramatise the unbridgeable gap between the returned soldiers and those who have not undergone the experience visualised in Act II.

Expressionist techniques, albeit separated from the ideological background of German expressionism, surfaced in some later plays about the War, particularly in Irish plays from the post-1970 period. In McCabe's *Gale Day*, passages from the court proceedings against Pearse and from his youth merge into scenes in a 'Dream Court' where characters from 'real life' change roles and everything takes on an atmosphere of unreality. In Rudkin's *Cries from Casement* the dream-like quality, often blending into nightmare, has been extended to the whole play. While the prime object is a posthumous exploration of Casement's controversial character rather than the pronouncement of general sentiments about the state of the world, all the persons whom the author employs to shed light (or cast additional shades) on Casement are anonymous representatives of groups or attitudes, distinguished by subtle variations of style or accent and frequently turned into grotesque caricatures. This description covers even the character of the 'Author' who, among the dramatis personae, wrestles with the unsolvable problem of understanding his subject. The scenic structure goes beyond the example set by expressionist drama in that the numerous 'stations' do not follow a chronological order and have to be arranged into some coherent pattern by the audience. Since the printed script follows the version produced for radio, no description of the scenery is provided, but it is clear that most of the scenes occur in some no-man's-land of the mind where traces of observable reality are negated or rejected by contradictory evidence.[132] Moreover, the author demands, in his 'stage' directions, a veritable cacophony of sounds and noises that form an acoustic background to the text. The illusion created by parts of Scene i, that of a public meeting, is dispelled by Scene ii during a dialogue between Casement and the notorious murderer Crippen who were both executed at Pentonville prison. Their bodies were thrown into the same limepit, and Rudkin derives some grim humour from the fact that, 50 years later when Casement's bones are to be taken to Ireland, it is not certain whether it is *his* remains that are dug up, with an indignant Crippen complaining: 'Hey! Hey! You two, watch it, *watch it*! My bleedin foot you got there, me leg ... Him you want, not me – Hey, watch it – *Watch it*! AHHH-!' (10). Black humour of this kind is familiar from earlier expressionist plays, as are the polemics directed against various nations and social groups. The pathos of Casement's concluding appeal for a new attitude towards Ireland, and also his acquiescence to his fate – 'Let me lie quiet now. Work for that dawn. Then come with spades, and bring me Home' (78) – would also fit into the pattern of the earlier plays, without, however, turning Rudkin's work into an unmodified expressionist drama.

McCartney's recent *Heritage* begins with a spectacular dream scene that would be difficult to imagine without the model function of expressionist drama:

THE STAGE IS LIT BY FIRE. A BOY DANCES SLOWLY AT FIRST TO THE BEAT OF A DRUM. THE DANCE GROWS MORE FRENZIED AS THE BEAT QUICKENS AND A FLUTE COMES IN. THE SOUND OF PEOPLE SHOUTING AND RUNNING IN ALARM.
FIRE CONSUMES THE BOY DANCER.
A SCREAM.
BLACKOUT.
SILENCE.

(1)

The emphasis on rhythm as an element on a par with the semantic dimension of the text is apparent especially in the linking passages

where Sarah, a character from the individual plot, doubles as the chronicler of the family stories and the historical events:

> Big engine
> Belching steam
> Green carriages
> New and shiny
> Not to carry our cheap cheap wheat
> But our men
> On the platform
> Tears
> Embraces
> Farewells
> Engine blasts
> One two
> One two [...]
>
> (70)

The staccato rhythm here and elsewhere serves admirably to outline not
only the physical scene of volunteers departing for the battleground in
Europe but also the desperate emotions on all sides underlying their
departure. Again, observed reality is distorted while it nevertheless
remains within the grasp of the audience.

7
The Documentary Mode

The 1960s saw the emergence of a new dramatic genre in the British theatre, the 'documentary play'.[133] Defined as 'group-created documentary on local subject matter'[134] and beginning with Peter Cheeseman's *The Jolly Potters* at Stoke-on-Trent in 1964, it flourished in particular in the north of England. The most famous example was Alan Plater's *Close the Coalhouse Door* (Newcastle, 1968) about 150 years of mining history in Durham, which eventually was even transferred to the West End. Documentaries are based on printed and oral sources of regional or local history, researched with the active participation of the local community and performed in a series of loosely structured scenes, enriched by traditional as well as original ballad material. History is here presented as remembered past turned into a dramatic present, the definition of 'history' being summed up as 'what the history books usually leave out'. The historical processes are exemplified with the help of partially individualised figures whose roles as representatives of a larger community are never in question. The sources of the documentary go back to 'the Living Newspaper productions of the 'thirties, the English Music Hall in its pre-war heyday, the satirical revues of the early Unity Theatre, the Pierrot tradition of the English seaside resorts, the socialistic convictions of the Manchester school [...]',[135] to which, in the case of the war play, should be added *Oh What a Lovely War* and, even earlier, Coward's *Cavalcade*. The subject matter was often the role of the working classes in the development of regional industries and their minor triumphs or major defeats in industrial conflicts, especially during the nineteenth century, while the authors intended to create an increased public awareness of past conflicts in their significance for the present. The creators of such documentaries distanced themselves from the tradition of the well-made play; they even went outside the local theatre buildings to produce their works on former industrial sites which provided a link to the subject matter of the plays.

The documentaries relevant to the present study appeared between the mid-seventies and the mid-nineties and were first performed outside the West End: D'Arcy and Arden's *The Non-Stop Connolly Show* in Liberty Hall, Dublin's trade-union centre; Rowbotham's *Friends of Alice Wheeldon* at Rotherham; Whelan's *The Accrington Pals* at the RSC's Warehouse; Hannan's *Elizabeth Gordon Quinn* at Edinburgh and Bryden's *The Big Picnic* in an engine shed at Glasgow; while *Oh What a Lovely War*, clearly a partial model for all of them, came out at Stratford in the East End. All of them rely on written sources as well as eyewitness accounts as the basis for the plot which is then extended through fictionalised scenes between characters from real life. The relationship between fictional and documentary elements was the crucial problem for the authors, and it is also the crucial factor in audience reception. Another factor the plays have in common is the use of extra-textual material – slides, projections, soundtracks and pieces from the local music tradition – to enhance the effect of the playscript.

The Accrington Pals follows the brief career of a battalion of volunteers in Kitchener's New Army from the beginning of the War to its destruction during the disastrous Somme offensive. The script emphasises the 'reality' of the events, and this is confirmed by historical studies.[136] Even the local women's march on the town hall is based on fact.[137] What distinguishes *The Accrington Pals* from other plays is the successful fusion of the 'documentary' side with the creation of credible, three-dimensional characters both among the soldiers and among the women they leave behind. In this respect, Whelan's play even surpasses *The Big Picnic* which it resembles in other respects: Bryden traces the events of the War through a group of volunteers from Govan, Glasgow, whose locally recruited battalion was virtually annihilated during the War. The extensive stage directions indicate that a great deal of the production was without dialogue, its role being partly taken over by ballads, hymns and folk songs.

Perhaps the most daring of the wartime documentaries is *Friends of Alice Wheeldon* where the author dramatises the different strands of the pacifist movement during the War. She takes great trouble in the Afterword to indicate those elements of the play she invented – a skilful strategy because if so little has been invented, the reader must assume that the rest is authentic. Even some of the discussions in the play are apparently based on fact: 'Here I used information from memoirs, speeches and articles about the kind of topics that concerned them.' Moreover, the localities were real: 'Hill Top Farm is still there.'[138] The author intends to reproduce faithfully the positions of the numerous small groups (the 'Glossary' in the appendix lists about 20 of them), which, for different reasons and by means of different strategies, opposed the War and, in particular, conscription. To this end, she creates lengthy discussion scenes between representatives who are distinguishable from one another by their ideological positions rather than by their personalities, while the plot remains secondary. 'Unrealistic' interpolations, familiar from documentary plays, appear in the form of inserts, such as the 'optional' news bulletins to be read by a voice offstage before Act III (165). The agitprop-like 'songs', which summarise certain positions and provide satirical side glances at the issues discussed in the 'realistic' scenes (their provenance faithfully documented in 'A Note on the Songs' by Tim Myers, 124–5) are reminiscent of the documentary genre. Nevertheless Rowbotham's method differs in that most of her documentary evidence has been worked into the plot and dialogue instead of being paraded as proof of the play's authenticity, but her purpose is the same: to use the stage for giving a wider public appeal to a subject of whose significance she is convinced.

While in Rowbotham's play the title character, despite the courtroom scene and the moving account of her death, remains in the background, in *Elizabeth Gordon Quinn* she is rather too much in evidence for the author's general concerns to be given sufficient stage space. One senses that the author himself did not fully achieve what he had attempted, that is, to present two important wartime issues of a documentary nature. One of them concerns the illegal strikes on Clyde-side begun by the tenement dwellers who refused to pay higher rents. The strikes then spread to the munitions works and the shipyards and brought 75,000 workers out on the streets (143). The other issue relates to front-line desertion and conscientious objection. Both of them are repeatedly upstaged by Mrs Quinn who consequently has the last word in the play while the 'documentary' issues peter out.

The most ambitious, albeit also the most partisan effort in the field of wartime documentaries is 'Part Six: World War and the Rising: 1914–1916' in the monumental *Non-Stop Connolly Show*. The authors' Preface provides detailed notes on the staging of the play which read like a description of a typical documentary play. The actors have to play many different roles and are to be assisted by stylised costumes, masks, traditional music and backcloths in the form of trade union banners; and the political content is to be foregrounded: it 'will work only if the actors are more concerned with understanding the political arguments and implications of the story than with "creating character" in the normal theatrical sense' (vii). Consequently the play is characterised by the constant alternation between snatches of semi-realistic dialogue and passages of verse, spoken by unrealistic figures such as Grabitall, various Demons and nine Shapes of Birds as well as type figures such as Docker, British General etc. and historical characters ranging as far afield as Lenin, Liebknecht and Rosa Luxemburg. Part 6 alone contains 39 scenes and a prologue, which renders it impossible to develop a coherent plot but helps to create sharply incised, snapshot-like pictures where arguments can be reduced to slogans and establishment figures to caricatures. All this, again as in traditional documentaries, is not without humour, but it is of the grotesque variety, simultaneously amusing and terrifying. A typical stage direction reads: '*The* WAR DEMON *taps his drum. The* CITIZEN ARMY *enter, raggedly marching. The* WAR DEMON *stops tapping, yawns, and stretches out as though bored and contemptuous*' (20). While most documentary plays do not shy away from polemics and partisanship, the authors here have taken to extremes their hagiographic approach to Connolly and the glorification of the Easter Rising as a central event of World War I. In this respect they have even gone beyond *Oh What a Lovely War* where the documentary mode has also been used excessively, albeit in a direction away from that pursued by D'Arcy and Arden, which is why it will be taken up once more as an 'Unconventional Solution'.

8
The War in Verse

Most authors of war plays seem to have considered the use of verse for their works as inappropriate, even improper or in bad taste, and this despite a long tradition of precedents, from *Henry V* to *The Dynasts*. Incidentally, Hardy's monumental work, although conceived as a closet play, was staged at the Kingsway Theatre on 25 November 1914, shortly after the outbreak of the War, in a version by Harley Granville-Barker, and might have served as a model for prospective dramatists; yet examples of dialogue in verse are few and far between. Apart from *The Non-Stop Connolly Show*, where one can never be certain whether the characters may suddenly break out into verse, only two plays stand squarely in the tradition of English blank verse drama: Phillips's *Armageddon* of 1915 and Zangwill's *The War God* of 1911, while a few others experiment tentatively with new departures. Since the categories are not mutually exclusive, some of these plays have already been discussed above and will here be considered solely as to the technique and quality of their verse.

As soon as the War broke out, Phillips who since the turn of the century had attempted to revive poetic drama in England, rushed into blank verse in his polemical full-length play *Armageddon*. Blank verse has, of course, always been considered an ideal compromise between prose on the one hand and more elaborate (and rhymed) verse forms on the other. Unfortunately Phillips foregoes one of its advantages, its easy flow through enjambment and long sentences, by separating his lines into a staccato effect. Moreover, he over-emphasises his adherence to the 'great tradition' of poetic drama through the excessive use of archaic appellation, inversion and abstract rhetoric. Here is Moloch, the 'Lord of War', planning his devastating campaign on earth:

> Rise, Madness! Mother that didst bring me forth
> In pangs before the making of the world,

> While Famine, like a midwife, eased thy throes.
> Arise now, Massacre! Thou favourite daughter,
> Got in adultery 'neath a moody moon;
> Awaken to the smell of infant-blood!
> What matter now the cause so ye be loosed?
> Here have I space at last and boundless field!
>
> (16)

Added to its other imperfections, the somewhat hysterical exclamations caused by Phillips's polemical attitude render his metrical composition less than easy to digest. His one-sided bias had peculiar consequences for the versification, because Phillips made one important reservation: scenes on the enemy side are kept in the 'lower' form of prose, while members of the Anglo-French camp, whether at home or on the front, are allowed to speak in verse. This created certain (unintentionally comic) problems for the dramatist when the two sides were shown in confrontation. In such cases, the language of the Germans is suddenly elevated to the 'higher' form of blank verse (33, 74). A similar problem was created by setting the Prologue and Epilogue in Hell. The mythological figures of Satan, Beelzebub etc., although clearly associated with the enemy, could hardly be prevented from conversing in verse, unless the author had been prepared to violate the traditions of verse drama which was his objective to propagate.

When, one year later, Zangwill wrote a spirited defence of poetic drama during wartime, he added some guarded reservations concerning Phillips's play. He criticised Phillips's 'hasty seizure of current matter' because the 'spirit is like to be as partisan as the matter is raw', and concluded: 'Superfluous, therefore, to revive Beelzebub or Belial [...] when life itself offers every element of pathos and mystery, of horror and devilry, that poetic dignity demands.'[139] In his own pre-War play *The War God* he had already demonstrated how he saw the role of blank verse in modern drama. His preface to the published edition, and the appreciation of his play by Archer which he quotes at length, read like another criticism of Phillips's approach. On the technique of alternating verse and prose, Archer had written: 'In spite of Elizabethan precedent, there is nothing more irritating than the drama which is couched in two mediums. It gives the verse passages an air of pompous self-consciousness [...].' Zangwill's own speech form he described as 'a peculiar art of writing smooth, easy, flowing blank verse, without contortions, without Elizabethan echoes. He makes the most ordinary talk (not even excluding slang) fall naturally and without incongruity into the iambic movement.'[140] To which should be added that Zangwill very skilfully avoids the commonplace in his characters' speeches by relegating what might have been all too prosaic to gestures and movements, documented in the stage directions. Also, his regular practice of dividing the pentameter line among two, three or even four speakers makes for a nervous energy that is admirably suited to the dramatic confrontation between various ideological positions. Had Zangwill possessed the imagination of a Drinkwater in the invention of unforgettable images, his play might have stood the test of time better than it did.

While Zangwill is at his best in short-lined confrontational dialogue but turns mawkish when his characters threaten to break out into soliloquies, Drinkwater in *X=0*, seemingly without effort, manages the transitions between pastoral poetry, philosophical reflections on the nature of war and straightforward descriptions of wartime activity, and the monologues of his four characters are at the heart of his play. The opening with its deceptive simplicity of syntax and vocabulary sets the tone for this unusual combination:

> So is the night often at home. I have seen
> White orchards brighten under a summer moon,
> As now these tents under the stars. This hour
> My father's coppices are full of song,
> While sleep is on the comfortable house –
> Unless one dear one wakes to think of me
> And count my chances when the Trojan death
> Goes on its nightly errand. [*The Sentinel passes.*]
>
> (141)

The pastoral scene easily merges into the contemplation of death as the central experience of war:

> There is now
> Nothing of hatred in the blood for them
> Whose death is all our daily use, but merely
> Consent in death, knowing that death may strike
> Across our tongues as lightly as those that lie
> For ever dumb because we might not spare.
>
> (142)

Drinkwater's verse, although based on unrhymed pentameter, is less regular than the traditional form, and the actors must have required elaborate coaching by the author before it could be spoken without being turned into commonplace prose.

A similar approach to versification is shown by Yeats in *The Dreaming of the Bones*: 'I was in the Post Office, and if taken / I shall be put against a wall and shot' (435) the Young Man says to explaining his behaviour, the second line, a regular pentameter, balancing the irregular, almost conversational first line. Yeats has, however, moved a further step away from the blank verse tradition in that he counterpoints the somewhat irregular pentameter lines of his 'characters' with the rhymed stanzas of the unrealistic Musicians where a pattern of three stresses can be dimly distinguished in their evocations of a ghostly atmosphere:

> At the grey round of the hill
> Music of a lost kingdom
> Runs, runs and is suddenly still.
> The winds out of Clare-Galway
> Carry it: suddenly it is still.
>
> (444–5)

The most unusual, as well as highly satisfactory, war play in verse is Fry's *A Sleep of Prisoners*, where four English soldiers, confined in a church, move in and out of various biblical roles in their sleep. Fry here has taken a further step away from the traditional verse forms. The division of the dialogue into lines is primarily based on syntactical units and unexpected images, in other words it is more a matter of semantics than of metre or rhythm. One of Fry's great achievements lies in the seemingly effortless transition from the soldiers' aimless patter to their partial insights into complex religious truths. In the beginning it is difficult to recognise the dialogue as verse:

ADAMS. How's the leg feel, Meadows?
MEADOWS. Ah, all right.
     I wouldn't be heard saying anything about one leg
     I wouldn't say about the other.
PETER. Where
     Did you get it, chum?
MEADOWS. I had it for my birthday.
     Quite nice, isn't it? Five toes, it's got.
PETER. I mean where was the fighting, you wit?
MEADOWS [*jerking his head*] Down the road.

                                  (8)

The transition is skilfully prepared for through utterances as the following:

> MEADOWS. Sometimes I think if it wasn't for the words, Corporal,
>   I should be very given to talking. There's things
>   To be said which would surprise us if ever we said them.
>
> (14)

It is exactly this that happens in the course of the religious dialogues, as when the same character pleads for a new, and optimistic, approach to God:

> The human heart can go to the lengths of God.
> Dark and cold we may be, but this
> Is no winter now. The frozen misery
> Of centuries breaks, cracks, begins to move;
> The thunder is the thunder of the floes,
> The thaw, the flood, the upstart Spring.
> Thank God our time is now when wrong
> Comes up to face us everywhere,
> Never to leave us till we take
> The longest stride of soul men ever took.
> Affairs are now soul size.
> The enterprise
> Is exploration into God.
>
> (55)

It is a far cry here, in the verse form as well as in the sentiments, from the polemical staccato lines of Phillips or the correct if pedestrian pentameter of Zangwill.[141]

In some other war plays verse is intermittently used as a deliberate contrast to prose sections. Sumner's short play *Jimmy Clay* is a highly original work that grows out of an irregularly rhymed ballad about a soldier as he lies dying on the battlefield, and it finally returns to the same situation. In Berkeley's *The White Château* a Chronicler sets the scene in rhymed verse and draws some generalised conclusions from the events to give them dignity and general significance. While here the device is largely successful, a similar practice in McCartney's *Heritage* sometimes leads to the impression that the printing of the 'chronicler's' lines in verse form may hide their essential prosaic nature, and that the verse may not be recognised on stage. Conversely, in Bell's rehearsal play

Symphony in Illusion, a frame action in prose is contrasted with a play within the play in verse, a device that is remarkably successful despite the irregularity and the somewhat commonplace nature of the verse lines. In Box's *'Bring Me My Bow'* the verse passages are nursery rhymes that have been inverted in their meaning to underline the anti-war stance of the play, while in Hamilton's *The Child in Flanders* the central nativity play consists of straightforward quotations from scripture and carols. Auden and Isherwood in *On the Frontier* juxtapose the individual action with agitprop-like songs by groups of workers, prisoners, soldiers etc. as well as with lyrical scenes between Eric and Anna who, in addition to their 'private' roles, are charged with drawing some conclusions from the catastrophes of history. The practice of interposing verse passages, usually in the form of songs, into prose sections has been taken to an extreme by Coward in *Words and Music* and, possibly following his precedent, by the joint authors of *Oh What a Lovely War*.

9
The Comic Side of the War

Many dramatists would have considered it flippant in the extreme to treat the War as anything but a deadly serious event. Yet there were exceptions, and some of these in their various functions – corrective, diverting, therapeutic or otherwise – allow interesting insights into public reactions to the War. It should be remembered in this context that categories of the comic are frequently employed rather carelessly. Terms such as 'comedy', 'farce', 'satire', 'caricature', 'burlesque', 'parody', 'irony' or 'grotesque' function on different levels and have to be approached with circumspection if they are to be useful in distinguishing between different modes of the comic in plays about the War.

Comedy has, of course, come to be used as an umbrella term for anything invoking laughter; however, the present practice of describing stand-up comedians as 'comedy' is causing additional terminological confusion. With reference to war plays, the term makes sense only if it refers to dramatic *structure*, describing a plot that revolves around one or a number of seemingly unsolvable problems, which, despite numerous impediments, are finally resolved in what is called a 'happy ending'. Traditionally, an ending is considered 'happy' if it leads to marriage between the principal characters. During wartime, the degree of improbability characteristic of all comedy plots is increased by the separation of lovers due to the men's front-line service. While comedies in general were *en vogue* on the stage during the war years, especially when embellished with song and dance as 'musical comedies', relatively few authors dared to dramatise a wartime situation; Barrie's *A Kiss for Cinderella*, Terry's *General Post*, Chambers's *The Saving Grace* and *Billeted* by Jesse and Harwood come to mind as the exceptions that prove the rule. While Barrie and Chambers evade the wartime reality by escaping into sentimentality, Terry confronts the situation with some social satire. *Billeted* is the most skilful in its accumulation of improbable but enjoyable complications until the engagement between one couple and the reconciliation of another brings about the 'happy ending'.

In general, comedies about wartime situations did not appear on the stage until the War was over and – a significant parallel to the happy ending on stage – until it had been won. Maugham's *Home and Beauty* with its unfeeling handling of the 'returned-soldier' theme became the first of such post-War comedies, except that here the traditional happy ending has been reversed because the two 'heroes' are happy when they finally *escape* from marriage. Berkeley's *French Leave* is perhaps the best example of a perfectly harmless post-War comedy that utilises wartime conditions for pure entertainment, employing such stock devices as sudden turns, mistaken identities, short-term love affairs, impending dangers and bizarre coincidences, while Zangwill in *We Moderns* mixes social criticism with farcical incidents and the conventional ending.

French Leave and *We Moderns* as well as the earlier *Billeted* and *General Post* employ motives and situations from *farce*, without becoming farcical in their entirety. True farce is almost always based on one individual situation, because the figures (it would be wrong to speak of 'characters') are types who are reduced to one dominant feature and are therefore incapable of realising the consequences of their actions, let alone of undergoing development. It is impossible for the audience to identify with such persons or to feel compassion towards them, and therefore *Schadenfreude* (malicious glee) is the appropriate emotion *vis-à-vis* a farce. Since the figures have little to express, the spoken word is reduced in exchange for gesture and mime and the predominance of inanimate objects which take on a life of their own. Consequently, the stage directions are of equal weight to the dialogue, and even the spoken text is largely composed of disguised stage directions. The wartime comedies listed above abound in scenes of the type described. In *French Leave* the night scene of Act II is an example of farce taking over the comedy plot, with extended stage directions like the following usurping the role of the dialogue:

> (*Re-enter* GRAHAM, *down the steps. He limps and bends down rubbing his left shin as he walks, and saying* 'Ooh! – Oo!' *he hobbles to chair* R. *of table and puts his left foot on it, pulls up his slacks to see what damage has been done, and turns his lighted torch on his calf. The light shows him* DOROTHY'S *scarf on the back of the chair. He at once forgets all about his damaged leg, and sits down, the scarf in his hand;* DOROTHY *and* GLENISTER *peep out at* R. *and* L. *sides of curtain and watch him.*)

(44)

Nevertheless, after a while the plot takes precedence again, and the characters in these comedies may even undergo some – if superficial – development.

Pure farce (in the tradition of the sketches of the music-hall and the curtain-raisers of the older professional theatre) is nearly always limited to short pieces; in the twentieth century it was almost exclusively produced by authors writing for the amateur stage. In the context of the First World War, however, such plays are rare; the only example that comes to mind is Calderon's deceptively titled *Peace*. Much more frequent are short plays that utilise some of the mechanisms of farce for didactic purposes, either in the form of a straightforward 'moral', as in Hankey's *A House-Warming in War-Time* and Brighouse's *Once a Hero* or in satirical reversal, as in Knoblauch's *A War Committee*, Thomson's *War Memorial* and Shaw's *Augustus Does His Bit*. Shaw's play demonstrates how the adaptation of the formal elements of farce allows a critical look at wartime behaviour by petty bureaucrats and shirkers of front-line service with a view to changing it, because laughing at Lord Augustus and his ilk implies a distancing from the attitudes personified by them.

Satire is a different comic approach altogether, an expression of the author's *purpose*, and it is therefore to be found in a number of war plays, for instance in *The Silver Tassie* where it is directed at the staff officers and the civilians, in *General Post* where it serves to denounce class snobbery and in *The Foundations* where it questions the class system. Satire is most effective where the criticised conditions are juxtaposed with a *satiric norm*, which can be embodied in a character (as in Jemmy the Plumber from *The Foundations*) if the norm is not obvious anyway from the general situation. Naturally, satire needs to be contemporary to the conditions it intends to change.

The approach most frequently employed in war plays to achieve a comic effect is that of *irony*. This is primarily a matter of *style*, used to demonstrate the author's attitude. Couched in simple terms, irony results from the discrepancy between what is said and what is meant, with the proviso that the recipient has an insight into the discrepancy (the seemingly innocuous statement 'Isn't it a lovely day today' becomes ironic when a glance out of the window confirms that it is raining hard). Several titles of war plays are ironic, the irony becoming apparent only when the title is juxtaposed with the play itself, as in *For Services Rendered*, *Progress*, *Luck of War* or the subtitle of *O'Flaherty V.C.: A Recruiting Pamphlet*. As part of a play's dialogue, irony can be 'personal', 'authorial' or 'structural'. Personal irony, as when Heine in Binyon's play announces Bombastes with the words 'Behold Europe's modern hero;

the flower of a great nation' (18), is a matter between two characters, whereas authorial irony concerns the *writer's* relationship to his characters. The latter is more frequent, especially in those works where the War or those responsible for it are criticised by the author. *For Services Rendered* has an excellent example of this type of authorial attitude, when Ardsley, unaware of the disasters that have befallen all his relations, sentimentalises over the happiness of resting in the bosom of his family and concludes: 'This old England of ours isn't done yet and I for one believe in it and all it stands for', whereupon the mentally deranged Eva sings, '*in a thin cracked voice*', the national anthem (181). A similar situation occurs at the end of *The Silver Tassie* where Mrs Foran, insensitive to Harry's suffering, brings down the curtain with 'It's a terrible pity Harry was too weak to stay an' sing his song, for there's nothing I love more than the ukelele's tinkle, tinkle in the night-time' (104). In these cases it would, of course, be difficult to speak of a 'comic' effect. In most instances, however, the bitterness in the authors' attitudes to their characters is mixed with an element of fun, as in Shaw's treatment of the two politicians Burge and Lubin, one of whom characterises himself as 'Joyce Burge [Lloyd George], pretty well known throughout Europe, and indeed throughout the world, as the man who – unworthily perhaps, but not quite unsuccessfully – held the helm when the ship of State weathered the mightiest hurricane that has ever burst with earth-shaking violence on the land of our fathers' (874).

Where the author's ironic attitude is not restricted to isolated expressions by individual characters but pervades the whole play, it would be appropriate to speak of *structural* irony. In Talbot's *Set Fair* the family's blindness towards the events that trigger off the War contrasts – painfully as well as comically – with the real events as they were familiar to every reader and spectator. In *The Silver Tassie*, the central character's downfall from football-hero to embittered cripple is deeply ironic, and so is the situation of the characters in *For Services Rendered*. Despite such examples, critics have sometimes complained of the *absence* of irony in English war plays, especially those set in the front line. A.C. Ward was the earliest to point out the immaturity of the characters in *Journey's End* and similar front-line plays and regretted that 'the author makes no dramatic or ironic use of this point.'[142] The fact that the defence of the nation was largely left to youngsters just out of school who commanded platoons, companies or even battalions might, indeed, have provided writers with a subject of highly ironic quality, but most authors of front-line plays were too deeply involved in the situations they recreated to realise the dramatic potential of the discrepancy between the emotional values at stake and the inability of the protagonists to cope with them. Whether a play with such a subject at its centre would still have justified the term 'comic' is of course a matter for debate.

The *grotesque*, another version of the comic, generally defined by the simultaneity of the ridiculous and the terrifying, is fairly rare in British war plays. Act II of *The Silver Tassie*, especially in the scenes with the Staff Wallah and the Visitor, is perhaps the nearest to the grotesque. Two varieties of the comic that are nearer the core of what is generally understood as 'comic' – *parody* and *burlesque* – are practically absent from British war plays. Parody, the imitation of literary models with the intention of rendering them ridiculous, can hardly be expected in this context, not only because it would have been out of place in the serious mood of most war plays, but also because few such plays were familiar enough to the general public to render a parody feasible. The one play that became famous from the start was *Journey's End*, and one indeed finds a brief parody of its basic situation in Coward's *Words and Music* (140–8), while its seriousness is mercilessly subverted when, for instance, the stage is subdivided by '*illuminated barbed-wire entanglements, over which the chorus, representing the Germans and the British respectively, are leaping gaily and pelting each other with coloured-paper streamers*' (145). Coward's scene then expands into a burlesque of the War in general. A similar irreverent burlesque of the British side did not occur until 60 years later, with the BBC series *Black Adder Goes Forth*.

The comic, then, does not play a prominent role in British war plays, even if one includes in the survey the distant relations of the heterogeneous family of comic modes. This is not to say, however, that there are no comic moments in these plays. In accordance with the tradition of what has been called the 'impure art' of British drama, serious issues are rarely free altogether from comic interpolations. Jokes can be expected even in the most terrifying situations. The archetypal witty remark relating to the War occurs in Hims's *The Breakfast Soldiers* where someone says: 'Shame about that archduke Ferdinand.... Shame he didn't duck [...]' (42), but similar expressions could be quoted from most of the works discussed here, where moments of harmless fun are set against a highly serious background. In Hamilton's *The Old Adam*, to cite only one example, the situation of the country being forced to fight a war without modern technology, is milked for its comic effects without losing sight of the central theme, the disastrous tendency in the 'old Adam' to go to war. Some plays even have a comic character, like Private Mason in *Journey's End*, whose entrances serve as comic relief. As a rule, this does not detract in any way from the essential seriousness of British war plays.

10
An Unconventional Solution

Nearly all the dramatists who turned to the War as a subject did so within the confines of established genres, even if they sometimes stretched their boundaries. For most of them, quite rightly, the mode of presenting the War was of secondary importance when compared with their attitude to the War itself. The one important exception is *Oh What a Lovely War*, which may at least partially account for the sensation it caused at the Theatre Royal, Stratford, in March 1963. It employs the conventions of a popular pre-World War I seaside entertainment, *'a pierrot show of fifty years ago with red, white, and blue fairy lights, twin balconies left and right and coloured circus 'tubs'* [...] (9), where actors-cum-singers in Pierrot costumes under the direction of a Master of Ceremonies take over all the roles in the script. There is no plot, and the only 'progression' is supplied by the historical events, from the pre-War declarations of politicians that 'War is unthinkable. It is out of the question' (15) through the various stages of mobilisation and some major events to a point in time before the end of the War, giving the impression of an interminable conflict drawn out beyond all human comprehension. The scenes are composed of a set of nine elements repeated in regular succession: a news panel providing headlines as they may have been used at the time, a screen behind the acting area on to which slides of front line photographs are projected, a band that plays popular tunes, popular songs written during the period of the War (the printed text carries almost a whole page of acknowledgements to previous writers), songs specifically written for this production, mimed allegorical tableaux illustrating political constellations (such as *'Belgium at bay, Germany threatening with a bayonet'*, 23), traditional patter by the Master of Ceremonies, brief scenes between allegorical figures representing, for instance, the nations involved in the conflict, brief scenes between individual characters who can be named (like Haig or Moltke) or nameless (like First, Second etc. Soldier). In the printed text, the scenes containing dialogue take up most of the pages, which gives a distorted impression of the stage spectacle that was equally dominated by visual and acoustic effects.

The unusual form of presenting the War can be accounted for, at least in part, by Joan Littlewood's unique approach. It was described thus by Brian Murphy:

> She said we are not doing a show about the First World War. We are finding a background for the songs, and these trace a period of history which can be presented without the realistic background that you would need in a film. Here we are, on the stage, The Clowns, and never in the course of the evening are we going to forget that the audience are out there.[...] Some of the scenes were dealt with very realistically, we had to work for hours and hours pretending to be in the trenches, getting the feeling of real boredom.
>
> The cast were completely involved in building up the script. We improvised lots of different scenes, read books and came up with ideas.[143]

Two points are particularly noteworthy here: the script was built around the songs, rather than the songs being used as ancillary material, and the cast contributed much of the script, which may account in part for the highly diverse elements in the show. The play's originality is only peripherally diminished by the fact that the idea of using a troupe of Pierrots originated in Coward's *Words and Music* 50 years earlier, 'where the slaughter of the First World War is represented by a chorus of clowns "pelting each other with coloured paper streamers"'.[144] It is, of course, uncertain whether Joan Littlewood knew of Coward's play or whether the idea originated independently with the two great show masters.

Part III Engaging Intellect or Emotions: Aspects of Attitude

1
'Nothing but the Truth'

It is one of the truisms of literary appreciation that the author's declared or implicit object in writing his or her work on the one hand, and the work's generally accepted theme established by popular reception and the concerted efforts of literary scholarship on the other, can diverge widely. Leaving aside the point, equally truistic, that critics can differ as to the 'true' meaning of a literary work, it is remarkable how often authors fail to appreciate the effect their work is going to have, or, conversely, how critics and general readers will mistake the author's intention. The war plays by British and Irish writers offer ample evidence of this phenomenon, *Journey's End* especially being an excellent case in point.

In an article for the *Daily Express* written soon after the initial reception of his play, Sherriff declared emphatically: 'Let me make myself clear. I have not written this play as a piece of propaganda. And certainly not as propaganda for peace. Neither have I tried to glorify the life of the soldier, nor to point any kind of moral. It is simply the expression of an ideal. I wanted to perpetuate the memory of some of those men.'[145] And when, nearly forty years later, he remembered his great success, he still remembered it as 'a war play *in which not a word was spoken against the war*, in which no word of condemnation was uttered by any of its characters'.[146] He described his characters as 'simple, unquestioning men who fought the war because it seemed the only right and proper thing to do. Somebody had got to fight it, and they had accepted the misery and suffering without complaint.'[147] He deliberately set his own play apart from those works where a protest was made against the conduct of the War or where its justification was called into question:

> [...] *Journey's End* happened to be the first war play that kept its feet in the Flanders mud. All the previous plays had aimed at higher

things: they carried 'messages', 'sermons against the war', symbolic revelations. The public knew enough about war to take all that for granted. What they never had been shown before on the stage was how men really lived in the trenches, how they talked and how they behaved.[148]

Sherriff even went one step further. Not only did he insist that *Journey's End* was *not* an anti-war play; he even admitted that originally it was not intended as a war play at all. As he describes it, the play began as a novel about two schoolboys, one of whom had good looks, charm, the ability for games and a gift for leadership, while the other admired him from afar (a situation still reflected in the relationship between Stanhope and Raleigh in the finished play). In the original plan, the plot continued beyond this point: when the boys left school, their position gradually became reversed; the school-time hero, spoilt by adoration, turned into a good-for-nothing, while the other grew into a successful businessman and supported his erstwhile hero who, in turn, despised him and accepted his assistance only from sheer necessity.[149] In other words, the original concept had no room for a wartime situation, nor did it terminate with the premature death of Raleigh.

So much for those critics who saw Sherriff, impelled by an irresistible impulse, making a dramatic protest against the War and those responsible for it, describing *Journey's End* as 'a brilliant indictment of the futility of war' and 'a protest against war which conveyed its harsh reality without tarnishing its humanity'.[150] The only exception from the general consensus appears to have been the reviewer in the *New Statesman* 'who called *Journey's End* "an orgy of the public-school spirit and Cockney humour" which failed to denounce the stupidity and cruelty of war and reduced it to a "slaughter-house for athletes and a school for gentlemen"'.[151] This statement apart, the initial reaction saw *Journey's End* as an anti-war play, and the delayed reception in literary and historical studies has generally confirmed this view.[152]

Looking at the play-text from a position some 80 years after the premiere, one is inclined to agree with Sherriff. There is little in the text to provoke an anti-war attitude, unless the reader or spectator comes to the play predisposed to see it in such a light. Not only is there no one who utters 'a word of condemnation' of the War; the War as such is never brought into perspective. Instead, the play depicts a specific situation for a number of individuals, and there is nothing to suggest that they should not have been exposed to such a position, because no one on stage or in the background can be made responsible for their plight.

While the question of responsibility is not asked by the characters, it is not suggested, however indirectly, by the author either.

What has been said here about *Journey's End* applies to the majority of the plays which have been categorised above as 'front-line plays'. Although in most cases we do not have personal testimonies of the kind that Sherriff offers, it is obvious that the authors' intention is to present credible situations and characters; the authenticity of the individual case is the criterion by which they would have wanted to see their works judged, while their attitude to larger issues remained non-committal. In their attempt to present the 'truth', the dramatists clearly reflected the position of the individual soldier at the front; numerous documents testify to the veracity of the picture that Sherriff and his colleagues presented.[153]

Where the playwrights or the critics speak of the 'truth' of these plays, it is what must be called an 'individual truth', limited to one specific situation. The authors' object was quite clearly to present a slice of life, hence their insistence on having got all the details right; and in the finished product it is the contrast between the concreteness on the individual level and the general opacity, even vagueness where the greater panorama of a 'world war' is concerned, that strikes one most. Despite the reservations concerning the 'realism' of such plays that have been voiced above,[154] the dramatists aimed for the immediacy of their characters' experience which they proceeded to convey to their audiences. If the War as such comes into view at all, it is seen as a natural disaster, a hurricane or earthquake rather than a man-made event that could, perhaps, have been avoided if some degree of sense had prevailed on all sides or if the victims had practised some resistance. Even where an author is on record elsewhere of being highly critical of the conduct of the War, he has kept his attitude out of his front-line play.[155] What is particularly notable is the absence both of patriotism and of anti-war propaganda and the refusal (on the part of the characters as well as the author) to voice any hatred of the enemy. When, in *Journey's End*, a captured enemy is brought onto the stage, the Sergeant-Major's first words are 'All right, sonny, we ain't going to 'urt you' (105). And before that Raleigh had asked rather naïvely, 'The Germans are really quite decent, aren't they? I mean, outside the newspapers?' (60).

In most of the plays discussed here the design to present the War 'as it really was' goes hand in hand with the undeclared attempt to enlist the audience's sympathies for the characters. Such an attempt succeeds where it is shown that the characters are unable to cope with the situation with which they are confronted; it fails where, as in Ackerley's

The Prisoners of War, their self-pity (apparently shared by the author) takes the upper hand. Plays of the type described here dominated the scene during the 1920s. *Journey's End* was preceded or followed by Schofield's *Men at War* (1920), Wall's *Havoc* (1923), Monkhouse's *Night Watches* (1925), Hodson's *Red Night* (1930) and MacGill's *Suspense* (1930), all of them without any indication of the author's stance towards the War, while in Brandane's *The Happy War* (1928) it is only the title that betrays an ironic distancing from a neutral attitude. It would, of course, be simplistic to claim that the twenties were the period of slice-of-life plays, wedged in between a period of propaganda plays during the preceding decade and a spate of *anti*-war plays in the thirties, but it is correct to say that by the beginning of the fourth decade the type of play represented by *Journey's End* had lost much of its attraction. In 1930, Ashley Dukes insisted that 'war realism is dead as far as the theatre goes, and war plays of personal experience have nothing more to say to us', and he went on to criticise the production of *Suspense* in no uncertain terms: 'We yawn recalling tiresome paragraphs to the effect that the author or producer or the actors or all of them once passed through such an experience, or at least found themselves in such a situation. What on earth that has to do with theatre or art is not explained.' On another war play, King-Hall's *B.J. One* of the same year, he added: 'The detail is capital – or it would be capital if the author ever understood how tiresome detail can be.'[156]

In the 1930s, the attitude described here still lingered in a few short plays for amateur stages, such as Peach's *Shells*, Hickey's two plays and Stewart's *The Home Front*, but the majority of the thirties plays, both short and full-length, turned away from the attempt to portray the War 'as it really was'. Even in Corrie's *Martha* (1937), non-committal although most of it is, a note of protest surfaces when Jimmy declares: 'I was gaun to say somethin' aboot the warmongers, but I'll haud my tongue' (25). Box's *Angels of War* is a particularly convincing illustration of the changes in attitude that occurred during the thirties, because these changes are dramatised in the play: while most of the scenes are 'slice-of-life' depictions of the situation in the ambulance drivers' camp, towards the end the girls begin to question 'why we ever came out here at all' (72) and even try to reassure themselves that 'there can never be another war after this. We've proved how futile and hopeless and pointless it is' (74). Not until the 1980s and 1990s, with Whelan's *The Accrington Pals*, Hannan's *Elizabeth Gordon Quinn*, Home's *A Christmas Truce*, Bryden's *The Big Picnic* and Murphy's *Absent Comrades*, did full-length plays again betray an attitude at all comparable to works like *Journey's End*, although now on a higher level of artistry.

2
The Patriotic Appeal

It was to be expected (and it would have been most surprising if it had been otherwise) that the outbreak of the War would produce a wave of patriotism, on the stage as elsewhere. Initially the Ministry of Propaganda (the Foreign Office News Department) attempted to encourage such an honourable attitude:

> It invited several prominent playwrights to help the good cause with theatrical tracts. These gentlemen, heroically sinking the artist in the patriot, wrote their little one-act pieces, exhorting us to do war-work, to eat less meat and so forth, and the result, so far as the art of drama was concerned, was the abomination of desolation. Unmitigated boredom swiftly brought this unhappy enterprise to an end, and the poor playwrights concerned must rejoice that oblivion hath scattered over it her poppy.[157]

Most of the patriotic play-texts that have survived from the period of the War deserve such a harsh judgement. Several of them appeal to the general public to change their attitude, either by ridiculing, in a simplistic manner, the behaviour they wish to correct, or by producing on stage a model of the changes they hope to bring about. Knoblauch, in *A War Committee*, satirises the useless work of those committees that only serve to satisfy people's self-importance. Hankey, in *A House-Warming in War-Time*, teaches her stage characters and, hopefully, her audiences to be less wasteful in their eating habits. *Patriotic Pence* by Porter and Bidder shows how a family sacrifice their amusements for shells and cartridges. Milne's *The Boy Comes Home* intends to pave the way for an appropriate reception of the returning soldiers.

Two issues surface repeatedly in patriotic war plays: the controversial question of recruiting and the equally important rejection of pacifist tendencies. Du Maurier in *An Englishman's Home* had already demonstrated before the War how vulnerable an Englishman's home was, and how important it was to give serious thought to greater defence efforts. This subject was taken up in *England Expects*—by Hicks and Knoblauch, apparently the 'first *new* war play to be produced'.[158] On the days of performance, recruiting officers were in attendance at the theatre, and the result seems to have justified the effort:

> Its crucial scene was one set at the Horse Guards in Whitehall, in which a recruiting sergeant appealed to the audience to join up, after which four actors planted in the stalls rushed to the stage, signed the book, and exited to a patriotic song from the sergeant. The scene was so persuasive, at one performance at least, that a member of the audience clambered up after the four actor-recruits, and had to be sternly sent back to his seat by the sergeant.[159]

Here is an instructive example of the proximity of these patriotic works to the agitprop. That the effectiveness of such crude appeals wore off once the initial enthusiasm had subsided, is underlined by the fact that there were no more recruitment plays of the type described, while works where the question of joining up is the subject of agonising conflicts for the individual, such as Monkhouse's *The Conquering Hero*, remained on the agenda. Winter's *Air Raid* of 1937 belatedly returned to the earlier mode, and the decision to join up here comes so unexpectedly that it would not have convinced the audiences of *England Expects*—.

Whereas the question of recruitment became obsolete once conscription was introduced in 1916, the rejection of pacifist tendencies grew into an increasingly serious issue when the War continued beyond the few months envisaged initially. Jones in *The Pacifists* perhaps unnecessarily complicates matters by splitting open the confines of allegory, but his purpose is clear: to give a warning to people of a liberal attitude who try to understand both sides of the conflict (with Shaw in a prominent position) while the world is threatened by unprincipled and power-hungry enemies, and his warning also comprises the danger of radicals inside the British camp if the responsible citizens themselves refrain from taking action. When his play became the worst flop of the 1917–18 season, Jones tried to rescue its thrust by attacking head on, in *The Times*, those against whom it was directed:

> To the tribe of Wordsters, Pedants, Fanatics, and Impossibilists [Jones's name for Shaw], who so rabidly pursued an ignoble peace, that they helped to provoke a disastrous war; who having provoked a disastrous war, have unceasingly clamoured against its effectual persecution; who throw dust in their own eyes, lest they should perceive the noonday truth; whom neither history, nor reason, nor thundering facts can teach; whom to convict of having been woefully and blindly wrong in the past, does but drive to be wilfully and madly wrong in the future; who might justly be regarded as pitiable figments of farce, if their busy mischief were not still seeking to bring about the tragedy of a delusive and abortive peace.[160]

The involved syntax here is in keeping with the somewhat hysterical sentiments which in the play had been partly neutralised by the farcical plot.

Such a comic side was totally absent from another anti-pacifist play that premiered soon after *The Pacifists*, Owen's melodramatic and polemical *Loyalty*. Here the patriotic message is unmistakable, because it is dramatised in the text: the owner of a radical newspaper is converted in the course of the play 'from Socialist pacifism to a fierce English patriotism',[161] a conversion that is expressed in such sentiments as 'I shall stand for English ideas – for English traditions – for English feeling and English manners and English sense and English policy, based on English character.'[162] The rejection of pacifism is, of course, also inherent in all the plays (discussed below) which extol British virtues and denounce the brutality, coarseness and general inferiority of the enemy.

Few dramatists went beyond the naïve approach to advocate or combat one specific issue, most importantly Zangwill in his pre-War *The War God* where the threat to British supremacy in the world is dramatised in no uncertain terms. It is personified in the character of Count Torgrim, the Chancellor whose Cato-like belief that Alba must be destroyed influences everything he does. The play's patriotic appeal is clearly to rouse the British public from an attitude of complacency and false security, although such an effect is partly obscured by the play's involvement in Gothia's internal politics. Given the intended effect, it is perhaps unavoidable that Germany alone is blamed for her expansion politics and the arms race, while the fact that Alba, too, has colonies, commercial interests and a strong navy is accepted as a matter of course.

At the other end of the chronological scale stands a play that is set at the same moment in time as *The War God* (in the immediate pre-War years) but was written and performed more than 30 years later and, indeed, after another world war. Rattigan's *The Winslow Boy* of 1946 can be read as an ideological justification for Britain's entry into the War: '[...] Rattigan's subtext is the significance of individual liberty versus global problems that threaten the stability of society itself (the coming First World War).'[163] With references to an imminent war, and with the Winslow family's struggle for the acceptance of the boy's innocence, the author suggests that it was a *moral* attitude more than anything else that took Britain to war, and the final verdict of the appeal court confirms the values for which Britain had decided to fight: 'Let Right be done' (127). Right – not Justice (which is a more technical process) stands at the end of the struggle, that, after great sacrifices for all concerned, ensures the liberty of the individual which the state and its institutions are not per- mitted to override. The implied contrast between Britain and her enemy nations on the Continent cannot be missed. *The Winslow Boy* must be seen as a patriotic appeal after the fact, much more convincing than most wartime plays but also perhaps one of the last patriotic appeals on the British stage.

3
Hun-Bashing

The line between patriotism and chauvinism, between honest loyalty, still to be admired today, and violent jingoism that causes nothing but embarrassment when looking back, is a thin one. The journalist Horatio Bottomley, his shady career in and out of Parliament and prison notwithstanding, was in the forefront of those who vilified the enemy with more than average venom. His periodical *John Bull* coined the term *Germ-huns* and 'was fond of speculating whether the enemy was human'.[164] Such an attitude was present in a number of wartime plays as in other walks of life. It was not, by the way, restricted to Britain. The American Clayton Hamilton, in an article on 'The Drama and the War', spoke out against 'the blonde beasts of the North' and 'the hordes of darkness', and, having first set aside the Spanish-American War as a 'chivalrous and almost charming sally', claimed that

> [...] in every world-historic war, without exception, one side has been emphatically right and the other side emphatically wrong. Such wars have tended always to debase and to deprave the spiritual instinct among the hordes that have been fighting on the side of evil; but they have tended simultaneously to uplift and sanctify the spirit of those nations that have striven to carry on the torch of truth and have offered up their lives, their fortunes, and their sacred honour to make reason and the will of God prevail.[165]

These sentiments were echoed, among others, by the Irish-born John Hartley Manners, author of *Peg o' My Heart*, who, after a minor career on the London stage, had settled in America. In the Foreword to his three short war plays he disqualified himself for any rational discussion by inveighing against the 'cowardly brutalities' committed by 'the Prussian hordes' and discrediting people who showed some sympathy with Germany after the War as 'a danger in civilised communities'. His own plays with their hysterical and wholly irrational outbursts of hatred have been briefly described above;[166] Manners intended them to prevent 'that business and social relations be resumed with Germany as in pre-war days', because civilisation must 'grasp the all-too evident fact that they are a race apart, unfit to associate with'. His purpose was 'to keep alive remembrance of some of the barbarous outrages perpetrated by the Hun on innocent and wretched peoples.'[167] This is one of the relatively few instances where 'Hun-bashing' continued after the War was over.

During the War, the consequences of such views made themselves felt in a considerable number of plays, not only in London but also in the provinces, as confirmed by J.C. Trewin: 'For a time, in up-dogs-and-at'em provincial melodrama, every villain had to be a German, preferably a Prussian. The country's stages resounded with the guttural invective of such characters as Gottlieb Hartz, Karl Schmidt, and a ubiquitous Prussian captain.'[168] Few of these plays went into print, but from the examples that have survived, one can gather that the chief areas of attack were threefold: the suspected presence of German spies in Britain, the German pretensions to cultural superiority and the German occupation of Belgium, while a few plays attempted a more comprehensive analysis of what was considered as the German national character.

Apparently not one of these plays was written by someone who had served at the front. The attitude of the front-line soldier was much more down to earth (if the pun may be allowed): 'Two general truths define the British soldier's relationship with his enemy on the Western front: the first is that he generally had a high regard for the Germans, and the second that the fighting man rarely felt a high degree of personal hostility towards them.'[169] Cecil Lewis, in *Sagittarius Rising*, even declared the term *Huns* to have been perfectly harmless:

> We always referred to our friends the enemy as 'Huns', [...] and nothing derogatory was, or is, intended. When they captured our pilots or observers they treated them with courtesy and gallantry, as I think we did them. I do not remember, except on one occasion over London in 1917, ever having any feelings of animosity against the Germans. They were simply 'the enemy'; their machines had black crosses, and it was our job to bring them down.[170]

While this view may be slightly euphemistic, perhaps caused by the still existing chivalry among the young pilots on both sides, it is clear that the boundless hatred of the enemy, coupled with a feeling of national superiority, was promoted by civilians, and, at least in the case of the drama, mostly by civilians of the older generation such as Caine, Barrie, Archer, Binyon and Phillips.

Barrie with his unfortunate *Der Tag* of December 1914 set the tone for much of what was to come. Although his chief object seems to have been to warn his compatriots that they are seen as complacent and defenceless by the Germans, his picture of the Emperor, in turn ruthless, fickle and conscience-stricken, and of the Chancellor and the Officer, so determined to go to war that they will even deceive their own Emperor, has contributed to the image of the 'typical' German on the stage. It was, of course, by far outdone by Binyon's *Bombastes in the Shades* and Phillips's *Armageddon*, both written at the beginning of the War. Bombastes is a *miles gloriosus* figure of the most intolerable nature whose bloodthirst equals his stupidity. His drunken entry confirms all the worst prejudices: 'Forward, swine! Where are the enemy?' (9). When he later claims that 'we are the most conscientious as the most intellectual of peoples; in our mailed fist we carry the standard of the noblest morality' (15), he reveals some English heterostereotypes of the German national character, disguised as Bombastes's autostereotypes. His blindness as to the most obvious facts (he does not even realise that he has arrived in the world of the shades) exposes him to Heine's sarcasm and the audience's laughter. It may have been Binyon's purpose to show how harmless the enemy actually is: with such an adversary, no world war would have been necessary.

Phillips's *Armageddon* is potentially more effective, because it depicts the enemy with deadly seriousness. The brutality of the German troops and the deviousness of the propaganda machine on the Berlin home front are emphasised not only by contrasting them with the heroism and humanity of the allied side but also by associating Germany and the Germans with the forces of darkness, assembled in Hell in the allegorical Prologue and Epilogue. It says a great deal for the down-to-earth attitude of English audiences that the play endured on the stage for a mere 14 performances.[171] The stage career of *Armageddon* in this respect was not an exception: '[...] judging by the short runs of the crude, jingoistic and overtly propaganda plays, the public were not totally deceived.'[172] Caine (who had already furnished ample proof of his rabid chauvinism in his book *The Drama of Three Hundred & Sixty-Five Days* of 1915) provided in *The Prime Minister* another frontal attack on alleged German character traits. Here the intended conversion of the audience to an anti-German attitude is prefigured on stage by the conversion of the title character, the personification of everything that is generous, just and benevolent, when he realises that it 'is the mad, bad blood in you that is deluging the world in crime' (153). It goes without saying that in the years immediately preceding the War many of the most influential figures on the German side, from Queen Victoria's grandson on the German throne to the leading politicians and military commanders, had provided British dramatists with ample justification for their negative images. The question here is how easily some writers succumbed to the temptation to simplify and generalise in order to stir up hatred.

This was particularly the case in popular melodramas with a wartime setting. Citing such (anonymous) titles as *In the Hands of the Hun*, Collins concludes from a survey of the manuscripts in the Lord Chamberlain's office: 'The greatest atrocities were attributed to the depraved antics of the German soldiery. This included the killing of mothers, beating of children and rape of young girls, the latter being the most common. In order to incite deep feelings of animosity the dramatists ensured that the crimes perpetrated were against the most innocent.'[173] Often these stories were later revealed to have been rumours without factual foundation or legends deliberately invented to discredit the enemy.[174]

The most popular element in such melodramas was the spy motif. Collins calculates that 'nearly 100 plays, many of which were one-act dramas involving espionage, were produced in Britain between September 1914 and November 1918. The spy play helped augment the propagandist's aims by instilling a distrust of anything German.'[175] Since the spy's first priority is disguise, it is easy to portray him, or her, as treacherous and untrustworthy, a characteristic then transferred to the national character as such. Howard's *Seven Days' Leave* had, according to the anonymous reviewer for *The Era*, 'a pair of the cleverest and most dangerous German spies. The Huns were after Captain Terry, and their plan was to convey him, properly drugged and trussed, to Germany by means of a submarine lying in wait close by, and there extort by torture the secret of some wonderful new guns.'[176] Here as elsewhere the notion of 'fair play' to which the German side does not adhere, is brought into play. Moreover, it is precisely the spies' cleverness which enhances the achievement of their British adversaries when they, as is regularly the case, discover and disarm the Germans. In *The Man Who Stayed at Home* by Worrall and Terry, the deception practised by the German spies is treacherous and contemptible, while a similar deception by their British opponent is laudable and patriotic. The reviewer of Page's *By Pigeon Post* in *The Era* specifically commended the actor playing the 'sinister' German for portraying 'the spy's depravity'.[177] In one case, Melville's *The Female Hun*, the spy has even succeeded in marrying a British General (the reviews do not reflect on the General's intelligence). The alternative to depicting the spy as supernaturally clever is, of course, to show him as abominably stupid. The reviewer of *The Era* commented on the spies in Mills's *The Luck of the Navy*: 'We have never met, to our knowledge, any spies in real life, but if they act at all like those in spy plays there is little danger to be feared from the aliens in our midst.'[178]

Another area where the criticism of the enemy frequently turned into chauvinistic exaggeration was the attempt by certain playwrights to debunk German pretensions to *cultural* superiority. While this was, without doubt, occasioned by wholly deplorable instances of a German superiority complex, extensively reported in the British press, the reactions in Britain, seen from a historical perspective, were equally regrettable:

> In December 1914 at the Manchester Hippodrome, there was a three-act play produced called *Kulture* [...] a Military Spectacular Aqua-Drama [...]. The denouement arrived with the opening of sluice gates which sent horses and cannon into the water, and houses collapsed under the cascading deluge. Thus the German army was pictured as being drowned. The remaining image was of a group of soldiers standing on a level below a Red Cross nurse who proffered a wreath of peace, and above her head there hung an illuminated halo under a collage of Allied flags. [...] The finale not only showed the triumph of good over evil but suggested, with the inclusion of the illuminated halo, that God was on the side of the Allies.[179]

Kulture was apparently an example of the old 'aquatic drama' (familiar from Sadler's Wells) turned to new propaganda uses and an instance of the battle for cultural superiority on the propaganda front. The description indicates that the play had nothing whatsoever to do with culture, German, British or international; the title simply promised an anti-German stance that the play was then amply to fulfil. At the same time, the misspelling of the German term shows the lack of information about the other country, which rendered it difficult to conduct a discussion on cultural superiority on any but the most primitive level.

Nevertheless Barrie, in *Der Tag*, made what under the circumstances must be seen as a brave attempt to open such a discussion, because the German Emperor is confronted not only with the deceitful Chancellor but also with the Spirit of Culture. She freely admits German claims to be a cultured nation, and merely makes the reasonable reservation that '[i]t has ever been your weakness to think that I have no other home save here in Germany' (26). Yet when the Emperor has signed the order for attacking France through Belgium, the Spirit of Culture returns, *'now with a wound in her breast'* (33) inflicted by the stroke of a pen, in other words, if Germany had not violated all international laws by invading Belgium, the country's claim to belong to the realm of Culture would still stand – a sentiment that goes considerably further than many commentators at the time would have been prepared to go (which makes it somewhat unfair to include Barrie's play under the heading 'Hun-bashing').

The prevailing general reaction to German cultural pretensions can be gathered from a phrase in *Bullets and Billets* by the immensely popular cartoonist, writer and occasional dramatist Bairnsfather: '[...] our men, superior, broad-minded, more frank and lovable beings, were regarding these faded, unimaginative products of perverted kulture [*sic*] as a set of objectionable but amusing lunatics whose heads had *got* to be eventually smacked.'[180] This attitude was confirmed in the play *Kultur at Home* by Besier and Spottiswoode that is graphically described in the *Times* review quoted above.[181] The reviewer disliked the triviality of the instances of English superiority over German manners and conventions and regretted that 'the exhibition of the English always showing "good form" and the German [*sic*] "bad" (i.e. English bad) "form" is in itself not the best form.'[182] The reviewer in the *Athenaeum* was probably more in agreement with public feelings when he saw *Kultur at Home* as 'the best play with particular reference to the war yet put on the stage', although in a highly ambiguous conclusion he attempted to reinstate his objectivity by warning that 'though our national failings have not reduced us to the falsehood and truculence evident in our enemies, those failings, being of a more insidious nature, may make our downfall should disaster ever befall us even more difficult to recover from.'[183] By the time of the writing of *Kultur at Home*, the term 'Kultur' had apparently taken on a broad (and vague) set of meanings, referring to various pejoratively connoted social *mores* and moral values exclusively associated with the enemy.

At the time, radical critics of Germany must have felt themselves on safer ground where they took the invasion of Belgium as their text. 'Poor little Belgium' (in Ireland 'Poor little Catholic Belgium') became the object of compassion and the occasion for Hun-bashing of a violent nature. In more recent years, the British entry into the War is seen to have had a variety of reasons, among which the defence of Belgian neutrality was only a minor one: 'It is clear that, whatever propaganda was milked from German violation of Belgian neutrality, British intervention was motivated by clear *raison d'état*.'[184] However, at the time propagandists in drama as in other fields had every right for their moral indignation.

Where their position is somewhat shaky is where German atrocities (especially *organised* atrocities) against the civilian population are concerned.
Yet writers who, during the War years, attacked the German side on the
account of outrages against civilians had an apparently incontrovertible
collection of witnesses on their side in the form of the 'Bryce Report'
(*Report of the Committee on Alleged German Outrages*), compiled on behalf
of the government by a committee led by the Right Hon. Viscount Bryce,
O.M.. The 70-page-long *Report*, complete with maps and references, gives
every appearance of authenticity.[185] It is not, of course, possible today to
test the veracity of the individual witnesses, nor is it the purpose of the
present study to do so. A balanced view of the *Report* is provided by Hynes
who states that 'some of the reported actions undoubtedly did occur.'
What is clear, however, is that the *Report* had enormous consequences for
the public attitude to the enemy, in drama as elsewhere. It 'fixed in
English minds, as "official" and therefore true, the idea of the German
soldier as a cruel savage, living and acting outside the limits of decent
human behaviour. [...] henceforth it became quite acceptable to express
a desire for the annihilation of Germans, the bombing of German civilians, the gassing of German troops.' Moreover, the *Report* 'released into
English imaginations a style, a language, and an imagery of violence and
cruelty that would in time permeate imagined versions of the war, and
become part of the record.'[186] A number of plays had a minor share in
these 'imagined versions'.

Galsworthy, for once unequivocally on the side of the propagandists,
described the invasion of Belgium as 'the masterpiece of cynicism –
perhaps the most cynical act and the greatest piece of folly the world
has ever seen', and added that this folly was committed 'by the State
which through a million tongues and pens claimed for itself leadership
of the civilised world, and the crown of human intelligence.' He did so
in his Foreword to a play by Crocker, *Pawns of War*, in which the author
melodramatised the situation in occupied Belgium.[187] It is set in a small
town where the burgomaster is taken hostage, and he and his son are
shot when the son has killed a German officer who has dared to approach
his sister. At the same time news comes through that the burgomaster's
other son (who, at the age of 14, has led a most improbable mission on
behalf of a Belgian General) has been killed, too, whereupon the burgomaster's wife goes insane. While the Belgians are shown as humane and
heroic if unable to defend their country, the German officers are
depicted as brutal, with the exception of the Commanding General who
is gentleman-like but duty-bound and incapable of deviating from his
orders. The attitude that the author wishes to convey is personified in

the burgomaster's daughter who eventually exclaims: 'Father. I've never held a weapon in my hand, but when I look at these men – I – could – kill … I want to kill them. I, myself.' (38).

Archer's *War Is War or the Germans in Belgium* is so similar to Crocker's play in its basic situation and in numerous details that one wonders whether Archer was aware of it when writing his own work. *War Is War* is again set in the burgomaster's household of a small Belgian community, with the burgomaster's daughter as the focus of identification for the audience. After a series of atrocities have been reported to the initially incredulous population, the burgomaster and other hostages are executed and the whole village burnt down because of a set of misunderstandings that would be purely farcical if they did not have such serious consequences. However, Archer goes beyond Crocker's play by ruling out any Belgian resistance to the occupation, which emphasises the innocence-versus-evil dichotomy of the play. It is underlined by the brutality of the reprisals which are totally out of proportion to the Belgian offences, and the callousness of the German officers, one of whom exclaims 'That's the way to treat the Belgian beasts' (67), while another boasts '[…] Germany can never meet an enemy that is her equal – an enemy she can respect. Where is she to find her peer, I won't say in bravery, but in culture, in morality, in chivalry?' (34). Here again the fictitious autostereotype is called into play to support the British heterostereotype of the enemy.

Archer must have felt that his presentation needed to be bolstered by documentary evidence, and he provided an extensive 'Postscript' (82–117) in which he lightly dismisses, as untrustworthy, a White Book published by the Berlin Foreign Office on violations of international law on the Belgian side, while he gives unreserved credence to its British equivalent, the *Bryce Report*. Archer must have subsequently felt justified in his view when Maurice Maeterlinck's *Le Bourgmestre de Stilmonde* of 1918 was, in the same year, brought to the Edinburgh Royal Lyceum in a translation by Alexander Teixeira de Mattos; it was acclaimed for 'its strong, indignant scorn of injustice, and its patriotic fervour.'[188] The play then came to the London Scala and (in 1921) to the London Lyceum; in 1925 it was revived at the Ambassadors, by which time, however, it had lost much of its black-and-white propaganda appeal and its 'passion of hate'.[189] Like Crocker's and Archer's plays, it is set in the household of a small-town mayor whose house is taken over by German officers. The burgomaster is finally executed as a hostage when one of the officers (described as 'un Prussien authentique, un hobereau féroce […] détesté de ses hommes qu'il maltraite et brutalise comme des chiens'[190]) is apparently shot by the burgomaster's son (aged 14).[191] Maeterlinck brought his prestige as the Nobel Prize winner of 1911 to the issue, and however chauvinistic and one-sided his play is, it must for a time have had considerable influence on public opinion in Britain. Incidentally, and quite apart from the propaganda issue, Maeterlinck's text is a prime example of how wooden and stilted the result can be if a *symboliste* poet condescends to write on the level of 'mere' psychological realism.

Two short plays from the 1930s that also deal with the conditions in occupied Belgium, Reid-Jamieson's *Eleven A.M.* and Atkinson's *The Chimney Corner*, while accepting the basic situation of a civilian population oppressed by foreign forces, focus less on the enemy than on the psychological consequences of the occupation and do not come under the present heading. 'Hun-bashing' was almost exclusively restricted to the War years and the immediate aftermath; moreover it was primarily pursued by dramatists of the older generation. Very few instances of inordinate denunciation of the enemy can be found in plays from 1920 onwards, and this although the War had enormous consequences, many of them of a negative nature, for the whole population. Surveying the complete range of British and Irish plays about the First World War, one cannot but be amazed that the role given to one-sided propaganda and chauvinistic sentiments was such a limited one.

4
Pacifism

A surprising number of British war plays show pacifist tendencies in the broadest sense of the term. In these cases there is normally no mistaking the authors' purpose because the writers have gone to great lengths to make their intention clear, even to the detriment of objectivity, dramatic structure and/or three-dimensional characterisation. The majority of these plays date from the 1930s, but even during the course of the War pacifist plays were written. Naturally, as long as the War lasted, the authors could not entertain any hope of seeing their works on the stage; as Collins explains: 'A study of shows sent to the Lord Chamberlain's office indicated that anyone considering writing a play which was critical of the government, and the war, would not submit the play for licence knowing that it would be rejected without a second thought.'[192] Many plays with a pacifist message were short plays, indicative of the degree of attention that pacifism found in amateur companies for which most short plays were written.

Pacifist war plays fall into two distinct groups. Works of the first group *analyse* the *causes* of the War, while plays in the second (and larger) group *demonstrate* its *consequences*. A possible third category, those plays that combine a pacifist message with a warning against another war, will be discussed below.

The outbreak of the War seems to have taken most people, even many of those in leading positions, by surprise. Therefore it was subsequently accounted for by an extremely wide spectrum of causes. Noel Annan, in the chapter on 'Pacifism' in *Our Age*, lists a whole range of explanations which, individually or collectively, have been suggested as the prime reasons for the beginning of the War.[193] Most of them are also reflected in British anti-war plays, but most frequently the blame here is attributed to the armaments manufacturers. As long as the War lasted, resistance to it came mainly from members of the Labour Party and other Socialist groups, but even here the critical voices were usually shouted down by those advocating unqualified patriotism.[194]

When the young journalist Fenner Brockway wrote his drastically titled *The Devil's Business*, he squarely placed the responsibility for the War on the international armaments-industry, which, according to Brockway, provided arms to both sides. Brockway was until his death in 1988 (at the age of 99) one of the leading British left-wing politicians and pacifists. Having been sent to prison in 1916 for opposing conscription, it would probably have amused (or enraged) him that he, who was later to become a founder of the Campaign for Nuclear Disarmament, would be made a life peer in 1964. *The Devil's Business* was the most straightforward expression in drama of a pacifist stance during the War, although Brockway very thinly disguised the nation and her Cabinet by inventing a fictitious setting and refusing the British politicians their proper names. The gist of Brockway's analysis is simple: 'Though Cabinets may govern nations the Armaments Trust governs Cabinets!' (25). The solution that he proposes is equally simple: in the words of the Premier, replying to the Armaments Manager, 'I would rather that we surrendered to the enemy than to you and the soulless traders in death whom you represent' (42). To support his thesis, Brockway provided an appendix ('The Justification of the Play') in which he revealed the international entanglement of various armaments firms as well as the role of former government officials who were employed by these firms because of their insider knowledge.

Compared to Brockway's courageous but one-dimensional solution to the problem of escaping from the War, Munro's post-War *The Rumour* is more complex. A war, this is the thesis that Munro sets out to demonstrate, does not 'break out' spontaneously; it is engineered by capitalist investors who wish to exploit the natural resources of a small and helpless state, 'a fair country' being turned into 'the happy hunting ground of a host of greedy adventurers' (104). They start a rumour that one country is preparing to attack another, which leads to countermeasures, war hysteria, a preventive strike, and general destruction. Such wholly respectable emotions as patriotism, sense of honour and existential fear are exploited to the full, while the 'enemy' is demonised to such an extent that it appears to be the inescapable duty for every decent person to attack him. The war is declared to be 'a holy war, fought by a people in righteous indignation [...] That, friends, is why we were joined in our sacred enterprise by our noble and disinterested allies, Great Britain and France!' (142). These do not act as honest brokers but manipulate the peace negotiations, settle the question of reparations to be paid by the loser and pocket the gains. Munro's suggested way out of the problem is to desist from such despicable manoeuvres, but the play's pervading attitude makes it less than likely that future wars can be avoided by a change in international politics.

The obverse of an 'analytical' anti-war attitude as represented by Brockway and Munro is the position of those playwrights who count the losses inflicted by the War rather than exploring its causes. In order to convey their pacifist message, such plays require a central character whose superior qualities render him, or her, an object of admiration for the audience. When this character is physically or mentally hurt by the War, the audience's compassion is turned into an indictment of the War as such. An interesting case is that of Thurston's *The Cost*, oddly subtitled *A Comedy* despite its serious nature. When John Woodhouse, after long and tortuous deliberations, decides to enlist and returns with a head wound, the nation has lost one of her most brilliant scholars. It is then only one short step from the audience's compassion for his personal situation and their regret for the country's loss to a general criticism of the War. *The Cost* is unique in that, despite its anti-war stance, it was produced at the Vaudeville in October 1914 and ran for 20 performances. Perhaps at the time the machinery for eliminating such 'defeatist' works was not yet in place, or the play's rather heavy-handed satire on wartime attitudes, especially the ridiculous 'sacrifices' which people at home are prepared to make, did in the production overshadow the tragic fate of the disabled philosopher.

Four short plays underline the fact that, despite Woodhouse's warning against the brutality and barbarism that will result from the War and will infect *everyone*, there was an undercurrent of pacifist thinking even during the war years. Shaw's *O'Flaherty V.C.* and Wentworth's *War Brides* of 1915, Malleson's *Black 'Ell* of 1916 and Drinkwater's *X=0* of 1917 reflect, in highly individual ways, Thurston's prophecy of barbarism as the unavoidable consequence of the War. In *War Brides* the criticism is directed at the attempt to assign the role of a mere 'breeding-machine' (31) to young women whose patriotic duty is understood as providing future soldiers for another war. Hedwig, who loses her husband and then kills herself and her unborn child, is clearly intended as the focus for the audience's compassion; her attitude is then transferred to the role of all women during the War. Shaw's O'Flaherty enlists the spectators' sympathies by his charm, his good sense and his down-to-earth attitude that stands in sharp contrast both to the villagers' illusions about the War and the bathos of the General's self-defeating rhetoric. Once he has been established as an alternative to the other characters who for a variety of reasons appear ridiculous, his statements about the War gain in weight beyond the specific situation in an Irish village. When he says, 'Dont talk to me or to any soldier of the war being right. No war is right; and all the holy water that Father Quinlan ever blessed couldnt make one right' (822), this becomes the play's central message far beyond the opinion of an individual character. It opposes everything that was sacrosanct at the time and radically undercuts the chauvinism of wartime propaganda.[195]

In *Black 'Ell*, apparently based on Malleson's own front-line experience, Harold Gould is established as the author's mouthpiece because he is the only one who has gone through the reality of the fighting which he describes in horribly brutal detail (52–3, 60–1), while the other members of his family have succumbed to the phraseology of the newspapers ('Ridding the world of the Hun', 43) and are unable to see the enemy as human beings. Harold's outcry against being treated as a hero ends in a Sassoon-like protest which serves as a call to others to help end the War: 'Well, you can shoot me … because I'm not going back … I'm going to stop at home and say it's all mad … I'm going to keep on saying it… somebody's got to stop sometime … somebody's got to get sane again … and I won't go back … I won't, I won't … I won't' (64). This outburst, grotesquely contrasted with the sound of three cheers for the returned soldier who sees himself as a murderer, embodies Malleson's purpose. The identity of the soldier's situation on both sides, so graphically described by Malleson, is expressed in a mathematical formula in $X=0$. Drinkwater, 'the most notable theatre lecturer to tour France',[196] had seen some of the realities of the War on a tour of the camps behind the front line. In contrast to Malleson's emotional outcry, Drinkwater's is a muted protest, muffled by the three-fold *Verfremdung* through the near-mythological setting, the reduction of the characters to nameless ciphers and the unrealistic verse form. Nevertheless, from today's perspective $X=0$ comes over as the most convincing of all anti-war plays from the War, because it presents an archetypal constellation ideally suited to the short form. Here the reader or spectator is under no patriotic obligation to identify with one of the two soldiers, and the sameness of their situation is brought home without being obscured by realistic details.

It took another decade before the two approaches in Malleson's and Drinkwater's plays, the realistic and the archetypal, were successfully combined in one work. *The Silver Tassie* is one of the great anti-war plays not only of this but of any war. Unlike Malleson's Harold Gould, O'Casey's Harry Heegan is incapable of articulating his protest, and the burden of the objection falls on the reader or spectator. It is not only the enormous gap between Harry's pre-War physical prowess and his post-War destitution, nor even his emasculation which is part of his injury, but his inarticulateness (which leads him to destroy the tassie and to lash out blindly at those on whose assistance he depends most) that leaves him the object of the audience's compassion. This compassion causes resentment, first at those who are responsible for Harry's fate, and then at war itself. Alternative attitudes to the War are offered in passing in some other characters, but they are quickly rejected because of their selfishness or lack of understanding. With Act II, through which he 'maintains a near-miraculous balance between the real and the symbolic',[197] O'Casey extends his protest to an unlimited number of further victims who share Harry's inability to realise how they are being manipulated. In this respect O'Casey went further than Wilfred Owen, whose unnamed victim in his poem 'Disabled' Harry otherwise resembles (he went to the War with the same thoughtlessness, and becomes paralysed like Harry; they even have a common background in football[198]). In the 1920s, only Pilcher in *The Searcher* came anywhere near O'Casey's uncompromising stance, but her short-cut solution of dispensing with all realistic detail and striving for an expressionist universality eliminates the empathy that O'Casey created for his central character, and reduces the force of her protest.

The 1930s were the period when a pacifist attitude found room in many plays, most of them short works designed for the amateur scene. By this time, the authors had gained enough distance from the war years to see the erstwhile enemy with a higher degree of objectivity and to dissociate themselves from the somewhat hysterical patriotism of earlier works. Beginning with Sylvaine's haunting *The Road of Poplars* of 1930, where a dead German soldier is described by his equally dead English counterpart as 'A good fellow. A friend of mine' (341), the enemy has now lost his diabolic qualities. Bell's *Symphony in Illusion* of 1932 illustrates the difficulties of making peace after it has been comparatively easy to make war; yet both in the frame action and in the play-within-the-play it is the character associated with an anti-war attitude, who is singled out to attract the audience's sympathies. Equally, in Brighouse's *A Bit of War* (1933) the girl Lorna who personifies a pacifist position is preferred by the author over her colleagues and is given the convincing arguments. Frequently the characters who support an anti-war attitude take their stance because they have suffered personal losses. Lorna has lost her fiancé at the front, while in Popplewell's *The Pacifist*, Mavis's father was gassed during the War. Mavis, the titular character, arouses the audience's sympathies when she courageously takes over a pacifist meeting while others are afraid to do so, and even calls off her engagement when her fiancé opposes her views on world peace and disarmament. The most convincing gesture is made by Mary Blake (whose father was killed in the War) in Box's *'Bring Me My Bow'* who foregoes a scholarship rather than writing a patriotic essay. In each case, individual sacrifices serve to enlist the audience's sympathies not only for this particular character but for the pacifist position he or she represents. Flather in *Jonathan's Day* even goes one step further, because he shows how Jonathan's memory can be honoured although he had been court-martialled for cowardice. It is his mother who saddles society with the blame for his death, and her courageous position in defending her dead son turns her into a pacifist heroine. More short plays written from a pacifist basis, such as the programmatically titled *Peace in Our Time* by Muriel and Sydney Box, will be discussed below.

Full-length plays with a pacifist message, written for the amateur theatre, were less numerous. Popplewell in Act III of *This Bondage* presents a diluted form of pacifism (much less direct than in her *The Pacifist*) because it comes at the end of a turbulent chronicle of the Feminist movement which includes phases of militant anti-authoritarianism as well as rabid nationalist poses. Profiteering from new inventions in the field of armaments is one of the issues under discussion here, and at least one character realises that 'Death is not the real tragedy of war, nor even pain. It's the *joy* of killing that debases, a joy sanctified in the last war by the churches, who tactfully described mass murder as "dying for one's country"' (153). Muriel Box, at the end of *Angels of War*, allows at least one of her characters the insight that all the suffering will have been in vain unless in retrospect the War is given some meaning, and she desperately pleads for the awareness 'that we were sacrificing all we wanted out of life to win this war – not because the winning of it mattered tuppence, but because it was a war that was going to end wars' (73). Again, the central message is less outspoken here than in the short plays written with her husband Sydney.

But even such a comparatively mild anti-war attitude seems to have been impossible to express in the commercial theatre. Coward's *Post Mortem* is a case in point. Despite the author's prestige (his *Cavalcade* of the same year ran for over 400 performances), his embittered attack on the attitude of post-War society to the War, apparently written with a tortured conscience, did not reach the commercial stage. The same is true of Auden and Isherwood's *On the Frontier* where the experience of World War I is seen as not having had the least effect on public attitudes to war in general. The one play with a clear pacifist message that made its way on to the commercial stage was van Druten's *Flowers of the Forest*, perhaps the most extended discussion on pacifism ever to be heard in the West End. The author presents a gamut of different views, including such hysterical statements as '[...] the Germans have got to be stamped out' (513) and '[...] the individuals we are fighting here aren't human beings. The Huns are monsters' (this from a C.of E. Vicar!, 509), but the central character is led to an insight into the value of *living* rather than dying for one's country. Her young lover who is dying of T.B. has just helped to publish a pacifist book, which triggers off a debate on people's behaviour during the War, but the final conclusion, for the characters on stage as well as for the audience, emerges effortlessly from the plot rather than from a mere discussion: war is 'an evil, like disease' (568). *Flowers of the Forest*, coming as it did from an author who is remembered as a writer of light comedy, was just as much a surprise as *Post Mortem* had been three years before from someone with Coward's reputation, and it is regularly ignored in summaries of van Druten's activities.

Pacifism in World War I plays from the post-World War II period was of course overshadowed by the recent past; to arouse indignation at conditions that had occurred before the majority of the audiences were born, was a difficult task. Most of these works come across in retrospect as confirming views that have been held anyway by their audiences, rather than trying to convince anyone of a new attitude. *Oh What a Lovely War*, generally received as an anti-war play, was a case of preaching to the converted. By 1963 it was agreed that the generals (on all sides) had made stupid mistakes, that the suffering in the trenches was out of all proportion to the initial enthusiasm on the home front and that the Versailles Treaty, motivated by *revanche* rather than justice, became one of the causes of another war. Goorney declares in *The Theatre Workshop Story* that the 'creation of an anti-war play was never in the minds of those connected with the production',[199] while audiences and critics alike saw it as confirming their critical attitude to World War I. The case of Sumner's *Jimmy Clay* is only slightly different: the author seems naturally to assume that his audiences will share his anti-war position. The grotesquely comic songs in both works appeal to those for whom a pacifist attitude is the only one possible, while there is no attempt at accumulating arguments in favour of such a position. Consequently, neither *Jimmy Clay* nor *Oh What a Lovely War* has a realistic character with whom the audience can identify. And in Macdonald's *Not about Heroes* it is again tacitly assumed that the position of Owen and Sassoon is the only one, and the play can then concentrate on the psychological relationship between the two poets rather than on their attitude to the War.

The only post-World War II play that deliberately sets out to *convince* its audience, to bring about an attitude that its spectators (or, in the case of the preceding novel, its readers) may not originally have held, is Jennifer Johnston's *How Many Miles to Babylon?* Its two central characters, despite their opposite social positions, are offered to the audience as models for identification. When they adhere to their personal code of values in opposition to everything that the War demands, and accept death as the only way out of the dilemma, they arouse sufficient sympathy, even admiration to satisfy the audience that, if these two individuals are in the right, the War must be in the wrong. That such an approach was still possible in the 1970s (the novel was first published in 1974) can be accounted for by the delayed reaction to the War in Irish public consciousness and the country's neutrality during World War II.

The one play that sums up the question of pacifism in British and Irish drama is Rowbotham's *Friends of Alice Wheeldon*, a chronicle of the pacifist movement during the War years as observed from the vantage point of 60 years into the future. With unprecedented attention to detail Rowbotham distinguishes between the various pacifist movements and their strategies. If the title character in her undogmatic anti-war attitude for parts of the play upstages all other groupings and arouses sympathies for the patently unfair treatment that she receives, this is nevertheless only one aspect of the play's message. The other, more significant in the present context, is that it brings to light, with a high degree of authenticity, a variety of pacifist positions not only as individual emotions but in their organised form. When this was recognised at last, due to Rowbotham's and other publications, it became understandable why even in British *drama* the role of pacifism was such a significant one.

5
Disillusionment

The distinction between 'pacifism', 'disillusionment' and the threat of another war is somewhat artificial. Writers of pacifist plays were disillusioned with the experience of the previous war and therefore opposed to the dangers of another. The difference lies in the emphasis; the allocation of plays to one of these sections is somewhat arbitrary. Thus one could again in the present section consider works that have been designated as 'pacifist'. While O'Flaherty's and Malleson's central characters gain an insight into the conditions that have led to their disillusioned state of mind, O'Casey's Harry Heegan is incapable of such a perception, and it is left to the audience to experience the loss of illusions. The latter is regularly the case in plays that have been grouped together here under the heading 'disillusionment'.

Sometimes even the titles reflect the pessimistic outlook that goes hand in hand with the destruction of deceptive beliefs: *Defeat* (Galsworthy), *Heartbreak House* (Shaw), *But It Still Goes On* (Graves) or, indeed, the deeply ironic *For Services Rendered* (Maugham) suggest, in various ways, the loss of values that had once been adhered to. Such an attitude seems to have begun to spread even before the War had come to an end. Galsworthy in particular foresaw that before long the War would be looked back upon as the beginning of a period of instability, social unrest and economic crisis. In his clear-sighted if simplified *The Foundations* of 1917 he demonstrated how shaky the basis of society would become once a return to 'normality' was attempted. In the title of his short play *Defeat* of the same year, he formulated a state of affairs that is not confined to the young prostitute but threatens to destroy the young officer's superficial optimism, too. In *Windows* (1922) he demonstrated in farcical terms that much of what he had predicted for the post-War period had indeed come true. The returned soldier escapes into sarcasm when the high principles he has brought back from the trenches do not stand up to the realities of civilian life: 'We went into the war to save the little and weak; at least we *said* so; and look at us now! The bottom's out of all that' (714). Moreover, the atmosphere of disillusionment is not restricted to individual expressions but is reflected in the plot, when the girl whom Johnny wishes to 'save' (ironically called Faith) refuses to behave as a victim of society. Worst of all, Johnny's idealism that he tries to practise on his family is treated by Galsworthy with heavy authorial irony, demonstrating that it leads to farcical behaviour, such as his going on hunger strike on the servants' staircase to force his mother to retain Faith as a servant.

From many plays it appears that the immediate post-War world was experienced as 'not Reconstructed, as the politicians had promised, not a land fit for heroes to live in, but a jumble of the same old problems, made worse by the war – unemployment, trade union discontent, Ireland, economic depression'.[200] Like Galsworthy in *The Foundations*, Dane in *A Bill of Divorcement* projected into the future the disillusionment that she predicted as a consequence of the War. To foresee that it would take Hilary 15 years to be cured of the effects of shell shock is a dismal prediction in itself, while assuming that he will find his wife divorced from him under a new law when he eventually returns, is another indication of the degree of disillusionment that seems to have prevailed at the beginning of the 1920s. Perhaps over-generalising from *A Bill of Divorcement*, Hynes describes the women of 'this new, unhappy world': '[...] the modern Women we meet in Twenties fiction and drama are not free and not self-affirming, but bitter, sad, cynical, wistful, lost. [...] the thing that they most evidently share is a feeling that lies behind all the other details – a feeling of personal failure, of worthlessness and waste. They are damaged women, as the male survivors of the war are damaged men.'[201] This judgement is borne out by Graves's *But It Still Goes On*, both by the individual characters and its general view of the world which 'still goes on' (although, it is implied, it makes little sense to do so).

In their accumulation of grievances about the society their characters have to live in, plays of the 1920s such as *A Bill of Divorcement* and *But It Still Goes On*, Granville-Barker's *The Secret Life* or Maugham's *The Sacred Flame* project an atmosphere of general discontent, occasionally even hopelessness – an atmosphere that is taken to a higher level of consciousness in the two works that, with radically opposing techniques, present the clearest analyses of the situation after the War: *Heartbreak House* and *Satan the Waster*. Shaw's imaginative wish-fulfilment in the explosion that destroys the house which represents England is perhaps the most radical judgement on the world that was emerging from the War, 'a Shavian apocalypse in which the destruction of an anachronistic, dying system of values comes, *and is desired.*'[202] If, in Shaw's analysis, the house, or ship, of England is a weird conglomeration of folly, nastiness, uncontrolled self-interest and amorality, it is only natural that the inmates themselves should wish for its destruction. In this respect, Shaw goes beyond those authors who in their plays merely create a vague sensation of uneasiness and disappointment. The same is true of *Satan the Waster* where every seemingly honest and patriotic effort that had gone into the War is deconstructed into a macabre dance staged by Satan for the benefit of the Muse of History and the Ages-to-come, a reversion that turns the term 'disillusionment' into an understatement.

To judge by some plays, the discontent and frustration with the outcome of the War persisted well into the 1930s. It is even tangible in Coward's caleidoscopic *Cavalcade* which is pervaded by a deep sense of insecurity although it has sometimes been interpreted as 'optimistic'. It is, however, much stronger in Mackenzie's *Musical Chairs* where even the title suggests an ineffectual struggle for positions. Both on the individual level and on the plane of economic analysis it offers a picture of depression which is hardly toned down by the author's half-hearted attempt to provide a hopeful (to avoid the term 'happy') ending. The clearest expression of an out-and-out disillusionment is, however, *For Services Rendered*. Set in a family where every single member has suffered from the War, it displays in a consistently pessimistic tone the destruction of every hope that the dramatis personae had harboured for the future, and then goes on to suggest that this one family is representative of all the ordinary people not only in Britain but in the 'enemy' countries as well. No other dramatist has been so devastatingly successful as Maugham in formulating the disillusionment of post-War society, the sharp contrast between the illusions at the beginning of the War and their destruction at the end. The words of Sydney Ardsley, blinded and embittered through his front-line experience, can serve as a blueprint of the attitude in plays of this kind:

> I know how dead keen we all were when the war started. Every sacrifice was worth it. We didn't say much about it because we were rather shy, but honour did mean something to us and patriotism wasn't just a word. And then, when it was all over, we did think that those of us who'd died hadn't died in vain, and those of us who were broken and shattered and knew they wouldn't be any more good in the world were buoyed up by the thought that if they'd given everything they'd given it in a great cause.

[...] we were the dupes of the incompetent fools who ruled the nations. I know that we were sacrificed to their vanity, their greed and their stupidity. And the worst of it is that as far as I can tell they haven't learnt a thing. They're just as vain, they're just as greedy, they're just as stupid as they ever were. They muddle on, muddle on, and one of these days they'll muddle us all into another war.

(164)

In Maugham's view, survival into the post-War world is an equal disaster to premature death, as much a part of the play's concluding catastrophe as death by suicide or fatal disease. No other commercial playwright showed such disregard for the feelings of his audiences, and produced such an uncompromising analysis as he saw it. As has been suggested above, Hims's *The Breakfast Soldiers*, produced more than 60 years later, returned somewhat surprisingly to the mood of the earlier play which it resembles in more than superficial details, the difference being however that both the author and the audiences had to hark back to the situation of the 1930s across the gulf created by the disaster of another war.

6
Another War to End All Wars?

From the early 1930s onwards, the issue of pacifism as seen in the context of the First World War was closely related to the ever-increasing threat of a new war. While the leading politicians in 1914 had encouraged their countrymen to go to war with the reassuring perspective that this would be the final effort to combat not only the enemy but the threat of war in general, in the 1930s their successors found themselves in the unwelcome position of having to advocate another effort that would finally put paid to the evil of wars. This dilemma is clearly reflected in a number of plays. Since they regularly make reference to the earlier War, they justify their treatment in the present context. Most of them have already been described in Part I under the heading 'Foreshadowing another War'. The point here is to clarify the authors' *attitudes* in envisaging another world conflict.

The first observation in this context, and one remarkable in itself, is that not a single play has been found which welcomes or advocates another war. Nevertheless one can note significant differences in the dramatists' attitudes. Some authors, to judge from their plays, seem (almost fatalistically) to have taken the outbreak of another war for unavoidable. Caine, in *The Prime Minister*, did so as early as 1918 when he envisaged an ultimatum issued to Germany which is followed by another war, with its dire consequences for the German expatriates in London. Dane in *Shivering Shocks* and Calderon in *Peace* almost nonchalantly place their insignificant plots in the context of preparations for another conflict. Hamilton in *The Old Adam* seems to accept that people will fight whatever the lessons they could have learned from earlier clashes and whatever the conditions they have to fight in. Even Muriel and Sydney Box, despite their anti-war attitude as evinced by other plays, in *Peace in Our Time* seem to have succumbed to the fact that a new confrontation is unavoidable because no one has got peace in his or her heart. And Auden and Isherwood, not surprisingly in view of the world situation of 1938, set their play *On the Frontier* in the middle of another war, with a *third* war already in the offing.

A second group of plays, far from being resigned to the inevitability of a new world conflict, encourages its audiences to combat all preparations – on the national as well as the private level – for another war. This is not the place to decide whether such attempts, given the realities of the international political constellations, were naïve, ill-judged or even deliberately misleading. Suffice it to say that several playwrights evidently saw it as their moral obligation to discourage all attempts at rearmament, and that they did so on the basis of their First World War experience. Their plays are often organised around a new invention that exceeds even the destructive power of those weapons that had proved so devastating during the earlier War. In Armstrong's *Eleventh Hour* it is an improved machine gun, surpassing even the instrument that must have been the greatest killer device between 1914 and 1918, in Box's *Fantastic Flight* and Fernald's *To-Morrow* it is gas, the most terrifying of all World War I inventions, while in Evans's *Antic Disposition*, Ervine's *Progress*, Dane's *Shivering Shocks*, Hamilton's *The Old Adam* and *Wings Over Europe* by Nichols and Browne (despite the hero's initial idealism) it is an invention that vaguely foreshadows bacteriological warfare, lethal radiation techniques or nuclear destruction, all of them described with little technical expertise but with a clear-sighted vision of their destructive power. Such plays derive their imaginative force from the horror that was caused by the sudden appearance of gas attacks during the earlier War. These devices are proffered with the clear intention of preventing their being put into practice in a future conflict.

To win over their audiences to their own conviction, some authors employ identification figures, i.e. characters that either embody their attitudes from the start or are converted to them in the course of the play. Mrs Meldon in *Progress* has the audience's sympathies on her side from the beginning because she has lost her only son during World War I. When she is confronted with her brother's callous and condescending attitude, it is easy to side with her and to feel that his invention should be suppressed. When, however, she is driven to kill her brother as the only means of protecting mankind from his discovery, her position is subjected to moral scruples: the centuries-old motif of tyrannicide, here applied to the dangerous scientist, opens up the discussion whether a smaller evil (murder) can be justified to prevent a greater one (destruction on an unheard-of scale). Popplewell's pacifist in the play of the same title is free from such moral ambiguities: she has clearly been designed to convert the audience to the author's pacifist stance. Inventing a character who accepts personal disadvantages in order to uphold his or her convictions is the clearest way to enlist the audience's sympathies and to transmit the ideological position that he or she embodies. When Mary Blake in Box's *'Bring Me My Bow'* refuses to write the essay that would have guaranteed her a place at Oxford, and resigns herself to a job in her mother's laundry, she makes a convincing stand for her convictions which must have impressed, perhaps even converted the play's audiences. The proof of the soundness of the author's principles here as elsewhere rests in the personal integrity of one of the characters.

In some other plays, it is not an individual character but the thrust of the plot as a whole that projects the author's attitude and convinces the audience of the superiority of such a stance. Armstrong in *Eleventh Hour* dispenses with a last-minute conversion (which would have been possible, given the course of the plot) and instead encourages the spectator to draw his own conclusions: that the only way to avoid future disasters is to withdraw all traditional or new weapons. Corrie, in *And So to War*, likewise allows the audience to take their own decision when the representative of Amalgamated Industries persuades the nation's leaders that expansion by war is a matter of life or death. Although everyone had earlier on agreed that 'The country still bleeds from the last war; we've had enough full stop!' (173), the voice of capital forces them, including the seemingly all-powerful dictator, to agree to a declaration of war.

Nowhere in these plays is there a serious discussion of the arguments that might be advanced *for* rearmament and the preparations for a future war. The tacit assumption is that a new war would be exactly like the earlier one – with the same confusions, the same futile sacrifices, senseless suffering and moral ambiguities, and, subsequently, the same disillusionment, and that therefore it must be avoided at all cost. The advocates of appeasement in the late 1930s had faithful allies in the authors of anti-war plays. When, in 1939, Britain once more declared war on Germany, such discussions became obsolete at one stroke, and the period of British plays about the First World War seemed to have come to an end abruptly.

7
Hope against Hope

It is a measure of the general disillusionment after the War that few plays derive a semblance of hope from the experience of the conflict. The belief that the world, or Britain, had become a better or a safer place to live in because of the War, seems not to have been shared by the majority of dramatists and, by implication, by their audiences. The War years are not, in retrospect, seen in a rosy light, although as a rule people tend to glorify a period of hardship they have survived, setting it against the present which appears bleaker and more sordid. Only one play successfully recreates the nostalgia for the War years that must have been felt by many. Chetham-Strode's *Sometimes Even Now* (the title in itself suggestive of a wistful attitude) looks back on the War as a period of sacrifices given freely and privation endured with a smile, and it draws an unfavourable comparison with the present of 1933: 'No one wants another war – but at any rate – we did live in the years when men *were* men. What *are* the gods of the present generation? Having a good time at other people's expense!' (453).

But to feel a degree of nostalgia for the past is not, of course, to derive hope from it for the future. Barrie's *The New Word* is one of the rare examples where the wartime experience helps to improve personal relationships, the 'new word' being the son's acknowledgement that a period of mutual sarcasm and resentment has been terminated by his imminent departure to the front. Roger's first appearance in uniform makes both father and son realise how much they have in common; however one wonders how long the feeling would last if they both had to return to the banalities of civilian life. A true happy ending is in store for the returned soldier in McEvoy's *The Likes of Her* where the coster-girl with the golden heart proves equal to all disappointments and guarantees, against all probability, a harmonious future. In Brighouse's *Once a Hero* the effect of the war experience may, one hopes, be more durable because it is less euphoric: in the case of Sir William and the erstwhile scoundrel Tim the War has revealed to others and to themselves who they really are, and such an understanding may lead to create a feeling of social responsibility. That the examples of an optimistic outlook are both scarce and rather trivial is in itself an indication of a widespread sceptical attitude. Significantly, religion plays practically no part in establishing a vision of a better future. The only exception is Hamilton's short play *The Child in Flanders*, where the three soldiers encounter a realistic nativity scene which in their dreams they transfer to the traditional Bethlehem tableau and leave the hut next morning being somehow transformed: against the noise of the big guns there is a suggestion of an 'Angel Choir' singing 'Alleluia'.

A hopeful perspective for the country as a whole arising out of an individual situation occurs in Box's *Angels of War* where at least one of the ambulance drivers, whose bickering takes up most of the play, realises that there is a desperate need to make peace work: 'Don't you realise how awful it would be if things weren't different after this? People used to take war for granted, but they won't any longer. They said it was a glorious adventure. But we can tell them a thing or two about it, can't we?' (74). It is, of course, one of the tragedies of Europe that, only a few years later, even such a moderate hope was crushed.

Perhaps the most optimistic of all World War I plays is King-Hall's *B.J. One* which derives hope for the future from the presentation of wartime events. This is clear from Act I where leading British and German industrialists, looking back on the War in 1929, conduct a discussion on the steel industry in the whole of Europe, planning to set up a cartel to eliminate ruinous competition and safeguard employment. The Act is suffused with an enthusiastic vision of the future: another war will not happen, people have learnt their lesson and will from now on understand the necessity of universal cooperation. Act II returns to the first meeting between the two protagonists who, in June 1914, serve as naval officers and celebrate their encounter in a spirit of mutual respect and even friendship, drinking to 'the eternal comradeship of our Navies!' (202). Even in Act III, set on a cruiser during the Battle of Jutland, this spirit survives: the British officers discuss the enemy with surprising detachment, weighing German war crimes against British ones and emphasising that such actions are 'inevitable in war' (210). Consequently the German officer, when he is rescued by the British, refuses to betray the movements of the German fleet *and* is highly respected for it. In production, the order of the Acts was apparently reversed (II, III, I), which must have placed additional emphasis on the hopeful outlook of the play, with the Battle of Jutland a mere episode, wedged in between the two 'optimistic' Acts. However, one suspects that in performance the ideological element in the play was largely neutralised by the spectacular battle scene. Unlike *B.J. One*, Nichols and Browne in *Wings over Europe* keep hope and despair in the balance until the end, which is the most one can say for the majority of the plays that deal with the future of the country. Where an optimistic attitude is expressed on a more general level, not associated with the actions of individualised characters, it can easily become so abstract and, indeed, irrational that little hope can be inferred from it. An archetypal example is Gandy's short play *In the House of Despair* where the Messenger of Spring lures the victims of the War back from the abode of Despair to a world of conflicts – there is nothing in the play to justify such a change of attitude, however much one may welcome it.

The most convincing (or should one say: the least unconvincing?) expression of a hopeful outlook can be found in Berkeley's symbolical play, *The White Château*. While in Robinson's *The Big House* the symbolic rebuilding of the country-seat is merely hinted at in the last few lines, in *The White Château* the reconstruction of the château (turned into a pile of rubble by the combined exertions of both sides) is the central event without which the preceding scenes would be meaningless. It is 'an act of faith' (857), all the more convincing because the owners themselves as well as the allegorical Workman have serious doubts as to the advisability of the reconstruction. Diane asks: 'Philip, are we trying to do an impossible thing?' (854), but is reassured 'If you look back you can only despair. Turn and look at the new Château' (854). While they stumble around the building site in the dark, they are reminded by the Workman that 'in all history there has been no war that did not pave the way for another' (857), and it seems for a moment that all efforts at rebuilding the house and the world must remain futile. Yet in the end Diane reaffirms her declaration of faith: 'I believe in the God in Man; in love; in the beauty of life; in the conquering struggle with evil; in the destiny of mankind. I believe there is a purpose in creation; a mighty scheme in the universe' (857–8), and the play ends with the wonderful curtain-line 'One sees a glimmer of light from time to time' (858). This would have been an eminently fitting conclusion not only to the play but also to the present chapter if it had not been for the catastrophe that was to engulf the world a mere 12 years after the writing of *The White Château*.

Part IV Popular Failures and Successes: Aspects of Reception

1
The West End

The War and its aftermath had enormous consequences for the *performance* of war plays. Within days of the outbreak of the War, the situation in the British theatres worsened dramatically. Restrictions on lighting, food, liquor, printing and public transport made the theatre less attractive for its traditional patrons. The threat of air raids caused anxieties and induced some theatres to substitute matinee shows for late-night performances. Young actors were put under pressure to enlist (and were actually called up once conscription was introduced).[203] Nevertheless, the West End stage recovered quickly; by Christmas 1914, 26 theatres were in operation as compared with 29 in the previous year.[204]

The most dramatic change occurred in the composition of audiences. Many pre-War theatregoers thought that the soldiers' sufferings at the front rendered the pursuit of pleasure in the theatre inappropriate or even immoral, and that self-denial could in some obscure way serve as a gesture of support for the troops. Instead, the theatres filled with soldiers (including Canadians, Australians and others) on leave from the front, and also with civilians whom the War had brought to London. Such a change had considerable consequences for the theatrical fare on offer in the West End: 'The theatre was [...] for both civilian and serviceman, a temporary release from the agonies of the war; and for this escape they looked, on the whole, to musical comedy and to the music hall with its songs, farcical one-act sketches and revues.'[205] The prototypical West End play of the war years and beyond was Asche's *Chu Chin Chow* which began its unlikely stage career in 1916 and clung on for five years, well beyond the end of the War, running for 2238 performances, in pre-*Mousetrap* times an incredible number.[206] As one critic described it, '*Chu*, with its moon and camels and picture-book East, became a habit. No doubt it was nougat but it was good nougat: it improved with keeping, and people went to it again and again.'[207]

Nevertheless it would be too simple to believe that theatre audiences insisted on nothing but escapism, avoiding the War in the theatre at all cost. According to Collins, nearly 120 war plays were passed by the Lord Chamberlain's office during the first year of the War, and while these numbers were reduced when the War lengthened beyond all expectation and audiences became aware of the real situation at the front, scripts of war plays continued to be submitted to the censor, and several of them actually reached the stage.[208] These fall into two groups: straightforward propaganda plays, designed to boost morale and to support specific causes, and sensational dramas in the tradition of the older melodrama, both types often overlapping where sensational effects were employed to generate patriotic feelings.

Propaganda plays were designed to encourage sacrifices on the part of the civilians, to support recruitment or to combat pacifist tendencies. The latter became a major concern once the War had gone beyond the initial patriotic fervour. The two most prominent anti-pacifist plays of the War years were Jones's *The Pacifists* and Owen's *Loyalty*, both first produced in 1917. *The Pacifists* could profit from its author's long-standing reputation as one of the leading pre-War dramatists, while *Loyalty* 'was accepted for production within three days of its completion, by the first management to which it was submitted, went into rehearsal within a week, and was produced (anonymously) three weeks later'.[209] Nevertheless, and although both plays were widely reviewed, they proved to be disappointing to the managements: '*The Pacifists* was the first flop of the 1917–18 theatrical season, and the worst: it closed after ten days', while *Loyalty*, 'in spite of its sound doctrine', ran for only three weeks.[210] Only the cliché-ridden *Kultur at Home* by Besier and Spottiswoode, with 109 performances, came anywhere near a box-office success. Clearly, to the majority of theatregoers *Chu Chin Chow* was the preferred choice; '[...] judging by the short runs of the crude, jingoistic and overtly propaganda plays', it appears that theatre audiences developed a healthy immunity to outspoken propaganda,[211] unless, that is, it was accompanied by a sensational plot and/or spectacular scenic effects.

In sensational drama, the most prominent plot element was the spy motif. According to Collins, nearly 100 plays involving espionage (many of them short plays) were produced in Britain during the war years. One of the reasons seems to have been that 'the locale for a spy could be home-based and involve everyone, military and civilian alike.'[212] Worrall and Terry's *The Man Who Stayed at Home*, described as 'good in a schoolboy's annual fashion', was among the most successful;[213] its long run of 584 performances (beginning in December 1914 at the Royalty, transferred to the Apollo in March 1916) is one of the incredible success stories in this field. Page's *By Pigeon Post* at the Garrick with 379 performances was nearly as popular and Hackett's *The Invisible Foe* (129) and *The Freedom of the Seas* (226) also proved how slight an effort was sufficient to achieve a run of several months.[214] Mills's *The Luck of the Navy* even survived the end of the War as well as the transfer from the Queen's to the Garrick and some scathingly ironic reviews, with a total of 406 performances. The Lyceum, now a far cry from the days of its glory under Irving and Ellen Terry, was particularly renowned for its scenes of excessive violence and highly improbable plots. Howard's *Seven Days' Leave* had, in the words of the *Times* reviewer, 'two German spies who [...] when brought to book, scowl and gnash their teeth like true Huns', and when even this did not satisfy the audience's demand for staged patriotism, 'the destruction of the U-boat by British destroyers [...] roused the audience to such a pitch of enthusiasm that they quite forgot to cough, this being the first time during the evening that they had omitted to do so.'[215] No wonder then that such a masterpiece ran for nearly one-and-a-half years (711 performances). However, other runs at the Lyceum were shorter, Melville's *The Female Hun* being the only one apart from *Seven Days' Leave* to reach triple figures (107), while *Jolly Jack Tar* by Hicks and Shirley at the Prince's closed after 67 nights. The critics of the national papers dutifully reported such plays, often with tongue-in-cheek irony at the expense of the audiences as well as the performers, reflecting the attitude of the more educated theatregoers (only the reviewers for *The Era* refrained from passing value judgements and stuck to providing extensive plot summaries).

Comedies with a wartime situation at the centre appear to have been an equally safe bet for box-office success. Terry's harmless *General Post* ran through most of 1917 and 1918 at the Haymarket, reaching 532 nights. Jesse's *Billeted* (236) and Chambers's *The Saving Grace* (166) also went beyond the break-even point, which at the time was lower than it is today, and so did Knoblock's suggestively titled *Home on Leave* (145). Among the established playwrights of the pre-War years, only Barrie with his sentimental *A Kiss for Cinderella* at Wyndham's (156 performances) reached triple figures with a war theme. However, by far the most successful wartime production, and one that still ranks among the 100 shows with the longest runs on the London stage, was *The Better 'Ole* by Bairnsfather and Eliot which lasted for 811 performances at C.B. Cochran's Oxford Theatre (in addition to 351 nights at the Greenwich in New York) – a success that is difficult to assess since the text was never published, although it was filmed in 1926 by Warner Brothers. In 1919, Bairnsfather boasted in his autobiography *From Mud to Mufty* that *The Better 'Ole* 'played in London for over a year, twice daily. Five touring companies toured and are touring as I write, and have played in the same town over and over again. It is an equal success in America, Canada and Australia, whilst among its minor activities it has toured India.'[216] Trewin, presumably speaking of the revival at the Regent in 1929, calls it a 'ramshackle drama' and a sign that 'dramatists remained afraid to take the war seriously.'[217]

Plays that were in any way critical of the war effort naturally stood little chance of reaching the stage for the duration of the War. The censors in the Lord Chamberlain's office were strict in detecting any hint of 'impropriety or anti-patriotic stage business', and 'it was also important to the military authorities that a character should not act in such a ridiculous fashion as to bring discredit on the Service or the King's uniform.'[218] With the Defence of the Realm Act (DORA) passed in August 1914, the authorities possessed another instrument to suppress undesirable publications, among them play scripts that were not designed for stage production. It was brought to bear, for instance, on Brockway's *The Devil's Business*, an attack on the international munitions industry. When it was published in October 1914, 'the police raided both the National Labour Press in Manchester, where the little pamphlet was printed, and the headquarters of the Independent Labour Party in London where it was being sold, and seized all available copies.' The London copies were destroyed, but fortunately for present-day readers the authorities in Manchester (who must have been somewhat obtuse in failing to recognise the play's explosive nature) found it unobjectionable and allowed some copies to be returned. Later, Brockway and other writers were imprisoned.[219] In 1916, all the copies of Malleson's book *Two Plays* were confiscated, doubtless because of *Black 'Ell* which he had written after being converted to pacifism and having joined the No-Conscription Fellowship as a consequence of his front-line experience.[220] It took more than 60 years before the atmosphere surrounding the persecution of anti-war militants was captured for the stage in Rowbotham's *Friends of Alice Wheeldon* of 1980.

The evidence accumulated here will indicate that serious plays with at least a limited degree of literary aspirations stood little chance of being produced during the war years. Authors who argued for artistic and intellectual quality on the stage must have sounded like voices in the wilderness. A writer in the *Athenaeum* who signed as H.F., deplored the deterioration of the London theatre since the beginning of the War, criticised the ubiquity of the revue, 'that incorrigible blackleg [...] the chief aim of which appears to be to hold all the legitimate expedients of the art of stage illusion up to ridicule', and regretted that 'our "legitimate drama" [...] now consists almost exclusively of light comedies.' His main appeal, however, goes beyond the questionable defence of stage illusion; he feared that the War experience would push aside all aesthetic considerations as well as all serious subjects that were not directly linked to the War: '[...] if we suffer the home fires to die out, we shall one day awaken to the shivering reality that, if there is nothing to live for, there was nothing to die for either.'[221]

Similar misgivings had already been voiced by P.P.H. (Howe?) in *The Outlook*. He set out to demolish a moralistic pamphlet by one Rev. G.S. Streatfeild who saw the War as a welcome opportunity to rid the stage of what he considered the immorality of the pre-War theatre. 'The present moment', Streatfeild argued rather pompously, harking back to Jeremy Collier, 'is one that invites us, summons us, to face the fact that the stage is a very potent force in the education of the people. [...] the outbreak of the war has apparently roused a healthier sentiment, so that there is, I believe, nothing on the boards at the present moment to which reasonable [!] exception could be taken [...]'. P.P.H., in ironically rejecting Streatfeild's set of values, confirmed the negative image of the theatre during the War: 'I wish I shared the fine healthy optimism of the author [...] as to the war's immediate effects. [...] I look down this morning's newspaper, and I find two good plays have enjoyed less success than they ought to have done, while about 26 musical comedies and revived old farces stand for the sobering and solemnising influence the war is exercising.'[222] A few weeks before the Armistice, E. Temple Thurston in an article for *The Era* concluded that the theatre during the War had served as an 'anæsthetic' and very little else: 'In four years the theatrical managers [...] have learnt to understand their function as anæsthetists.' Thurston decided it was about time that the theatre (re)discovered its responsibility for society: 'A thousand problems, moral and social, will arise out of the war, and these must be dealt with, not only by the authorities, not only by the State, but by the dramatist and author, who must and will say what is in their minds.'[223]

Zangwill, in his plea for a poetic tragedy about the conflicts arising out of the War, again stressed the deficiencies of the stage during the War years, lashing 'the British cult of brainlessness on the stage' where 'patriotism [...] was the last refuge, not of a scoundrel, but of a comic singer.' The War, in his view, has 'deepened this sense of a wasted or perverted instrument.' Zangwill claims that 'the drama, whose life is clash, is the truest of all literary forms', but in his call for such works suggests that so far they do not exist:

> What we need from our stage is a drama that helps us to move habitually on the high plane to which we are roused by the death and heroism of our soldiers and our sons, by the agony and aspiration of our country. [...] A nation whose greatest actors are drawn off to the music-halls is not likely to disentangle itself from commercialism when the hour for heroism strikes; a nation that feeds its spiritual fires upon the slag and ashes of dead formulæ is not likely to burn with a clear flame.[224]

These pessimistic views were echoed in an article by A.B. Walkley that appeared immediately after the end of the War. Walkley set out to prove or refute the argument that 'the war has gravely menaced, if not destroyed, the art of the theatre', and while, in somewhat rambling fashion, he does not arrive at a clear-cut answer, his conclusions, expressed in such phrases as 'The theatre has been swamped by the *simples*', are predominantly negative. In particular he argues that 'Where the art of the theatre did really suffer at the hands of the "simple" public was in its so-called "war" plays' – not only, as he adds, because better plays were barred from the stage by the taste of the masses, but because the reality of the War sat uncomfortably close to the reality presented on stage: 'The war will have to await recollection in tranquillity before it can provide pure art.'[225] In this respect he agreed with the anonymous *Times* critic who wrote in 1917, before the Armistice: 'The great war play has still to be written – it looks now as if the greatest dramatic theme in history will have to wait for proper treatment until peace has again returned to the world.'[226]

Walkley was not far out in his prophecy. When hostilities ended, the theatre-going public (judging by the list of box-office successes) wanted nothing so much as a comedy with a happy ending. This statement is borne out by such works as Berkeley's *French Leave*, which in 1920 ran for 283 nights at the Globe, Hoffe's *The Faithful Heart* (1921; 194 performances at the Comedy), McEvoy's *The Likes of Her* (1923; 228 performances at the St Martin's) and Darlington's silly *Alf's Button* (1924; 111 performances at the Prince's). Dane's *A Bill of Divorcement*, which in 1921 began a long run of 401 nights at the St Martin's, had at least a serious theme, the current debate on the new divorce legislation in conjunction with the wide-spread experience of shell shock, but it shied away from the tragic consequences of the plot in a glaringly artificial conclusion. Not until the late 1920s did some of these authors turn to a more serious treatment of the War, as did Berkeley with his symbolic *The White Château*; needless to say, it did not come anywhere near the popularity of his *French Leave*, although as early as 1929 it was included by one editor among the 'great modern British plays'.[227]

An even more instructive example is that of Maugham who opened the series of harmless post-War comedies in 1919 with his *Home and Beauty* where the seriousness of the underlying issues is ignored to an extent that, with hindsight, appears equally embarrassing for the author and his audiences. Its premiere at the Playhouse on 30 August 1919, the beginning of a run of 235 performances, was almost immediately followed by the Broadway opening (under the title *Too Many Husbands*). Subsequent revivals included a long-running production at the Adelphi in 1937 (when another war was already in the offing), a post-World War II production at the Arts and St Martin's (1950), another at the National Theatre (1968) and yet another at the Lyric (2002). The BBC adapted the play for television in 1979, and there were two Hollywood films (*Too Many Husbands* in 1940 and *Three for the Show* in 1955).[228] One likes to think that Maugham, when he wrote *The Unknown*, tried to make amends for the facetiousness with which he had treated the returned-soldier theme in *Home and Beauty*. His theological discussion on the responsibility for the War, with the famous/infamous line 'And who is going to forgive God?', resulted in the play being described as 'the most discursive and mirthless of Maugham's plays'.[229] Needless to say, *The Unknown* remained as obscure as suggested in the title despite a brief 1920 run of 77 performances at the Aldwych, and it was not until the end of the decade that another Maugham play about the consequences of the War achieved some popularity. *The Sacred Flame* at the Playhouse in 1929, having first been tried out at Washington and on Broadway, ran for 209 nights, but it is safe to assume that at least part of its success was due to the whodunnit element in the plot which obscured the serious plight of the paralysed soldier hero. When Maugham, at the end of his career as a playwright, turned to an uncompromising indictment of the War, a plot without any loopholes for his audiences to escape into sentimental regrets, he suffered a humiliating defeat, because *For Services Rendered* had to be taken off after a short run (considering Maugham's status as a playwright) of 78 nights despite a cast which included Flora Robson, Cedric Hardwicke and Ralph Richardson: 'There were no epigrams or happy endings to make a West End audience go home smiling.'[230] Not until late in the century, with the revival of *For Services Rendered* at the

National, did the theatre-going public discover that Maugham had written one of the finest plays about World War I.

The first commercially successful play about the situation at the front was Wall's *Havoc* which, after the production by the Repertory Players at the Regent (1923), was revived in the following year at the Haymarket and ran for 174 performances (as well as being filmed with George O'Brien in the central role), a sensational series considering the type of play it is. Apparently by 1924 large audiences were prepared to accept 'realistic' front-line scenes which resulted in blindness or death for some of the characters. What they were not yet ready to accept (and what they were not offered in Wall's play) was a general criticism of the War. The soldiers in the play grumble at the inconveniences, even the horrors of their experience, but they do not question the military strategies, let alone the objectives of the War; the conflict is treated by them (and also by the author) as an unavoidable catastrophe.

Such an attitude was confirmed when, five years later, Sherriff's *Journey's End* reached the commercial stage at the Savoy after having been produced on a Sunday night by the Incorporated Stage Society at the Apollo with the young Laurence Olivier in the role of Stanhope. From the Savoy it later moved to the Prince of Wales's. The play ran for 594 performances (plus 485 nights on Broadway), which earned it an honourable place in the all-time list of long runs on the London stage, a list that is otherwise dominated by titles such as *The Mousetrap, Oh! Calcutta!* and *No Sex Please, We're British*. It has been estimated that about half a million people saw it at the Savoy alone.[231] The play was soon translated into various languages; a German version called *Die andere Seite* and directed by Heinz Hilpert was produced as early as August 1929 at the Deutsches Künstlertheater, Berlin, and subsequently at 40 other theatres. Translations proliferated, 'and when the Japanese and the Rumanians and the Russians came in, together with Lithuania, Finland, Estonia and Latvia, the total added up to 27 different languages, including Irish and Afrikaans, Hindustani and Siamese.'[232] Touring companies took the play to the remotest corners of Britain and to many parts of the world:

> Throughout the summer and autumn of 1929 the play went on building up, until fourteen companies were playing it in English and seventeen foreign versions were running in Europe. It was running in America and Canada, Australia and South Africa; an English speaking production had established itself in Paris; and a modest little company had sailed off into the blue with the right to perform the play anywhere it fancied east of Suez.[233]

When Coward travelled in the Far East in 1929–30, he encountered a straggling repertory company in Singapore who were doing *Journey's End* (apparently the one mentioned by Sherriff), and generously helped them out by playing Stanhope for a few nights. When, four years later, Coward produced his revue *Words and Music* (1932), it needed only a few short phrases from a character called Stanhope – 'Three years of Hell. Will it never end? God! I am tired. Only wine can keep me going' (144) – to conjure up the setting and atmosphere of Sherriff's play which Coward shortened into a 'Teutonic Dream' (140) and mercilessly burlesqued in a riot of absurdities.

Journey's End provoked countless reactions. It was agreed by most critics (those who had been through a front-line experience as well as those who had been too young to be in the trenches) that Sherriff's depiction of the situation in the dugout was true to life. Many writers confessed themselves to have been deeply moved; Hugh Walpole wrote that after the final curtain, 'in common with the rest of the audience I went out into the street ennobled and simplified by a supreme experience.'[234] Very few contemporaries dared to question such an impact; when G.A. Martelli, writing in the *Cornhill Magazine* in 1929, detected 'a hint of falseness and sentimentality' in the play,[235] he was called to order by T.C. Fowle in the same magazine.[236] A.C. Ward in *The Nineteen-Twenties* was one of the few contemporaries who found some degree of 'sentimentality, falsification, hysteria' in *Journey's End*; while praising Sherriff's 'dramatic craftsmanship', he asserted that the dialogue displayed 'public-school standards', that Sherriff had failed to make 'dramatic or ironic use' of the characters' immaturity, that he did not 'cause the audience to meditate upon the circumstance that her War was being fought and her national destinies swayed by young men who had been given no chance to reach emotional maturity.'[237] With the benefit of hindsight the analogy to the public-school system was later reiterated by many writers. Hynes saw in *Journey's End* 'the same idolizing, the same adolescent emotionalism, the same team spirit and self-sacrifice, the same hovering note of homosexuality', which, taken together, made the play 'a canonical example of the Myth'.[238]

For the majority of Sherriff's contemporaries, however, the play's 'truthfulness' overshadowed all other considerations, aesthetic, ideological or otherwise; as one critic declared categorically: 'We are spared nothing in this play. This is war as it really was.'[239] Even those who took exception to Sherriff's presentation, did so with reference to its 'truthfulness'. In the forefront of these was Frank Fox, an ex-officer with front-line experience, who singled out *Journey's End*, together with Remarque's

All Quiet on the Western Front ('the German masterpiece of muck'), for a bitter attack on recent war-literature: '[...] this war literature, which comes now in a sewer spate, gives not a true but a foully libellous picture; it represents partly an ignorant and neurotic view, partly a profit-seeking pandering to the pruriency of a section of the public which is willing to pay for libels on the men and women of whose fame they have a mean-spirited jealousy.' Fox objected to *Journey's End* primarily on account of Stanhope's alcoholism and Hibbert's cowardice: 'it portrays conditions in regard to drink and to "nerves" which were impossible',[240] in other words, he denies the authenticity of Sherriff's portrayal which had earned him so much praise. Fox's protest was echoed by Douglas Jerrold in a 50-page pamphlet characteristically entitled *The Lie about the War*. Although reasoned more dispassionately than Fox's emotional outburst, it repeats the assertion that *Journey's End* (on which it touches only in passing) and other war books are statistically incorrect;[241] what they show may have happened, but it is the exception and carries the grave danger of being generalised by an uninformed public.

What apparently did not, at the time, worry either the general public or the critics, was that Sherriff's characters gave no thought to the causes and the justification of the War, and that they were joined in this by the author. As in other plays, the War is being treated here as one great calamity, inevitable if senseless, and deep regret for the unhappy fate of the dramatis personae is the only reaction the audience is expected to feel. When some reviewers saw the play as a protest against this particular War and against all wars, this was clearly not Sherriff's intention.[242] In January 2004, 75 years after the original production, *Journey's End* opened once more in the West End (this time at the Comedy; the third revival within 15 years), prior to an extended run in four West End theatres and 30 cities across the UK.[243] Even then, it was still greeted with the same enthusiasm as the first premiere. The veteran W.F. Deedes reminisced in the *Daily Telegraph*: 'It is 70 years [*sic*] since I saw RC Sherriff's play [...] It made a more lasting impression on me than any play I have seen since.'[244] The *Times* welcomed the play back with a long story on the original show and on the present director's excitement about Sherriff's text, and it was still amazed that a play which was 'a handy standby for schools and am-dram' but had 'no leading lady' could successfully return to the West End.[245] It even suffered still from the same misunderstandings, as when the *International Herald Tribune* assumed that 'Sherriff's specific view of the Great War was that it made no sense.'[246]

The original production had coincided with a turning point in the public reaction to the War. Desmond McCarthy, writing in 1929, was one of the first to realise that to 'the historian the year 1929–30 will chiefly be remembered as that in which men's emotions first began to turn against the idea of war'.[247] The 'realistic' presentation of individual experience was repeatedly replaced, or at least supplemented, on the stage as well as in fiction, by an often aggressive indictment of the War which had been the cause of so much suffering.

The outstanding example of such a change is O'Casey's *The Silver Tassie*. It was premiered at the Apollo in 1929 (ironically on the same stage where *Journey's End* had been tried out by the Stage Society) at a time when the long run of *Journey's End* was still continuing at the Savoy, and it was seen by its author as an anti-*Journey's End*. Originally, *The Silver Tassie* had been written for the Dublin Abbey Theatre, and O'Casey had even created the major parts for certain Abbey actors. However, it was rejected under the overbearing influence of Yeats, which resulted in what has gained some notoriety as the '*Tassie* controversy'. Yeats wrote an arrogant letter which began with the condescending 'My dear Casey' and went on to state some rather questionable reasons why the Abbey could not produce the play. Adding insult to injury, Yeats suggested to Lady Gregory that O'Casey himself might withdraw the manuscript to spare him the 'disgrace' of having had a play of his rejected by the Abbey, a letter that Lady Gregory rather undiplomatically passed on to O'Casey. Understandably enraged by such a suggestion, O'Casey sent a violent rejoinder in which he demolished most of Yeats's arguments. Then, in a typical overreaction, he submitted the whole correspondence to several newspapers; it was printed in *The Irish Statesman* whereupon Yeats threatened to sue O'Casey for breach of copyright. By then the press not only in Ireland but also in Britain and America had taken up the battle with delight, Shaw had joined in on O'Casey's side, and it took some time until the two protagonists allowed themselves to be mollified by Lady Gregory and Mrs Shaw into letting the matter drop. O'Casey had the concluding satisfaction that neither his English publisher nor his English producer seemed unduly worried by the Dublin rejection, and *The Silver Tassie* was both published and performed in London within a year of the controversy.[248]

Once *The Silver Tassie* had reached London, O'Casey turned his wrath from Yeats to Sherriff. In his autobiographical volume *Rose and Crown*, published in 1952, he still remembered

[...] the false effrontery of Sherriff's *Journey's End*, which made of war a pleasant thing to see and feel; a strife put spiritually at a great distance; a demure echo, told under candlelight, at a gentle fireside, of a fight informal; a discreet accompaniment to a strident song, done on a lute, played low; the stench of blood hid in a mist of soft-sprayed perfume; the yells of agony modulated down to a sweet pianissimo of pain; surly death, or death exultant, fashioned into a smiling courtier, bringing himself in with a bow; a balmy breath of blood and guts; all the mighty, bloodied vulgarity of war foreshortened into a petty, pleasing picture.[249]

By contrast, O'Casey saw his own play as going 'into the heart of war' by juxtaposing the individualised plot of Harry Heegan who sets out as a hero and returns as a cripple, with an expressionist second act where all traces of individuality have been removed and where the War as such is displayed in harsh reality. Here it was impossible for the audiences to restrict their reactions to compassion for the stage characters; the War itself came under attack, and all those who did not accept O'Casey's verdict reacted with dismay or resentment, as in a statement from the *Catholic World*: 'O'Casey's play fails [...] because he has produced a drama that does not satisfy the man in the street. The man in the street knows that the Great War was something more than mere blood and brothels. [...] the plain man will turn from this play to that other war play, *Journey's End*.[250] However, there was no stopping the transition from psychological realism to a generalised anti-war stance in some of the plays of the thirties for which O'Casey had paved the way.

Incidentally, O'Casey had a pioneering function in another field, too. When in 1926, two years before *The Silver Tassie*, his tragedy about the Easter Rising, *The Plough and the Stars*, had a respectable run of 133 performances at the Fortune, it introduced the West End public to an Irish view of the War in which the 1916 rebellion loomed larger than the Somme or Gallipoli.

In the 1930s, the subject of the War seems to have lost much of its attraction for a wider theatre audience. Only four West End productions ran for more than 100 performances, one of these beings a revival of *Home and Beauty* in 1937. The longest running production which dealt (at least in part) with the War was Coward's *Cavalcade* with 405 nights, while *Words and Music* by the same author closed after 164 performances. In both cases, the author's prestige as actor, director, composer, librettist and dramatist must have contributed to the success. *Cavalcade* was sometimes criticised for being excessively patriotic; it is more correct to say that it balanced the positive sides of the War years against the negative and avoided any overtly partisan statement. That Coward was also capable of a straightforward indictment of the War, becomes clear from *Post Mortem*, the play he wrote on his way home from Singapore after having acted in *Journey's End*. In his autobiography he calls it 'an angry little vilification of war', adding that 'my mind was strongly affected by *Journey's End*' and that 'I wrote *Post Mortem* with the utmost sincerity [...] In fact I tore my emotions to shreds over it.' Such an astoundingly frank confession by one of the most professional playwrights of all times, who always knew what his audiences wanted and acted accordingly, is followed by the admission that an adherence to one's convictions can lead to aesthetic failure: 'There is, I believe, some of the best writing I have ever done in it, also some of the worst. [...] I passionately believed in the truth of what I was writing; too passionately.'[251] Even Coward's popular name could not save *Post Mortem* from being ignored by the commercial stage; ironically it was premiered in January 1944, during another world war, by English prisoners in a POW camp at Eichstätt, Germany (the first professional production was by BBC 2 in September 1968).

One of the most amazing events of the theatre in the 1930s was the long run (314 performances) of Mackenzie's *Musical Chairs* at the Criterion, a play that is every bit as pessimistic as Maugham's *For Services Rendered* which had closed after a ten weeks' run in the same season, and this although *Musical Chairs* does not have the distinction of Maugham's craftsmanship and clarity of vision. No other war play during the thirties, with the exception of *Cavalcade*, came anywhere near the popular appeal of *Musical Chairs*. Even Chetham-Strode's *Sometimes Even Now*, with its skilful character portraits and its nostalgic look at the war years, a play one would think might have captured the mood of the early 1930s, could not rival the success of *Musical Chairs*. Another skilfully constructed play with a multiplicity of viewpoints, van Druten's *Flowers of the Forest*, probably was not acceptable to the majority of theatregoers because it ends on a clear pacifist message, calling war 'an evil, like disease' which *can* be stopped if it is realised that this is 'our duty' (568).

After the end of the Second World War, the earlier War did not possess sufficient topicality for West End managements to encourage speculations on a profitable investment – with two significant exceptions. Rattigan's *The Winslow Boy*, although set *before* the War, has various references to an imminent war and was considered by many as an ideological justification for Britain's entry into the First (and, by implication, into the Second) War. That such a justification was welcomed by the general public can be seen from the long run of 476 performances at the Lyric in 1946 and from the play's subsequent career on numerous provincial stages.

Theatre Workshop's *Oh What a Lovely War* appealed to a wide public for the opposite reason. First produced during the period of Cold War disillusionment, it could only be seen as a rejection of all justifications for this war and any war. Whatever Joan Littlewood and her co-workers had originally intended ('The creation of an anti-war play was never in the minds of those connected with the production'[252]), it came over as an attack on war, endorsed by thousands of theatregoers who patronised the play once it had been moved from the shabby Theatre Royal at Stratford East to Wyndham's in Charing Cross Road. Apparently 15 managements had offered such a transfer to the West End,[253] an indication of the popular resonance not only of the play's new technique but also of its timely appeal to anti-war sentiments. It ran at Wyndham's for 507 performances, almost catching up on the record for a serious war play set by *Journey's End* more than 30 years before. By the time it was sent on the 'Big Top Tour' through the British provinces before opening at the Roundhouse (Arnold Wesker's old Centre 42) in 1998, its 'message' could be described in the Programme as 'a reminder of the horror and futility of the four years of trench warfare',[254] an interpretation that had been forced on the production by the general reception. To many, *Oh What a Lovely War* appeared to be, quite literally, the last word on World War I, and it was left to some provincial theatres to discover, in their productions, new aspects of the War.

2
Professional Theatre in the Provinces

During the course of the War, the provincial theatres contributed relatively little to the history of the war play. The four flagships of the repertory-theatre movement before the War (setting aside for the moment the exceptional role of the Dublin Abbey Theatre) were the Gaiety Theatre, Manchester, the Scottish Repertory Theatre in Glasgow, the Liverpool Repertory Theatre and the Birmingham Repertory Theatre. All four of them suffered – albeit in different ways – from the War. The Glasgow enterprise folded with the beginning of hostilities – not, it should be added, exclusively because of the War (after some initial difficulties, it had been remarkably successful, and 'The Glasgow shareholders', as one critic put it, 'having recovered their losses, decided to take no further risks'[255]); yet the radical changes that wartime conditions imposed had undoubtedly a share in the collapse. Miss Horniman's company at the Gaiety, Manchester (where Monkhouse's *The Choice* had been premiered in 1910) struggled on until 1917 when it was dissolved. Again, the seeds of disintegration had been sown before the War when the sensational success of Stanley Houghton's *Hindle Wakes* in 1912 and its transfer to London had taken some of the company's best actors to the West End, never to return. However, the War contributed substantially to the demise of this remarkable venture. At the beginning of the War Miss Horniman 'believed herself faced with the alternatives of a wider popular appeal or of closing the theatre' and chose the former, declaring defiantly: 'No, I am not going to be smashed because a lot of men are rushing at each other's throats. [...] The Gaiety will go on as usual – and ignore the war. I am going to do cheery plays, though. The more sober brethren will go on the shelf – until you start mafficking, then they'll be done to restore youth's sanity.'[256] In the end even the recourse to 'cheery plays', in effect the lowering of artistic standards, did not prevent the disbanding of the company, and the Gaiety became another 'lodging-house theatre' (Miss Horniman's term), the home for travelling companies speculating on the drawing powers of faded London attractions. The downfall from its former glory can be measured by the fact that in October 1917, *after* the end of the repertory experiment, the Gaiety was used for a trial run of Chambers's sentimental *The Saving Grace* before it went to the Garrick in the West End. It is true that some of the authors commonly associated with the 'Manchester school of dramatists' wrote war plays, but these were premiered outside Manchester, such as Cannan's *The Right to Kill* (an adaptation of a French novel), performed in 1915 at His Majesty's Theatre, London, or Brighouse's short *Once a Hero*, produced in 1922, after the closing of the Gaiety, at Southend, and in particular Monkhouse's *The Conquering Hero*, premiered in Leeds and at the Aldwych in 1924.

The same fate as the break-up of the Manchester company could easily have befallen the Liverpool Repertory Theatre, but by concentrating on 'cheery plays' it managed to survive, having to shed the name 'Repertory Theatre' for the innocuous title 'The Playhouse' to dispel the gloom that was associated with the term 'repertory'. Between 1914 and 1922 Liverpool did not premiere a single new play, and the plays the company did produce were far removed from the ambitious programme that Basil Dean, the theatre's founder, had formulated in 1911.[257] Not until 1922, with Galsworthy's *The Sun*, did Liverpool produce a serious war play. Barry Jackson's remarkable venture at Birmingham did not have to change its programme to the same extent. It had the backing of its famous patron, and since it was not designed to concentrate on new plays and artistic risks alone, it did not have to retrench to the same extent, continuing instead to produce its catholic programme with Shakespeare and Shaw as the two centrepieces and an occasional world premiere, especially from the pen of its prominent director, John Drinkwater.[258]

Drinkwater was also the author of the one great war play to be premiered by the repertory theatres during the War. His *X=0* was first produced in Birmingham as part of a triple bill with two other short plays on 14 April 1917; it was twice revived in other triple-bill combinations and ran for 21 performances. Although it was considered highly topical as 'an indictment of the wastefulness of war',[259] it appears not to have caused a patriotic outcry, partly perhaps because of the high esteem its author enjoyed, partly because it was 'merely a one-act play' and partly also because it expressed a widespread feeling of disillusionment after the Somme debacle. Today, *X=0* stands out as one of the few war plays from the War years to have stood the test of time, and in the universality of its archetypal situation it applies equally to all later wars. Although Drinkwater's work at Birmingham was later eclipsed by his West End successes with his biographical/historical plays, it is for his idealistic stance in pieces like *X=0* that he deserves to be remembered today.

Few other war plays were produced in the provinces during the war years: Jones's *The Pacifists* at the Southport Opera House (apparently a trial run for the production at the St James's Theatre), Lonsdale's short play *The Patriot* at Clapham Junction in 1915, Malleson's short play *'D' Company* at Oxford in 1914 and Clifford Mills's *The Luck of the Navy* at the Theatre Royal, Bournemouth as a trial run for the performance at the Queen's in 1918, a list that documents the minimal contribution of the provincial theatre to the British war play.

After the end of the War, and well beyond the Second World War, the situation did not change dramatically. While a considerable number of new repertories were established, the idealistic impulse that had characterised the pioneering theatres before the War seems to have been absorbed, to a large extent, by the beginnings of the amateur movement. Most of the reps had to resort to 'weekly repertoire', a system clearly hostile to any attempt at artistic excellence, because they found little interest among potential theatregoers. In 1934, the historian of the early repertory-theatre movement complained that 'There are very few things which the British public is less anxious to consume than a really good play. Indeed our public may be said to loathe and detest first-rate drama even more than it abominates good music, modern art, or fine literature.'[260] Under such conditions it was not surprising that new, serious and challenging plays remained the exception in the provinces.

The most significant among the full-length plays to be premiered outside London was *On the Frontier* by Auden and Isherwood (Cambridge, Arts Theatre, 1938). Hamilton's *The Old Adam* was first produced at the Birmingham Repertory Theatre in 1924 under the unattractive title *The Human Factor* before its 1925 London production under its new title at the Kingsway Theatre. A few plays were given brief trial runs before being taken to London: Berkeley's *French Leave* at Eastbourne before going to the London Globe in 1920, McEvoy's *The Likes of Her* at Battersea before opening at the St Martin's in 1923, Darlington's 'extravaganza' *Alf's Button* at Portsmouth before reaching the Prince's via the Hippodrome, Golder's Green, in 1924 and Monkhouse's *The Conquering Hero* at Leeds before being transferred to the Aldwych in 1924. Sylvaine's excellent *The Road of Poplars* was staged at Liverpool from where it went to the London Coliseum in 1930. From the outset the Liverpool Playhouse had made it a special policy to produce short plays whenever possible, usually as curtain-raisers, and it continued to do so after the end of the War, alone among professional theatres in Britain, under William Armstrong (Director from 1922 to 1941). Between 1911 and 1934 it premiered nearly 100 short plays (a record that could only be challenged by the Dublin Abbey Theatre), among them such remarkable war plays as *The Road of Poplars* (1930) and *The Sun* (1922).[261]

The initial impetus for changes in the provincial theatres came from the founding of the Council for the Encouragement of Music and the Arts (C.E.M.A., the forerunner of the Arts Council) soon after the beginning of the Second World War, which, for the first time, recognised the state's obligation to support the theatre. A second step was the Local Government Act of 1948, which authorised local councils to set aside a modest share of tax money for the encouragement of 'entertainment'. The repertory theatres also profited from the collapse of the commercial touring network with the advent of television. When the majority of the touring-date theatres, the Empires and Pavilions were demolished or converted into bingo halls, this left more breathing space for the struggling local companies. A newly awakened pride in local traditions and institutions in the provinces eventually culminated in a wave of theatre building, beginning with the Belgrade in Coventry (1958), which released the repertory companies from their existence in shabby backyards and brought them into the limelight of civic centres and arts complexes where they found better artistic and financial conditions to produce new plays. In many cases these plays were commissioned to celebrate specific historical events, as in the new genre of the 'local documentary'.

This had direct consequences for the production of World War I plays after the Second World War. While Fry's *A Sleep of Prisoners*, premiered at the Oxford University Church in 1951, was still the exception that proved the rule of the scarcity of remarkable plays in the provinces, from the 1960s onwards the best war plays originated outside London: Wilson's *Hamp* was acted in 1964 both at the Theatre Royal, Newcastle, and the Edinburgh Lyceum; MacDonald's *Not about Heroes* was performed by the Dundee Repertory Company at the Netherbow Theatre, Edinburgh, in 1982; Hannan's iconoclastic *Elizabeth Gordon Quinn* was premiered at Edinburgh, too (Traverse Theatre, 1985); Home's *A Christmas Truce* (1989) was first produced by the Horseshoe Theatre Company at the Haymarket Theatre, Basingstoke; Bryden's epic *The Big Picnic* was done in 1994 in the Harland & Wolff engine shed at Govan, Glasgow; Hims's *The Breakfast Soldiers* appeared at the Contact Theatre, Manchester in 1996 before moving to the Finborough Theatre, London and McCartney's *Heritage* came out at the Traverse Theatre, Edinburgh, in 1998. Even *Oh What a Lovely*

War (1963) must be numbered among these war plays originating from theatres outside the West End. In addition, most of the works by Irish authors (which make up the bulk of post-World War II plays) were first produced either in Dublin (Abbey, Peacock, Gate, Eblana, Focus) or at Belfast (mostly in the Lyric). This is true of plays concerned with the specific situation in Ireland as well as front-line plays set in Flanders.

The shift from West End productions to premieres in the provinces (if, for the present purpose, the term 'provinces' may be extended to the theatres in Ireland) is one of the most remarkable aspects of the production side of war plays. It seems that, after 1945, the First World War as a rule is no longer considered commercially viable by the West End managements, while theatre audiences in the provinces are still eager to return to the earlier War which was, after all, at the root of developments that spanned the whole of the twentieth century and beyond.

3
The Amateur-Theatre Movement

The founding of the British Drama League (later British Theatre Association) in 1919 was arguably the most important event in the history of non-professional theatre in Britain.[262] Naturally, there had been amateur plays before this, ever since the clergy turned over the performance of religious drama to the civic authorities. In *A Midsummer Night's Dream* the existence of a group of amateur actors is accepted without surprise by the Court of Athens and, by implication, by Shakespeare's London audiences. School performances, often in Latin, became a regular feature of the English educational system from the Age of Humanism and the New Learning. Later, private theatricals were the highlights of the winter season at English country houses.

Such historical evidence notwithstanding, it was not until the end of World War I that such activities came to be organised at a national level. When the amateur theatre turned into a mass movement, not least due to the emotional upheaval caused by the front-line experience of thousands of soldiers and the subsequent revulsion against the streamlined mass products of the commercial stage, the members of local theatre groups found that they had to provide their own texts, because the plays produced by the West End theatres or the provincial repertory companies proved to be unsuitable or unavailable or both. For a variety of reasons the standard play form of the amateur theatre became the *short play* (sometimes rather nonsensically called the 'one-act play', which would be comparable to calling the short story a 'one-chapter novel'). The enthusiasm of the amateurs (in the 1930s there were more than 25,000 amateur-theatre societies in Britain, most of them organised in the Drama League) created a mass demand for short plays unprecedented in the history of the genre. The standard bibliography[263] lists some 30,000 titles for the years up to 1964. Many of the authors were members of amateur groups, although some professional playwrights, such as Shaw, Barrie, Galsworthy or O'Casey, and later Coward and Rattigan, also sought to profit from the publicity and the fees to be earned in the amateur market.

Often the plays were written for specific purposes and did not lay claim to literary distinction, but the amateur theatre also produced an impressive crop of texts that are excellent by any standard. Most of this material (by obscure as well as well-known writers) has not found its way into the canon of Eng Lit, partly because the critics of the national press rarely condescend to notice amateur performances, partly because the majority of such plays were published in acting editions or anthologies designed for the amateur market alone and partly also because the short play has always suffered from its reputation, often unjust, as a simpler, facile and 'minor' form of drama. Nevertheless, it was to this genre that the amateurs turned in the 1920s. Part of its appeal lay in the fact that the short play had already become a significant factor in the international movement against the commercial theatre, triggered off by small theatres in Russia, Germany, France and, slightly later, in America. The wave had reached Britain via the Dublin Abbey Theatre and had found an initial resonance in the pre-World War I repertory theatres of the provinces.

The popularity of the short play with the amateur companies was not, however, founded on exalted notions of anti-commercial idealism alone. There were also various practical reasons for such a preference. The short play was not only less demanding in scene design, stage technique and casting; it also became the standard format for the drama festivals (variously named Festival of Community Drama, National Festival of Community Theatre and, from 1979, All-England Theatre Festival) which (beginning in 1926) were organised by the British Drama League. These were run on a competitive basis, not unlike the soccer cup. From local festivals where adjudicators, in compliance with a set of standardised rules, selected the best productions, the winners moved on to further stages, the best of them reaching the English and eventually the British final, an event that for several decades became an important institution in the British cultural scene. While in 1926 seven groups were entered, in 1949 there were over 1000 and in 1978 (after television had done considerable damage to the amateur theatre) still more than 600. In addition, many amateur societies participated in other festivals which also required short performance duration. Naturally it would be wrong to assume that the amateur theatre does not produce full-length plays; some societies run their own theatre where they regularly stage full-length plays. In the field of the war play, the Huddersfield Thespians in 1930 premiered Hodson's *Red Night: A War Play in a Prologue and Four Acts*, and even Sherriff's *Journey's End* emerged from an 'amateur' background, because the only play-writing experience Sherriff had, came from producing plays for the stage group of his rowing club. Yet the majority of amateur companies concentrated on the short play.

Plays for the amateur theatre were published in dozens of anthologies, especially in the 1920s and 1930s, many of them edited by John Hampden or J.W. Marriott. To judge by their publication history, they must have reached thousands of companies; Hampden's *Ten Modern Plays* was reprinted in 1964 for the twenty-fifth time.[264] Like other collections, it contained Drinkwater's *X=0*, a play that, judging from the number of reprints, was the most popular of all war plays. What is next to impossible to establish is where and when such plays were performed and what reactions they provoked. Reports on amateur productions are few and far between, and those that do exist cannot be taken as representative.

This is also true of the *war plays* which formed a relatively large group among these works. In very few cases is it possible to locate productions. *Over the Top* by E. and D.E. Hickey was first produced by the actors of the Research Department of the General Electric Company, probably in 1934; Thomson's *War Memorial* was premiered by the Edinburgh Philosophical Institution Dramatic Society in 1929; and Peach's *Shells*, a prototypical front-line play, was in all probability premiered by the Village Players of Great Hucklow in Derbyshire, because Peach, who had founded the group in 1927 and remained its director in 'benevolent dictatorship' until 1971,[265] had most of his plays first performed there. The *year* of a play's first production is often equally difficult to establish, except where the texts were published in series such as J.W. Marriott's *The Best One-Act Plays of* …(which contained, for 1934, both *Over the Top* by E. and D.E. Hickey and *Eleven A. M.* by Reid-Jamieson), or *8 New One-Act Plays of* …, edited until 1935 by John Bourne and afterwards by William Armstrong, which printed several war plays: Box's *Fantastic Flight* (1934), Talbot's *Set Fair* and Evans's *Antic Disposition* (1935), Corrie's *And So to War* and Grant's *The Last War* (1936), and Winter's *Air Raid* (1937). Some of these plays made bigger news: Pakington's *All Camouflage* won first prize in a play-writing competition organised by the Liverpool Playhouse Circle in 1931, and in 1936, when a new war was already looming on the horizon, Grant's *The Last War* and Corrie's *And So to War* reached the Finals of the British Drama League Community Theatre Festival at the Old Vic.

The best documented amateur-production, however, took place *during* the War: Shaw's *O'Flaherty V.C.* was premiered by a group of officers of the 40th Squadron R.F.C. at Treizennes in Belgium in February 1917, with the actor-manager Robert Loraine, then on active service, in the title role. It says a great deal about the tolerance of the military authorities (unless it was sheer obtuseness) that they allowed such an iconoclastic work to be produced at the front. Shaw himself attended a dress rehearsal and was deeply shocked when a few weeks later Loraine was wounded in combat. Admittedly, the play had not been intended for an amateur production but for the Dublin Abbey Theatre, where the premiere had been scheduled for 23 November 1915. It was conceived at Coole Park, the country home of Lady Gregory, where Shaw had been invited (he was even permitted to cut his initials on the famous autograph tree), and he had a Coole setting in mind for the finished play.[266] However, when in 1915 the text reached St John Ervine, at the time manager of the Abbey, the British officer commanding the Dublin district contacted a Trustee of the Abbey, warning him that if there were riots as a consequence of the production, the theatre's licence would be revoked. Unfortunately Yeats was away in London, and Lady Gregory in America, which left Ervine to take the decision alone, and, not wishing to jeopardise the existence of the Abbey, he withdrew Shaw's play, a decision he later regretted.[267] Thus the unofficial censor in Dublin made it possible for this 'dangerous' play to be performed near the front line! In 1920, to complete the play's early stage history, it was produced at the Lyric, Hammersmith, by the Stage Society, and on 20 November 1924 Shaw made it his first radio broadcast.

In contrast to the publicity inevitably surrounding a play by Shaw, most amateur productions took place in relative obscurity. It is, then, perhaps less important to notice individual performances than to identify certain trends in the plays, most of which must have been written on demand and in close contact with the societies for which they were destined. What is immediately striking when one takes a look at the list of plays in Part VI, is the uneven distribution of short plays. They dominated in two periods: during the War itself and in the 1930s, while at other times they were easily outnumbered by full-length plays destined for the West End or the provincial reps. The four War years saw nearly 30 short plays (admittedly some of them written by well-known authors and performed by professionals, but the majority evidently intended for amateurs). In such plays, the amateur theatre reacted to situations that concerned the ordinary citizen, such as patriotic propaganda, the real or imagined spy threat, wartime shortages, the conditions in the hospitals, and, in particular, the return of the soldier from the front.

The dominance of the short play in the 1930s can be explained by a variety of reasons: the existence of numerous amateur companies had created a huge demand for new plays; the wave of short-play anthologies gave amateur writers a realistic chance to see their works in print and to expect a limited but steady income from them; the bonus given to *original* plays at festivals encouraged companies to attempt new works, and the threat of another disastrous war must have been an incentive to take the current discussion about pacifism and the 'just war' to the stage. To judge from the printed material, many amateur societies must have engaged in a lively, and possibly controversial, discussion on serious issues that one would not perhaps associate with amateur theatricals.

One immediate consequence of the War in this field should not be overlooked: 'In the 1921 census there were 19,803,022 females in England and Wales, and only 18,082,220 males [...] More than a million women – one in nine of the child-bearing group – would not marry or bear children. For them, the war would be a continuing reality in their lives until they died.'[268] Many of them found some kind of compensation for what they felt as the loss of a purpose in life, in the local Women's Institute, and the theatre groups of W.I.s (and also other companies chronically short of men) created a demand for 'plays for women only'. Such 'all-women plays' have been much maligned or ridiculed; one critic claimed that they, 'with notable exceptions, do not come up to the standard of mixed cast plays. This is due, to some extent, to the rush by playwrights to cash in on a ready market and the lack of discrimination by those who perform these plays.'[269] This may be true in general; however, where such writers and performing groups turned to the subject of the War (which, after all, was the prime reason for the demand for all-women dramas), they produced some outstanding plays, for instance those printed in the volume *Ladies Only* by Muriel and Sydney Box,[270] including the remarkable *Peace in Our Time*. Several other plays also reflect the situation in which they were produced, for instance Popplewell's *The Pacifist* that uses a Women's Institute meeting as its setting or Bell's anti-war *Symphony in Illusion*, a 'rehearsal-play' in which an all-women cast prepares for the production of a short play, then performs it and finally clears the stage. Bell is highly successful in establishing links between the frame plot and the play-within-the-play, creating roles for amateur actresses who play amateur actresses performing an amateur play. Other war plays 'for women only' include Stewart's *The Home Front* with its archetypal situation of a world without men and Wentworth's well-intentioned but naïve *War Brides*. The outstanding war play for women, however, is Box's *'Bring Me My Bow'*, where a realistic frame plot is skilfully interwoven with a dream sequence that serves to underline the author's pacifist stance. In the specific context of the war play, therefore, all-women plays cannot be dismissed as negligible.

Part V 'Good' versus 'Bad' War Plays: Aspects of Evaluation

1
Literary Standards

Writing about literature regularly entails making value judgements. While the newspaper review of a play in performance will usually be openly, often blatantly, judgemental, a reference to the same play in a historical study may be more guarded, perhaps even sublimated in its subtlety, but in both cases the evaluation will be based on a set of criteria that the writer considers essential to determine the play's quality. Even the process of selection, for instance in a literary history, is subject to value decisions, and when, in a study like the present, one play is discussed at some length while another is dismissed in a single sentence, this is clearly due to judgements based on certain standards. While such criteria are not always openly declared and have to be guessed at between the lines, while, moreover, the critic may not even be fully aware of them, they are nonetheless implicit in every literary judgement.

That there exists a general hesitation to disclose one's evaluative criteria, may in part be due to the fact that such criteria, when put into so many words, tend to appear rigid, even fossilised and lay themselves open to criticism, if not to ridicule. Many twentieth-century writers on literary evaluation therefore seem to see it as their primary object to dissect, demolish and reject previous theories, while they appear hesitant in the extreme to state any positive criteria.[271] Yet to forego any attempt at formulating standards is not a viable alternative. Such an attitude (which would come dangerously close to the naïve *de gustibus* argument) would invalidate any idea of a literary canon, however provisional and open to correction. Leaving everything to the 'test of time' is, of course, no adequate way out, because literary history presents numerous examples where the 'test of time' has not prevented valuable works from sinking into oblivion or negligible ones from being celebrated as masterpieces.

For the present purpose it seems in order to lay open (however diffi-cult) the standards on which value judgements in the preceding pages have been based. Looking back over the history of literary evaluation (explicit or implicit), one can identify a set of six criteria which have been regularly applied to substantiate value judgements. They have been variously formulated, their definitions vary, and sometimes one or two of them are given priority over the others, but in essence they encom-pass the whole range of literary judgements. These criteria are *originality, authenticity, universality, actuality, complexity* and *homogeneity*.[272] In highly simplified terms, 'originality' is brought into play when a certain work is praised for offering a new approach that has not been attempted before; 'authenticity' refers to its immediate, spontaneously convincing plausi-bility and its ability to cause the suspension of disbelief; 'universality' underlines a text's achievement in transcending the borderlines between different cultures, nations, epochs, classes and age groups; 'actuality' stresses the specific topicality and relevance to a present-day audience; 'complexity' refers to a high degree of concentration in structure, style and thought and to the multiplicity of experiences a literary text can *simultaneously* convey to the reader, and 'homogeneity' emphasises the functionality of every single element in a literary work, its appearance as an artistic organism in which each part performs a vital role.

These criteria not only underlie the appreciation of literature on the highest critical level but also come into play in our commonplace reac-tions to literary texts in the most basic forms of reception, for instance our response, in the stalls, to a play in performance. In negative terms, the test of 'originality' is applied when a certain work is condemned as derivative or 'old hat', 'authenticity' when it is blamed for its improba-bilities, 'universality' when it is seen as provincial or dated, 'actuality' when its relevance for the immediate present is called into doubt, 'com-plexity' when it appears all too simple and obvious, and 'homogeneity' when it does not present a consistent or uniform appearance and 'falls apart'. Other terms which are sometimes advanced in discussions on lit-erary evaluation, such as credibility, consistency and objectivity, can without difficulty be subsumed under these six criteria. It goes without saying that the apportioning of such criteria still leaves a wide margin for subjectivity and differences of opinion, but this should not serve as an excuse for foregoing altogether the attempt to objectify literary judgements.

It will have been noticed in the present study that the differences in quality among the plays under discussion are exceptionally great, because the selection of the textual *corpus* was not based on excellence but on the plays' subject matter – the First World War. Consequently, plays of outstanding merit have sometimes been discussed side by side with works that appear as the last word in foolishness or banality. Moreover, this study offers ample evidence that texts can be seen as successful under one or two of these criteria while failing in others. The highest literary quality is, of course, achieved where a play can be praised for complying with every one of them; at the same time, a number of plays can be dismissed as lacking in excellence under any conceivable standard. While it would be impossible at this stage to resume the discussion of the whole body of war plays under the aspect of evaluation, a few examples may be in order – not, it must be stressed, to repeat or revise previous judgements, but to underline the qualities, not always recognised by preceding criticism, which they possess. It would be unjust to omit excellent short plays from this appraisal, although in some respects they cannot compete with the best full-length plays.

The outstanding example of *originality* in the field of war plays is undoubtedly *Oh What a Lovely War*. It was original both in its genesis, with the whole company contributing to the text, and in the finished product, a sequence of heterogeneous elements that nevertheless produces a unified impression. The effect on the audience in particular was unique: although the events of World War I were burlesqued and presented with apparent flippancy (of which the title is an example), the audiences reacted with the feeling that such a war must never happen again. On a smaller scale, few other works come anywhere near the originality of *Oh What a Lovely War*. Rudkin's *Cries from Casement* explores Casement's character by means of acoustic effects in the widest possible sense and by an idiosyncratic application of expressionist techniques – a stylistic *tour de force* utterly foreign to other war plays. Within the scope of the short play, Grant's *The Last War* (despite the inconclusive ending) is a highly original version of a post-World War I situation, with the animals passing judgement on mankind after the unspeakable crimes the world has been subjected to in the War. Not unlike *The Last War*, in Hamilton's *The Old Adam* the basic idea – modern technology being immobilised on both sides of the front, which leads to a war fought with medieval weapons – is highly original, and so is the resulting moral, that human beings will fight whatever the conditions, whereas the play resulting from this idea is relatively conventional.

A few plays deserve to be singled out for their originality in one particular area. Van Druten's *Flowers of the Forest* has been praised above because it brought a multilayered discussion of pacifism, long familiar in the non-commercial theatre, to the West End. Rowbotham in *Friends of Alice Wheeldon,* unique among World War I plays, dramatises the whole spectrum of pacifist movements during the War; despite the reservations that have been voiced concerning the play's homogeneity in plot, structure and characterisation, its originality of subject matter is undisputed. Johnston's *How Many Miles to Babylon?* links the discussion about the conflict between individual and collective values during the War with the relationship between Irish landowners and tenants and the role of Irish soldiers in Flanders, foreshadowing their position in a future war of independence – at the time an unusual combination of ideas as far as Ireland was concerned. The originality of these plays stands out even more clearly when they are contrasted with the banality and conventionality of some other works that fail to produce new ideas or to give them a convincing shape.

Authenticity is primarily a matter of the immediate credibility of dialogue, plot and characters, and it comes into play especially in the context of the presentation of front-line scenes. The 'crisis of representation', frequently discussed with reference to 'realistic drama', is of particular relevance here. In the field of dialogue, MacGill's *Suspense* is an outstanding example, due, no doubt, to the author's personal experience as a Private at the front. However a biographical background to the scenes depicted is by no means a guarantee for believability, as can be seen from the stilted 'tank' plays by Hickey, and in a more general sense from other front-line plays which suffer from an artificially structured plot and two-dimensional characters. The atmosphere of a front-line situation has been captured remarkably well in Williams's *One Goes Alone,* while Chetham-Strode's *Sometimes Even Now* is successful in re-creating dialogue, atmosphere and characters both from the wartime home front and from the post-War period. Surprisingly, two recent plays whose authors cannot have had personal experience of the War, Whelan's *The Accrington Pals* of 1981 and Murphy's *Absent Comrades* of 1997, are noteworthy for a convincing delineation of wartime scenes, although the two works could hardly be more different: *The Accrington Pals* showing a broad panorama of front-line and home-front scenes, *Absent Comrades* concentrating on a single situation in the trenches. That 'authenticity' is not merely a matter of the presentation of observable reality can be demonstrated from a number of 'ghost' plays, especially Barrie's *A Well-Remembered Voice,* where the unseen ghost is successfully evoked in the Father's reactions, and Sylvaine's *The Road of Poplars* where the ghosts of the dead soldiers marching past the lonely farmhouse are as 'real' to the audience as anything in 'realistic' drama.

Most of the war plays that have been discussed here are firmly anchored in a specific historical situation; they cannot be transferred to other periods and locations, because the First World War was so very different from all previous wars. Only in a few cases is the situation of the suffering soldier at the front or the grieving mother at home divested to such an extent of specific details that the experience becomes *universal*. Even where the plays are set in a fictitious time or country, the proximity to real locations is in most cases so great that it is impossible to disregard the specificity of time and place. Two short plays come closest to transcending the limits of an individual situation. Stewart's programmatically titled *The Home Front* has already been described as an archetypal play: without relinquishing the hold on observable reality and psychological individuality, the play depicts the sufferings 'at home' in a way that it could be transferred without difficulty to other wars in other countries and at other times. This is even more true of Drinkwater's $X=0$ where the setting described in the subtitle, *A Night of the Trojan War*, not merely serves to evade wartime censorship but underlines the play's relevance for all times. In this case it is the plot, too, that in its universal simplicity – I am killing your friend while you are killing my friend, and both of us will be the poorer for it – outlines the eternal experience of war, ancient, medieval or modern.

The *actuality* of the war experience and the plays based on it is somewhat restricted because later wars – both the 'mobility war' 1939–45 and the 'high-tech wars' in the Middle East and elsewhere – were so very different from the fighting in the trenches that is still remembered as the archetypal situation of the 'Great War'. Where World War I plays come closest to the actuality of the twenty-first century is in the fear of destructive forces launched by an unseen enemy on an unsuspecting world, symbolised by the threat of poison gas or other unspecified inventions. By merely substituting 'nuclear warfare' or 'biological warfare' for the threat of 'gas-attacks', one is frighteningly close to the contemporary situation. All the plays that deal with the sinister figure of the scientist who sells his inventions to the highest bidder irrespective of ethical considerations have therefore a dangerous ring of immediate relevance to them. These plays – Ervine's *Progress* and *Wings Over Europe* by Nichols and Browne are pertinent examples – involve the audience in moral decisions that are far removed from the all too simple dichotomy between the 'world of freedom' and the 'world of evil'. The bacteriologist in Evans's *Antic Disposition,* the discoverer of radiation techniques in Hamilton's *The Old Adam*, the owner of the world's largest works for the production of poison gas in Box's *Fantastic Flight* and even the inventor of a new machine gun in Armstrong's *Eleventh Hour* are closely related to the scientists who in more recent plays – by Morgan,

Dürrenmatt, Zuckmayer, Kipphardt and many others – threaten civilisation with their inventions or suffer intolerable conflicts of conscience and loyalty.

In no other field of literary evaluation is the gap between 'bad' and 'good' plays as great as in the field of *complexity*. The range extends from the superficiality of Calderon's *Peace* and the one-sidedness of Phillips's *Armageddon* (to name two titles from a wide selection of works that suffer from a deplorable lack of complexity) to the intricacies of religious associations in Fry's *A Sleep of Prisoners* or the multilayered significance in Lee's *Satan the Waster*. Lee's play (which would also deserve an entry under 'originality' and 'universality') is the outstanding example of allegorical complexity not only among war plays but in the whole field of early twentieth-century drama. However, in its self-defeating sophistication of argument the play deprives itself of the chance to make itself heard and seen by a wider audience. In this respect it is not dissimilar to Zangwill's *The War God* and Rudkin's *Cries from Casement*.

A number of plays appear complex because of the juxtaposition of highly divergent viewpoints. Desmond's *My Country* (although lacking in authenticity of characterisation and plot construction) successfully presents a whole gamut of positions *vis-à-vis* the War. Where 'complexity' denotes the encounter of ideas embodied in credible characters rather than the confrontation of abstract concepts or beliefs, it is much more likely to be effective on the stage, as seen in McGuinness's *Observe the Sons of Ulster* and McCartney's *Heritage*. A high degree of complexity can also be attested to plays that take dramatic objectivity to the point where the decision for or against the various positions is left to the audience, without being influenced by the author's taking sides; Monkhouse's *The Conquering Hero* or Ervine's *Progress* are cases in point.

A certain degree of *homogeneity* is essential for all drama (although some works, like Pinero's *The Enchanted Cottage* and Hannan's *Elizabeth Gordon Quinn*, have been criticised for inconsistencies in plotting and characterisation). However, the functionality of every element can be more intense in some works than in others. An outstanding example is O'Casey's *The Plough and the Stars* where the mutual interdependence of 'form' and 'theme' is particularly noteworthy. As described above, O'Casey's play on the one hand offers a closely woven network of realistic detail and highly individualised character portrayal, while on the other it provides a convincing image of a large population under the extreme conditions of an insurrection in a modern city. An unusual case of homogeneity is also Bell's *Symphony in Illusion* where the two levels, the frame action of the women's drama group and their play-within-the-play, are related by clever interlocking devices, producing an intricate image of the difficult relationship between reality and illusion. Both O'Casey's four-act work and Bell's short play are telling examples of the effective interaction of 'form' and 'theme', the plays' thematic concerns being successfully expressed through formal devices.

It will have been noticed that a few works have so far been omitted from the discussion, although from what has been said before they deserve the highest praise. In the field of full-length plays these are Shaw's *Heartbreak House,* Berkeley's *The White Château,* O'Casey's *The Silver Tassie* and Maugham's *For Services Rendered.* These four, more than any others, satisfy the standards of literary evaluation. It would be tedious to enumerate their compliance with every one of the six criteria, and it must suffice to list in brief form their chief marks of distinction as a mere summary of what has been said above in greater detail.

Heartbreak House is an exceptionally complex analysis of British society at the time of the War with all its contradictions, based on credible individual characterisation which, however, the play transcends to exhibit a comprehensive (if not universal) image of a world at war with *itself* as well as with the enemy. To envisage pre-War society as a ship of fools, with a built-in destructive force and with a shipwreck as the inescapable outcome, is an exceptionally original thought. Despite its seemingly disparate elements, the play presents an intricate web of associations, suggestions and allusions which form a homogeneous if eccentric universe. That many of Shaw's ideas, and many traits of the pre-World War I world he paints, have not lost their relevance even today, is part of the play's continued attraction.

While *Heartbreak House* was written during the War, demonstrating Shaw's independence of thought in the middle of convulsions which threw many other writers off balance and led established dramatists like Barrie, Pinero, Jones, Archer and others to produce sub-standard work, Berkeley's, O'Casey's and Maugham's plays present a post-War summing-up of the consequences the War had for individual characters and for British or Irish society at large. Berkeley's play is the least pessimistic of these. It is based on closely observed reality, the actual château in the various stages of its destruction and reconstruction together with its inhabitants, conquerors, destroyers and rebuilders. It is, however, also a complex and highly symbolic image of a world that needs rebuilding. In this respect, it reaches beyond the specific situation of the 1920s and illuminates a typical post-War world of the past as well as of today. Berkeley's unusual device of promoting the château to the role of dramatic hero emphasises the play's originality, while he is least successful in the category of homogeneity, because the various elements, ranging from tea-time gossip to pathos-filled verse passages and from everyday characters to highly unrealistic figures such as the Workman who sees himself as the representative of Mankind, are so diverse that they fail to integrate into one artistic concept.

For Services Rendered is in many ways the opposite of *The White Château*. In its presentation of a family irrevocably stricken by the War, it comes over as absolutely authentic on the individual level, while at the same time this family presents itself as a universal group of war victims whose sufferings can be transferred without difficulty to other settings and to present-day post-war situations. While it might be argued that Maugham's play lacks in complexity of the kind that makes *Satan the Waster, A Sleep of Prisoners* or *The White Château* such exceptional war plays, it is daring (and 'original') in the extreme (especially in the world of the West End theatre) in its undiluted pessimism and consequently its uncompromising condemnation of the War.

The categories of originality, authenticity, universality, actuality, complexity and homogeneity are complied with to an unprecedented degree in *The Silver Tassie*. To begin with, O'Casey is more successful than any other in combining the authenticity of specific characters and experience with the universality of a person who embodies the victimisation of the individual by this War, and any war. The Heegan family and their friends are credible characters in their engaging as well as unpleasant traits, while Harry, a football hero and a cripple, a thoughtless volunteer and a helpless war victim, is believable as a person as well as immediately acceptable as a representative figure. The universality of his fate is underlined by the fact that the play carries not the slightest reference to the 1914–18 War; it is not even clear on what side the soldiers are fighting. These legionnaires would be as much at home in the 'vasty fields of France' of *Henry V* or in the turbulence of Schiller's *Wallensteins Lager*, or, to emphasise the play's actuality, in a desert encampment in the Middle East. In contrasting the soldiers' front-line experience with the world of petty quarrels and shallow emotions at home, O'Casey achieves a higher degree of complexity than most. His greatest accomplishment, however, lies in the original conception of the second act with its nightmarish extinction of individuality and its emphasis on the universal experience of loneliness, fear and deprivation.

2
'Literary' versus 'Historical' Evaluation

If applying standards of evaluation to a certain group of works is a difficult process under any conditions, it is even more so in the case of war plays, because here the *literary* evaluation competes, and more often than not comes into conflict with, the evaluation of the *historical* event which forms their subject matter, the War itself. The First World War has undergone a series of highly divergent evaluations. Historians have differed widely both as to its justification and as to its conduct by the military leadership. While this is not the place to reiterate the discussions on the alleged inevitability of the War and its consequences, conducted among historians from many countries over the past century, it can be said with some confidence that there seems to be a general agreement now in the evaluation of the War. It is fairly clear today that the War could have been prevented by the politicians on all sides, in Russia, France and Britain as well as Germany, Austria and Turkey, if some degree of disinterestedness and clearer foresight of the consequences had prevailed. As it was, an unholy mixture of imperial arrogance, desire for revenge, economic greed, national inferiority feelings, lack of self-confidence and sheer stupidity, combined with the machinations of the international armaments industry, led to the destruction of millions of lives and the devastation of whole countries. It seems also to be agreed that in the conduct of the War enormous mistakes were committed (the terms 'Gallipoli' and 'the Somme' stand for some glaring errors on the British side). Moreover, most historians would concede today that the harsh conditions of the Versailles Treaty bore considerable responsibility for the rise of Fascism in Germany, Austria and elsewhere, leading to an even greater catastrophe just 20 years later.

All this has indirect consequences for the evaluation of plays about the War. If the outbreak of the War was not unavoidable, its conduct by the authorities was faulty, and its consequences devastating for the whole of Europe and beyond, those plays are bound to appear most valuable which argue that the War should not have happened, that the sacrifices demanded by the military leaders were unnecessary and that another war must be avoided at all cost – in other words, a pacifist attitude becomes another criterion to assess war plays, while a pro-war position appears as a negative touchstone. Such a subjective element is inescapably present in the appraisal of British and Irish war plays that has been attempted above. Plays that condemn the War and its management or deplore its results are – from a present-day point of view – bound to appear more 'successful' than others that were in agreement with the temporary war aims or with the one-sided condemnation of the enemy.

This caveat should be borne in mind when it is argued here that some of the 'best' war plays are *anti*-war plays. This is not to say that pacifism automatically produced better plays. Some pacifist works are just as shrill and one-sided as those others that have been described above as 'Hun-bashing'. It is, perhaps, the plays which refrain from apportioning the blame for the War on individuals or on a certain country, and simply condemn 'war' without any restrictions, that from a present-day point of view appear as the most successful. This is true, for instance, of Drinkwater's *X=0*, Shaw's *O'Flaherty V.C.*, Bell's *Symphony in Illusion*, Sydney Box's *'Bring Me My Bow'* and, among the full-length plays, of Johnston's *How Many Miles to Babylon?*, van Druten's *Flowers of the Forest*, Maugham's *For Services Rendered* and, more than any other, of O'Casey's *The Silver Tassie*. The final word in this survey should, then, be left to Shaw's titular character in *O'Flaherty V.C.* who declares bluntly, with the evident approval of the author, that 'No war is right.'

Part VI British and Irish Plays about the First World War: Two Checklists

1
Alphabetical Listing by Author

The following checklist records the plays which have formed the basis for the present study. The information is as complete as could be obtained, but in some cases even the most reliable sources, such as the *British Library Catalogue* and Allardyce Nicoll's invaluable 'Hand-list of Plays' in his *English Drama 1900–1930: The Beginnings of the Modern Period* (Cambridge UP, 1973), 451–1053, yielded incomplete and in some cases inconsistent data, or none at all.

The first line gives the author's name, the main title and the year of the first production or publication, whichever occurred earlier. Short plays ('one-act plays') have been marked by an asterisk. The second line states the place, the theatre, and the year of the first production. Where no production details are given, it can be assumed that the play has remained unperformed, except possibly in an unrecorded amateur production. The third line attempts to give full bibliographical details, including the play's subtitle and the place, publisher and year of publication. Where collected or complete editions of the author's works are available, these rather than the play's first printing have been listed. Where no publication dates have been included, it can be assumed that the play has remained unpublished. Although I was fortunate to obtain a number of unpublished plays in typescript, others have remained inaccessible to me; they have been marked 'not seen'.

All quotations from individual plays in the text of this study have been taken from the editions listed here; all page references in the text are to these editions.

Needless to say, the definition of any bibliographer's work – an attempt, usually futile, to minimise incompleteness and unreliability – applies to this checklist as well.

Ackerley, Joe Randolph, *The Prisoners of War* (1925)
First produced London, Playhouse, 1925
J.R. Ackerley, *The Prisoners of War: A Play in Three Acts* (London: Chatto & Windus, 1925)

Archer, William, *War Is War or the Germans in Belgium* (1919)
William Archer, *War Is War or the Germans in Belgium: A Drama of 1914* (London: Duckworth, 1919)

* Armstrong, Anthony, *Eleventh Hour* (1933)
Anthony Armstrong, *Eleventh Hour: A Drama in One Act*, in: R. H. Ward (ed.), *Ten Peace Plays* (London: Dent, 1938), 43–61

* Atkinson, M.E., *The Chimney Corner* (1934)
M.E. Atkinson, *The Chimney Corner: A Play for Women in One Act*, The Year Book Press Series of Plays (London: Deane, n.d.)

Atkinson, W.S., *'Glory Hole'* (1932)
W.S. Atkinson, *'Glory Hole': A Play of the Great War of 1914–18* (typescript dated 1932 in the British Library)

Auden, W.H., and Christopher Isherwood, *On the Frontier* (1938)
First produced Cambridge, Arts Theatre, 1938
W.H. Auden and Christopher Isherwood, *On the Frontier: A Melodrama in Three Acts*, in: *Plays and Other Dramatic Writings by W. H. Auden, The Complete Works of W. H. Auden*, vol. I (Princeton UP, 1988), 357–418

Bairnsfather, Bruce, and Arthur Eliot, *The Better 'Ole* (1917)
First produced London, Oxford Theatre, 1917; London, Regent, 1929
[filmed by Warner Brothers in 1926]
[not seen]

* Barrie, J.M., *Der Tag* (1914)
First produced London, Coliseum, 1914
J.M. Barrie, *Der Tag: A Play* (London: Hodder & Stoughton, 1914); also in *Daily Telegraph* (22 Dec. 1914)

* Barrie, J.M., *The New Word* (1915)
First produced London, Duke of York's, 1915
J.M. Barrie, *The New Word*, in: *The Plays of J. M. Barrie* (London: Hodder & Stoughton, rev. ed. 1942), 853–73

Barrie, J.M., *Rosy Rapture, Pride of the Beauty Chorus* (1915)
First produced London, Duke of York's, 1915
[not seen]

Barrie, J.M., *A Kiss for Cinderella* (1916)
First produced London, Wyndham's, 1916
J.M. Barrie, *A Kiss for Cinderella*, in: *The Plays of J. M. Barrie* (London:
Hodder & Stoughton, rev. ed. 1942), 875–943

* Barrie, J.M., *The Old Lady Shows Her Medals* (1917)
First produced London, New Theatre, 1917
J.M. Barrie, *The Old Lady Shows Her Medals*, in: *The Plays of J. M. Barrie*
(London: Hodder & Stoughton, rev. ed. 1942), 963–92

* Barrie, J.M., *A Well-Remembered Voice* (1918)
First produced London, Wyndham's, 1918
J.M. Barrie, *A Well-Remembered Voice*, in: *The Plays of J. M. Barrie* (London:
Hodder & Stoughton, rev. ed. 1942), 1061–82

* Barrie, J.M., *La Politesse* (1918)
First produced London, Wyndham's, 1918
[not seen]

* Barrie, J.M., *Barbara's Wedding* (1927)
First produced London, Savoy, 1927
J.M. Barrie, *Barbara's Wedding*, in: *The Plays of J. M. Barrie* (London: Hodder
& Stoughton, rev. ed. 1942), 1167–82

Barry, Sebastian, *White Woman Street* (1992)
First produced London, Bush Theatre, 1992
Sebastian Barry, *The Only True History of Lizzie Finn, The Steward of
Christendom, White Woman Street* (London: Methuen, 1995), 135–81

Barry, Sebastian, *The Steward of Christendom* (1995)
First produced London, Royal Court Upstairs, 1995
Sebastian Barry, *The Only True History of Lizzie Finn, The Steward of
Christendom, White Woman Street* (London: Methuen, 1995), 67–133

* Bell, James Wallace, *Symphony in Illusion* (1932)
James Wallace Bell, *Symphony in Illusion: An Allegory in One Act*, in:
J. W. Marriott (ed.), *The Best One-Act Plays of 1932* (London: Harrap,
1933), 67–90

Berkeley, Reginald, *French Leave* (1920)
First produced London, Globe, 1920, after four weeks in the provinces, beginning at Eastbourne, Devonshire Park, 1920; transferred from Globe to Apollo
Reginald Berkeley, *French Leave: A Light Comedy in Three Acts* (London: French, 1921)

Berkeley, Reginald, *The White Château* (1925)
First produced BBC, 1925; London, Everyman Theatre, 1927
Reginald Berkeley, *The White Château*, in: J. W. Marriott (ed.), *Great Modern British Plays* (London: Harrap, 1929), 807–58

Besier, Rudolf, and Sybil Spottiswoode, *Kultur at Home* (1916)
First produced London, Royal Court, 1916; transferred to Strand
[not seen]

* Binyon, Laurence, *Bombastes in the Shades* (1915)
Laurence Binyon, *Bombastes in the Shades: A Play in One Act*, Oxford Pamphlets 1914–1915 (London: Oxford UP, 1915)

Box, Muriel, *Angels of War* (1935)
First produced by Mrs Worthington's Daughters on UK tour, 1981
Muriel Box, *Angels of War: A Play in Three Acts*, in: *Five New Full-Length Plays for All-Women Casts* (London: Lovat Dickson & Thompson, 1935), 7–74; also in: Claire M. Tylee (ed.), *War Plays by Women: An International Anthology* (London, New York: Routledge, 1999), 115–39

* Box, Muriel and Sydney, *Peace in Our Time* (1934)
Muriel and Sydney Box, *Peace in Our Time*, in: Muriel and Sydney Box, *Ladies Only: Six One-Act Plays with All-Women Casts* (London: Harrap, 1934), 15–30

* Box, Sydney, *Fantastic Flight* (1934)
Sydney Box, *Fantastic Flight*, in: John Bourne (ed.), *8 New One-Act Plays of 1934* (London: Lovat Dickson, 1934), 55–77

Box, Sydney, *The Woman and the Walnut Tree* (1935)
Sydney Box, *The Woman and the Walnut Tree: A Modern Morality Play in Six Scenes*, in: *Five New Full-Length Plays for All-Women Casts* (London: Lovat Dickson & Thompson, 1935), 295–375

* Box, Sydney, *'Bring Me My Bow'* (1937)
Sydney Box, *'Bring Me My Bow'*, in: John Bourne (ed.), *Twenty-Five Modern One-Act Plays* (London: Gollancz, 1938), 199–225

* Brandane, John, *The Happy War* (1928)
John Brandane, *The Treasure Ship, Rory Aforesaid, The Happy War* (London: Constable, 1928), 226–48

* Brighouse, Harold, *Once a Hero* (1922)
First produced Southend, Ambassadors', 1922
Harold Brighouse, *Once a Hero: A Comedy in One Act* (London: Gowans & Gray, 1922)

* Brighouse, Harold, *A Bit of War* (1933)
Harold Brighouse, *A Bit of War: A Play in One Act* (London, New York: French, 1933)

* Brockway, A. Fenner, *The Devil's Business* (1915)
A. Fenner Brockway, *The Devil's Business: A Play, and its Justification* (Manchester: National Labour Press, 1915)

Bryden, Bill, *The Big Picnic* (1994)
First produced Govan, Glasgow, Harland & Wolff Engine Shed, 1994
Bill Bryden, *The Big Picnic, Theatre Scotland*, III, no. 10 (Summer 1994), 28–43

* Bulkeley, H.J., *The Scouts* (1917)
H.J. Bulkeley, *The Scouts*, in: Bulkeley, *Four War Plays for School Children* (London: Routledge, n.d. [1917]), 33–64

* Bulkeley, H.J., *The Hospital Hut* (1917)
H.J. Bulkeley, *The Hospital Hut*, in: Bulkeley, *Four War Plays for School Children* (London: Routledge, n.d. [1917]), 65–92

* Bulkeley, H.J., *Home!* (1917)
H.J. Bulkeley, *Home!* in: H.J. Bulkeley, *Four War Plays for School Children* (London: Routledge, n.d. [1917]), 95–126

Caine, Hall, *The Prime Minister* (1918)
First produced London, Royalty, 1918
Hall Caine, *The Prime Minister: A Drama* (London: Heinemann, 1918)

* Calderon, George Leslie, *Peace* (1922)
George Leslie Calderon, *Peace: A Farce in One Act*, in: George Calderon, *Eight One-Act Plays* (London: Grant Richards, 1922), 11–28

Cannan, Gilbert, *The Right to Kill* (1915)
First produced London, His Majesty's, 1915
[translation, with Frances Keyser, of an adaptation of the French novel *L'homme qui assassina*]
[not seen]

* Carroll, Paul Vincent, *The Coggerers* (1939)
Paul Vincent Carroll, *The Conspirators* [*The Coggerers*], in: Paul Vincent Carroll, *Irish Stories and Plays* (New York: Devin-Adair, 1958), 109–29

Chambers, Charles Haddon, *The Saving Grace* (1917)
First produced Manchester, Gaiety, 1917; London, Garrick, 1917
C. Haddon Chambers, *The Saving Grace: A Comedy in Three Acts* (London: Heinemann, 1918)

Chetham-Strode, Warren, *Sometimes Even Now* (1933)
First produced London, Embassy, 1933
W. Chetham-Strode, *Sometimes Even Now: A Play in Three Acts*, in: *Famous Plays of 1933* (London: Gollancz, 1933), 369–464

* Corkery, Daniel, *Resurrection* (1918)
Daniel Corkery, *Resurrection, Theatre Arts Magazine* (1918); (Dublin: Talbot Press, n.d. [1940?])

* Corrie, Joe, *And So to War* (1936)
Produced in the Finals of the British Drama League Community Theatre Festival, London, Old Vic, 1936
Joe Corrie, *And So to War: A Satirical Comedy*, in: William Armstrong (ed.), *8 New One-Act Plays of 1936* (London: Lovat Dickson, 1936), 167–96

* Corrie, Joe, *Martha* (1937)
Joe Corrie, *Martha*, in: Jean Belfrage (ed.), *Let's Raise the Curtain: Twelve Modern One-Act Plays* (London: Collins, 1937), 9–27

Coward, Noël, *Cavalcade* (1931)
First produced London, Drury Lane, 1931
Noël Coward, *Cavalcade*, in: Noël Coward, *Plays: Three* (London: Eyre Methuen, 1979), 125–99

Coward, Noël, *Post Mortem* (1931)
First produced by British soldiers at POW camp, Eichstätt, Germany, 1944; first professional production BBC 2, 1968
Noël Coward, *Post Mortem*, in: Noël Coward, *Plays: Two* (London: Eyre Methuen, 1979), 277–361

Coward, Noël, *Words and Music* (1932)
First produced London, Adelphi, 1932
Noël Coward, *Words and Music*, in: Noël Coward, *The Collected Plays*, vol. II (London: Heinemann, 1950), 93–188

Crocker, Bosworth [Mary Arnold Lewisohn], *Pawns of War* (1918)
Bosworth Crocker, *Pawns of War: A Play* (Boston: Little, Brown & Co., 1918)

Curtis, Richard, and Ben Elton, *Black Adder Goes Forth* (1995)
TV Series, BBCV 5714 (1995)

Dalton, Maurice, *Sable and Gold* (1918)
First produced by Munster Players, Cork, Father Matthew Hall, 1918
Maurice Dalton, *Sable and Gold: A Play in Three Acts* (Dublin: Maunsel & Roberts, n.d.)

Dane, Clemence [Winifred Ashton], *A Bill of Divorcement* (1921)
First produced London, St. Martin's, 1921
Clemence Dane, *A Bill of Divorcement*, in: J. W. Marriott (ed.), *Great Modern British Plays* (London: Harrap, 1929), 645–95

* Dane, Clemence [Winifred Ashton], *Shivering Shocks or, The Hiding Place* (1935?)
Clemence Dane, *Shivering Shocks or, The Hiding Place: A Play for Boys*, in: Philip Wayne (ed.), *One-Act Comedies* (London: Longmans, 1935), 115–40

D'Arcy, Margaretta, and John Arden, *The Non-Stop Connolly Show* (1975)
First produced Dublin, Liberty Hall, 1975; London, Almost Free Theatre, 1976
Margaretta D'Arcy and John Arden, *The Non-Stop Connolly Show: A Dramatic Cycle of Continuous Struggle in Six Parts* (London: Pluto Press, 1977–8)

Darlington, William Aubrey Cecil, *Alf's Button* (1924)
First produced Portsmouth, Theatre Royal, 1924; Hippodrome Golder's Green; London, Prince's Theatre, 1924

William Aubrey Cecil Darlington, *Alf's Button: An Extravaganza in Three Acts* (London: Jenkins, 1925)

Daviot, Gordon [Elizabeth Mackintosh], *The Laughing Woman* (1934)
First produced London, New Theatre, 1934
Gordon Daviot, *The Laughing Woman: A Play*, in: *Famous Plays of 1933-34* (London: Gollancz, 1934), 369–471

Desmond, Shaw, *My Country* (1921)
Shaw Desmond, *My Country; A Play in Four Acts*, Plays for a People's Theatre, no. 11 (London: Daniel, 1921)

Dowling, Sean, *The Bird in the Net* (1961)
Sean Dowling, *The Bird in the Net: A Play in Three Acts* (Dublin: Duffy, 1961)
[not seen]

* Down, Oliphant, *Tommy-by-the-Way* (1918)
First produced London, Alhambra, 1918
Oliphant Down, *Tommy-by-the-Way*, in: Down, *Three One-Act Plays* (London, Glasgow: Gowans & Gray, 1923), 59–78

* Drinkwater, John, *X=0* (1917)
First produced Birmingham, Repertory Theatre, 1917
John Drinkwater, *X=0: A Night of the Trojan War*, in: *The Collected Plays of John Drinkwater*, vol. I (London: Sidgwick & Jackson, 1925), 139–55

Dryden, Theresa I. [Mrs. W. Dymond], *The Breath of War* (1915)
First produced by Mossel Bay Dramatic Society, n.d.
Theresa I. Dryden, *The Breath of War* (Mossel Bay: Mossel Bay Advertiser, n.d. [1915?])

Du Maurier, Guy Louis Busson, *An Englishman's Home* (1909)
First produced London, Wyndham's, 1909
A Patriot, *An Englishman's Home* (London: Arnold, 1909)

Ervine, Brian, *Somme Day Mourning* (1994)
First produced Belfast, Shankill Community Theatre Company, 1994

* Ervine, St. John [John Greer Irvine], *Progress* (1922)
First produced London, Little Theatre, 1922

St. John G. Ervine, *Progress*, in: Ervine, *Four One-Act Plays* (London: Allen & Unwin, 1928), 31–52

* Evans, Cicely Louise, *Antic Disposition* (1935)
Cicely Louise Evans, *Antic Disposition*, in: John Bourne (ed.), *8 New One-Act Plays of 1935* (London: Lovat Dickson & Thompson, 1935), 147–76

Fernald, C.B., *To-Morrow* (1928)
First produced London, Arts Theatre, 1931
C.B. Fernald, *To-Morrow: A Play: In Three Acts of Drama and an Epilogue of Discovery* (London: Benn, 1928)

* Flather, Horace, *Jonathan's Day* (1938)
Horace Flather, *Jonathan's Day: A Play in One Act*, in: R. H. Ward (ed.), *Ten Peace Plays* (London: Dent, 1938), 23–41

Fry, Christopher, *A Sleep of Prisoners* (1951)
First produced Oxford, University Church, and London, St. Thomas's Church, Regent Street, 1951
Christopher Fry, *A Sleep of Prisoners*, in: Fry, *Plays* (London: Oxford UP, 1971), 1–57

Gallivan, G.P., *Decision at Easter* (1959)
First produced Dublin, Gate, 1959
G.P. Gallivan, *Decision at Easter: A Play in Three Acts* (Dublin: Progress House, 1960)

* Galsworthy, John, *Defeat* (1917)
First produced London, Lyric Hammersmith, 1920
John Galsworthy, *Defeat: A Tiny Drama*, in: *The Plays of John Galsworthy* (London: Duckworth, 1929), 953–62

Galsworthy, John, *The Foundations* (1917)
First produced London, Royalty, 1917
John Galsworthy, *The Foundations*, in: *The Plays of John Galsworthy* (London: Duckworth, 1929), 461–512

Galsworthy, John, *Windows* (1922)
First produced London, Royal Court, 1922
John Galsworthy, *Windows*, in: *The Plays of John Galsworthy* (London: Duckworth, 1929), 687–736

* Galsworthy, John, *The Sun* (1922)
First produced Liverpool, Playhouse, 1922
John Galsworthy, *The Sun*, in: *The Plays of John Galsworthy* (London: Duckworth, 1929), 963–9

* Gandy, Ida, *In the House of Despair* (1937)
Ida Gandy, *In the House of Despair*, in: Jean Belfrage (ed.), *Let's Raise the Curtain: Twelve Modern One-Act Plays* (London: Collins, 1937), 57–82

* Grant, Neil, *The Last War* (1936)
Produced in the Finals of the British Drama League Community Theatre Festival, London, Old Vic, 1936
Neil Grant, *The Last War: A Fantasy in One Act*, in: William Armstrong (ed.), *8 New One-Act Plays of 1936* (London: Lovat Dickson, 1936), 197–222

Granville-Barker, Harley, *The Secret Life* (1923)
Harley Granville-Barker, *The Secret Life: A Play in Three Acts* (London: Chatto & Windus, 1923)

Graves, Robert, *But It Still Goes On* (1930)
Robert Graves, *But It Still Goes On: A Play in Three Acts*, in: Graves, *But It Still Goes On: An Accumulation* (London: Cape, 1930), 211–315

Gregory, H., *Prisoners of War* (1934)
H. Gregory, *Prisoners of War: Krieg Gefangeners (German): A Play* (London: Stockwell, n.d. [1934])

Griffith, Hubert, *Tunnel Trench* (1924)
First produced London, Repertory Players at Prince's Theatre, 1925
Hubert Griffith, *Tunnel Trench: A Play in Three Acts and Seven Scenes* (London: Allen & Unwin, 1924)

Hackett, Walter, *The Invisible Foe* (1917)
First produced London, Savoy, 1917
[not seen]

Hackett, Walter, *The Freedom of the Seas* (1918)
First produced London, Haymarket, 1918
Walter Hackett, *The Freedom of the Seas: A Play in Three Acts* (London, New York: French, 1929)

* Hamilton, Cicely, *The Child in Flanders* (1919)
First produced Bethnal Green, Excelsior Hall, 1919
Cicely Hamilton, *The Child in Flanders: A Nativity Play in a Prologue, Five Tableaux, and an Epilogue*, in: J.W. Marriott (ed.), *One-Act Plays of To-day: Second Series* (London: Harrap, 1925), 237–67

Hamilton, Cicely, *The Old Adam* (1924)
First produced Birmingham, Repertory Theatre [under the title *The Human Factor*], 1924; London, Kingsway Theatre, 1925
Cicely Hamilton, *The Old Adam: A Fantastic Comedy* (Oxford: Blackwell, 1926)

* Hankey, Mrs. Arthur, *A House-Warming in War-Time* (1917)
Mrs Arthur Hankey, *A House-Warming in War-Time: A Play in One Act* (Hove: Combridges, n.d. [1917])

Hannan, Chris, *Elizabeth Gordon Quinn* (1985)
First produced Edinburgh, Traverse Theatre, 1985
Chris Hannan, *Elizabeth Gordon Quinn: A Serious Melodrama*, in: Alasdair Cameron (ed.), *Scot-Free: New Scottish Plays* (London: Nick Hern Books, 1990), 105–46

Harvey, Frank, *The Last Enemy* (1929)
First produced London, Fortune Theatre, 1929
Frank Harvey, *The Last Enemy: A Play in Three Acts and Seven Scenes* (London: Allen & Unwin, 1930)

* Hickey, E., and D.E. Hickey, *Over the Top* (1934)
First produced by Research Dept., the General Electric Company, n.d.
E. and D.E. Hickey, *Over the Top*, in: J.W. Marriott (ed.), *The Best One-Act Plays of 1934* (London: Harrap, 1935), 191–220

Hickey, E., and D.E. Hickey, *The Belly of Hell: A Play in Three Acts* (1935?)
First read London, Little Theatre, n.d.
[not seen]

* Hickey, E., and D.E. Hickey, *Youth in Armour* (1940)
E. and D.E. Hickey, *Youth in Armour* (London: Nelson, 1940)

Hicks, Seymour, and Edward Knoblauch, *England Expects—* (1914)
First produced London, Opera House, 1914
[not seen]

Hicks, Seymour, and Arthur Shirley, *Jolly Jack Tar* (1918)
First produced London, Prince's Theatre, 1918
[not seen]

Hims, Katie, *The Breakfast Soldiers* (1996)
First produced Manchester, Contact Theatre, and London, Finborough
Theatre, 1996

Hodson, James Lansdale, *Red Night* (1930)
First produced by Huddersfield Thespians, 1930
James Lansdale Hodson, *Red Night: A War Play in a Prologue and Four Acts*
(London: Gollancz, 1930)

Hoffe, Monckton, *The Faithful Heart* (1921)
First produced London, Comedy Theatre, 1921
Monckton Hoffe, *The Faithful Heart: An Original Play* (London:
Heinemann, 1922)

* Hogg, Cyril Wentworth, *The Story of Corporal Bell* (1915)
Cyril Wentworth Hogg, *The Story of Corporal Bell: A Play for Present Times:
In One Act* (New York, London: French, 1915)

Home, William Douglas, *A Christmas Truce* (1989)
First produced by Horseshoe Theatre Company, Basingstoke, Haymarket
Theatre, 1989
William Douglas Home, *A Christmas Truce: A Play* (London: French, 1990)

Howard, Walter, *Seven Days' Leave* (1917)
First produced London, Lyceum, 1917
[not seen]

* Jennings, Gertrude E., *Waiting for the Bus* (1919)
Gertrude E. Jennings, *Waiting for the Bus: A Play in One Act* (London,
New York: French, 1919)

* Jerome, Jerome K., *The Three Patriots* (1915)
First produced London, Queen's, 1915
[not seen]

Jesse, F. Tennyson, and H.M. Harwood, *Billeted* (1917)
First produced London, Royalty, 1917

F. Tennyson Jesse and H.M. Harwood, *Billeted: A Comedy in Three Acts* (London: French, 1920)

* John, Gwen, *Luck of War* (1917)
First produced London, Kingsway Theatre, 1917
Gwen John, *Luck of War: A Play in One Act* (London: Gowans & Gray, 1922)

Johnston, Dennis, *The Scythe and the Sunset* (1958)
First produced Dublin, Abbey, 1958
Denis Johnston, *The Scythe and the Sunset: A Play in Three Acts*, in: *The Dramatic Works of Denis Johnston*, vol. I (Gerrards Cross: Smythe, 1977), 83–166

Johnston, Jennifer, *How Many Miles to Babylon? A Play in Two Acts* (1993)
First produced Belfast: Lyric, 1993

* Jones, Henry Arthur, *The Knife* (1909)
First produced London, Palace Theatre, 1909
Henry Arthur Jones, *The Knife*, in: Walter Prichard Eaton (ed.), *One-Act Plays for Stage and Study: Second Series* (New York, London: French, 1925), 327–46

Jones, Henry Arthur, *The Pacifists* (1917)
First produced Southport, Opera House, 1917; London, St. James's, 1917
Henry Arthur Jones, *The Pacifists: A Parable in a Farce* (London: Blackie, n.d. [1955])

King-Hall, Stephen, *B.J. One* (1930)
First produced London, Globe, 1930
Stephen King-Hall, *Three Plays and a Plaything* (London: Nicholson & Watson, 1933), 167–254

* Knoblauch, Edward, *A War Committee* (1915)
First produced London, Haymarket, 1915
Edward Knoblauch, *A War Committee and The Little Silver Ring* (New York, London: French, 1915)

Knoblock, Edward, *How to Get On* (1915)
First produced London, Victoria Palace, 1915
[not seen]

Knoblock, Edward, *Long Live England* (1915)
First produced London, Botanical Gardens, Regent's Park, 1915
[not seen]

Knoblock, Edward, *Mouse* (1915)
First produced London, Royalty, 1915
[not seen]

Knoblock, Edward, *Home on Leave: A Play in Three Acts* (1916)
First produced London, Royalty, 1916
[not seen]

* Kramskoy, Adrian, *Good Morning – And Welcome To The Last Day Of The Final Test At The Berlin Oval* (1978)
Adrian Kramskoy, *Good Morning – And Welcome To The Last Day Of The Final Test At The Berlin Oval*, in: E.R. Wood (ed.), *The Tenth Windmill Book of One-Act Plays* (London: Heinemann, 1978), 54–77

Lee, Vernon [Violet Page], *The Ballet of the Nations* (1915)
Vernon Lee, *The Ballet of the Nations: A Present-day Morality* (London: Chatto & Windus, 1915)

Lee, Vernon [Violet Page], *Satan the Waster* (1920)
Vernon Lee, *Satan the Waster: A Philosophic War Trilogy with Notes & Introduction* (New York: John Lane, 1920), 1–110

Lonsdale, Frederick, *The Patriot* (1915)
First produced Clapham, Grand Theatre, 1915
[not seen]

McCabe, Eugene, *Pull Down a Horseman* (1966)
First produced Dublin, Eblana Theatre, 1966
Eugene McCabe, *Pull Down a Horseman / Gale Day* (Dublin: Gallery Books, 1979), 9–34

McCabe, Eugene, *Gale Day* (1979)
First produced RTE and Dublin, Peacock Theatre, 1979
Eugene McCabe, *Pull Down a Horseman / Gale Day* (Dublin: Gallery Books, 1979), 35–70

McCartney, Nicola, *Heritage* (1998)
First produced Edinburgh, Traverse Theatre, 1998

Nicola McCartney, *Heritage*, A Traverse Theatre Programme Playscript (Edinburgh: Traverse Theatre, 1998)

MacDonald, Stephen, *Not About Heroes* (1982)
First produced by Dundee Repertory Company, Edinburgh, Netherbow Theatre, 1982; Glasgow, Tron Theatre, 1982; London, King's Head, 1983
Stephen MacDonald, *Not About Heroes: The friendship of Siegfried Sassoon and Wilfred Owen* (London: Faber, 1983)

McEvoy, Charles, *The Likes of Her* (1923)
First produced Battersea, Town Hall, and London, St. Martin's, 1923
Charles McEvoy, *The Likes of Her*, in: J.W. Marriott (ed.), *Great Modern British Plays* (London: Harrap, 1929), 859–902

MacGill, Patrick, *Suspense* (1930)
First produced London, Duke of York's, 1930
Patrick MacGill, *Suspense: A Play in Three Acts* (London: Jenkins, 1930)

McGuinness, Frank, *Observe the Sons of Ulster Marching Towards the Somme* (1985)
First produced Dublin, Peacock, 1985
Frank McGuinness, *Observe the Sons of Ulster Marching Towards the Somme* (London: Faber, 1986)

Mackenzie, Ronald, *Musical Chairs* (1931)
First produced London, Arts Theatre Club, 1931
Ronald Mackenzie, *Musical Chairs: A Play in Three Acts*, in: *Famous Plays of 1932* (London: Gollancz, 1932), 9–88; and in: *Plays of a Half-Decade* (London, Southampton: Camelot Press, 1933), 859–926

MacMahon, Bryan, *Seven Men: Seven Days. Stage Version of a Golden Jubilee Pageant in Honour of the Easter Rising* (1966)
First produced Dublin, Croke Park, 1966

Mac Mathúna, Seán, *The Winter Thief / Gadaí Géar na Geamh-Oíche* (1992)
First produced Dublin, Peacock, 1992
[not seen]

* Malleson, Miles, *'D' Company* (1914)
First produced Oxford, New Theatre, 1917
Miles Malleson, *'D' Company and Black 'Ell: Two Plays* (London: Hendersons, 1916), 7–31

* Malleson, Miles, *Black 'Ell* (1916)
First produced London, Gate Theatre, 1926
Miles Malleson, *'D' Company and Black 'Ell: Two Plays* (London:
Hendersons, 1916), 33–64

* Manners, J. Hartley, *God of My Faith* (1917)
J. Hartley Manners, *God of My Faith: A Play for Pacifists in One Act*, in:
J. Hartley Manners, *Three Plays* (New York: Doran, 1920), 45–70

* Manners, J. Hartley, *All Clear* (1918)
J. Hartley Manners, *All Clear: A Protest*, in: J. Hartley Manners, *Three Plays*
(New York: Doran, 1920), 9–44

* Manners, J. Hartley, *God's Outcast* (1919)
J. Hartley Manners, *God's Outcast*, in: J. Hartley Manners, *Three Plays* (New
York: Doran, 1920), 71-92

Maugham, W. Somerset, *Home and Beauty* (1919)
First produced London, Playhouse, and New York, Booth Theatre [under
the title *Too Many Husbands*], 1919
W. Somerset Maugham, *Home and Beauty: A Farce in Three Acts*, in:
Maugham, *Plays*, vol. III (London: Heinemann, 1932), 225–324

Maugham, W. Somerset, *The Unknown* (1920)
First produced London, Aldwych, 1920
W. Somerset Maugham, *The Unknown: A Play in Three Acts*, in: Maugham,
Plays, vol. VI (London: Heinemann, 1934), 1–89

Maugham, W. Somerset, *The Sacred Flame* (1928)
First produced Washington, Belasco Theatre, and New York, Henry Miller
Theatre, 1928; London, Playhouse, 1929
W. Somerset Maugham, *The Sacred Flame: A Play in Three Acts*, in:
Maugham, *Plays*, vol. V (London: Heinemann, 1934), 221–319

Maugham, W. Somerset, *For Services Rendered* (1932)
First produced London, Globe, 1932
W. Somerset Maugham, *For Services Rendered: A Play in Three Acts*, in:
Maugham, *Plays*, vol. VI (London: Heinemann, 1934), 91–181

Melville, Walter, *The Female Hun* (1918)
First produced London, Lyceum, 1918
[not seen]

Millar, Robins, *Thunder in the Air* (1923, revised 1928)
First produced London, Duke of York's, 1928
Robins Millar, *Thunder in the Air: A Play in Three Acts* (London, New York: French, 1928)

Mills, Clifford, *The Luck of the Navy* (1918)
First produced Bournemouth, Theatre Royal, and London, Queen's, 1918; London, Garrick, 1919
[not seen]

* Milne, A.A., *The Boy Comes Home* (1918)
First produced London, Victoria Palace, 1918
A.A. Milne, *The Boy Comes Home*, in: J. W. Marriott (ed.), *One-Act Plays of To-day* (London: Harrap, 1924), 12–35

Minney, R.J., and Osbert Sitwell, *Gentle Caesar* (1942)
R.J. Minney and Osbert Sitwell, *Gentle Caesar: A Play in Three Acts* (London: Macmillan, 1942)

* Monkhouse, Allan, *The Choice* (1910)
First produced Manchester, Gaiety, 1910
Allan Monkhouse, *The Choice*, in: Monkhouse, *War Plays* (London: Constable, 1916), 65–96

* Monkhouse, Allan, *Shamed Life* (1916)
Allan Monkhouse, *Shamed Life*, in: Monkhouse, *War Plays* (London: Constable, 1916), 1–32

* Monkhouse, Allan, *Night Watches* (1916)
Allan Monkhouse, *Night Watches*, in: Monkhouse, *War Plays* (London: Constable, 1916), 33–63

Monkhouse, Allan, *The Conquering Hero* (1923)
First produced Leeds, Albert Hall, and London, Aldwych, 1924
Allan Monkhouse, *The Conquering Hero: A Play in Four Acts*, Contemporary British Dramatists II (London: Ernest Benn, 1923)

Munro, C.K. [C.W.K. McMullan], *The Rumour* (1922)
First produced London, Stage Society at Globe, 1922
C.K. Munro, *The Rumour: A Play in Four Acts. Stage Version* (London: Collins, 1927)

* Murphy, Bill, *Absent Comrades: A One-Act Play* (1997)
First produced Dublin, Focus Theatre, 1997

Murphy, Tom, *The Patriot Game* (1991)
First produced Dublin, Peacock, 1991
Tom Murphy, *The Patriot Game*, in: Murphy, *Plays: One* (London: Methuen, 1992), 92–142

Nichols, Robert, and Maurice Browne, *Wings over Europe* (1928)
First produced New York: Theatre Guild at Martin Beck Theatre, 1928
Robert Nichols and Maurice Browne, *Wings over Europe*, in: Burns Mantle (ed.), *The Best Plays of 1928–29 and the Year Book of the Drama in America* (New York: Dodd, Mead, 1929), 88–119 [extracts]

O'Brien, Flann [Myles na Gopaleen], *Thirst* (1942)
First produced Dublin, Gate, 1942
Flann O'Brien, *Thirst*, in: O'Brien, *Stories and Plays* (London: Hart-Davis, MacGibbon, 1973), 99–113

O'Casey, Sean, *The Plough and the Stars* (1926)
First produced Dublin, Abbey, 1926; London, Fortune, 1926
Sean O'Casey, *The Plough and the Stars: A Tragedy in Four Acts*, in: O'Casey, *Collected Plays*, vol. I (London: Macmillan, 1949), 159–261

O'Casey, Sean, *The Silver Tassie* (1928)
First produced London, Apollo Theatre, 1929
Sean O'Casey, *The Silver Tassie: A Tragi-Comedy in Four Acts*, in: O'Casey, *Collected Plays*, vol. II (London: Macmillan, 1949), 1–111

Owen, Harold, *Loyalty* (1917)
First produced London, St. James's, 1917
Harold Owen, *Loyalty: A Play in Four Acts* (London: Hodder & Stoughton, 1918)
[not seen]

Page, Austin, *By Pigeon Post* (1918)
First produced London, Garrick Theatre, 1918
[not seen]

* Pakington, Mary, *All Camouflage* (1931)
Mary Pakington, *All Camouflage: An Episode of the War in One Act* (London: Deane, 1931)

* Peach, Lawrence du Garde, *Shells* (1937)
Lawrence du Garde Peach, *Shells*, in: Peach, *Collected Plays*, vol. IV
(Manchester: Countrygoer Books, 1955), 109–124

Phillips, Stephen, *Armageddon* (1915)
First produced London, New Theatre, 1915
Stephen Phillips, *Armageddon: A Modern Epic Drama in a Prologue Series of
Scenes and an Epilogue Written Partly in Prose and Partly in Verse* (London,
New York: John Lane, 1915)

Pilcher, Velona, *The Searcher* (1929)
First produced London, Grafton Theatre, 1930
Velona Pilcher, *The Searcher: A War Play. Reading Version* (London:
Heinemann, 1929)

Pinero, Arthur Wing, *Mr. Livermore's Dream: A Lesson in Thrift* (1916)
First produced London, Coliseum, 1916
[not seen]

Pinero, Arthur Wing, *Monica's Blue Boy* (1918)
First produced London, New Theatre, 1918
[not seen]

Pinero, Arthur Wing, *The Enchanted Cottage* (1922)
First produced London, Duke of York's, 1922
Arthur Pinero [*sic*], *The Enchanted Cottage: A Fable in Three Acts* (London:
Heinemann, 1922)

Plunkett, James, *The Risen People* (1958)
First produced Dublin, Abbey, 1958
James Plunkett, *The Risen People* (Dublin: Irish Writers' Co-operative, 1978)

* Popplewell, Olive, *The Pacifist* (1934)
Olive Popplewell, *The Pacifist*, in: John Bourne (ed.), *8 New One-Act Plays
of 1934* (London: Lovat Dickson, 1934), 161–89

Popplewell, Olive, *This Bondage* (1935)
Olive Popplewell, *This Bondage: A Chronicle Play of Enquiry into the Actions
and Re-Actions of Feminism from 1891 to the Present Day*, in: *Five New Full-
length Plays for All-Women Casts* (London: Lovat Dickson & Thompson,
1935), 75–159

* Porter, Mrs. Horace, and George Bidder, *Patriotic Pence* (1917)
Mrs Horace Porter and George Bidder, *Patriotic Pence or The Home Fairy: a Musical War Savings Play for Young People* (London: Evans, n.d. [1917])

Rattigan, Terence, *The Winslow Boy* (1946)
First produced London, Lyric, 1946
Terence Rattigan, *The Winslow Boy*, in: Rattigan, *Plays: One* (London: Methuen, 1981), 81–178

Reid, Christina, *Tea in a China Cup* (1983)
First produced Belfast, Lyric Players Theatre, 1983
Christina Reid, *Joyriders & Tea in a China Cup: Two Belfast Plays* (London: Methuen, 1987), 1–35

Reid, Christina, *My Name, Shall I Tell You My Name* (1988)
First produced by BBC Radio 4 1988; full-length version: first produced Dublin, Theatre Festival, 1989, and London, Young Vic, 1990, by Yew Theatre Company
Christina Reid, *My Name, Shall I Tell You My Name*, in: Claire M. Tylee (ed.), *War Plays by Women: An International Anthology* (London, New York: Routledge, 1999), 213–22

* Reid-Jamieson, Marion, *Eleven A.M.* (1934)
Marion Reid-Jamieson, *Eleven A.M.*, in: J. W. Marriott (ed.), *The Best One-Act Plays of 1934* (London: Harrap, 1935), 269–90

Robinson, Lennox, *The Big House* (1926)
First produced Dublin, Abbey, 1926
Lennox Robinson, *The Big House: Four Scenes in Its Life*, in: Christopher Murray (ed.), *Selected Plays of Lennox Robinson*, Irish Drama Selections I (Gerrards Cross: Smythe; Washington DC: Catholic University of America Press, 1982), 137–98

Rowbotham, Sheila, *Friends of Alice Wheeldon* (1980)
First produced Rotherham, Arts Centre, by DAC Theatre Company
Sheila Rowbotham, *Friends of Alice Wheeldon* (London: Pluto Press, 1986), 109–206

* Rubinstein, H.F., *Arms and the Drama* (1923)
H.F. Rubinstein, *Arms and the Drama*, in: Rubinstein, *What's Wrong with the Drama? Five One-Act Plays* (London: Benn, 1923), 91–110

Rudkin, David, *Cries from Casement as His Bones Are Brought to Dublin* (1973)
First produced as a BBC radio play, 1973; first stage production London, Royal Shakespeare Company, 1974
David Rudkin, *Cries from Casement as His Bones Are Brought to Dublin* (London: British Broadcasting Corporation, 1974)

Rye, Elizabeth, *The Three-Fold Path* (1935)
Elizabeth Rye, *The Three-Fold Path: A Play in 7 Scenes*, in: *Five New Full-length Plays for All-Women Casts* (London: Lovat Dickson & Thompson, 1935), 229–294

Schofield, Stephen, *Men at War* (1920)
Stephen Schofield, *Men at War: A Play in Two Scenes* (London: Daniel, 1920)

* Shaw, George Bernard, *O'Flaherty V.C.* (1915)
First produced by Officers of the 40th Squadron R.F.C., Treizennes, Belgium, 1917
Bernard Shaw, *O'Flaherty V.C.: A Recruiting Pamphlet*, in: *The Complete Plays of Bernard Shaw* (London: Hamlyn, 1965), 819–28

* Shaw, George Bernard, *Augustus Does His Bit* (1916)
First produced London, Stage Society at Court Theatre, 1917
Bernard Shaw, *Augustus Does His Bit: A True-to-Life Farce*, in: *The Complete Plays of Bernard Shaw* (London: Hamlyn, 1965), 839–48

Shaw, George Bernard, *Heartbreak House* (1919)
First produced New York, Theatre Guild at Garrick, 1920; London, Court Theatre, 1921
Bernard Shaw, *Heartbreak House: A Fantasia in the Russian Manner on English Themes*, in: *The Complete Plays of Bernard Shaw* (London: Hamlyn, 1965), 758–802

* Shaw, George Bernard, *The Gospel of the Brothers Barnabas* [Part II of *Back to Methuselah*] (1922)
First produced New York, Garrick Theatre, 1922
Bernard Shaw, *The Gospel of the Brothers Barnabas*, in: *The Complete Plays of Bernard Shaw* (London: Hamlyn, 1965), 869–91

Sherriff, R.C., *Journey's End* (1928)
First produced London, Incorporated Stage Society at Apollo, 1928; London, Savoy, 1929

R.C. Sherriff, *Journey's End: A Play in Three Acts*, in: *Famous Plays of To-day* (London: Gollancz, 1929), 10–136

* Smyth, Ethel, *Entente Cordiale* (1928)
Ethel Smyth, *Entente Cordiale: A Post-War Comedy in One Act*, in: Ethel Smyth, *A Final Burning of the Boats etc.* (London: Longmans, 1928), 234–63

* Stewart, Hal D., *The Home Front* (1937)
Hal D. Stewart, *The Home Front*, in: Jean Belfrage (ed.), *Let's Raise the Curtain: Twelve Modern One-Act Plays* (London: Collins, 1937), 83–101

Stoppard, Tom, *Travesties* (1974)
First produced London, Royal Shakespeare Company at Aldwych, 1974
Tom Stoppard, *Travesties* (London: Faber, 1975)

* Sumner, Derry, *Jimmy Clay* (1978)
Derry Sumner, *Jimmy Clay*, in: E. R. Wood (ed.), *The Tenth Windmill Book of One-Act Plays* (London: Heinemann, 1978), 1–17

* Sylvaine, Vernon, *The Road of Poplars* (1930)
First produced Liverpool, Playhouse, and London, Coliseum, 1930
Vernon Sylvaine, *The Road of Poplars*, in: Constance M. Martin (ed.), *Fifty One-Act Plays* (London: Gollancz, 1934), 313–46

* Talbot, A. J., *Set Fair* (1935)
A.J. Talbot, *Set Fair*, in: John Bourne (ed.), *8 New One-Act Plays of 1935* (London: Lovat Dickson & Thompson, 1935), 125–46

Temple, Joan, *The Widow's Cruise* (1926)
First produced London, Ambassadors', 1926
Joan Temple, *The Widow's Cruise: A Comedy in Three Acts*, Contemporary British Dramatists, vol. 41 (London: Benn, 1926)

Terry, J. E. Harold, *General Post* (1917)
First produced London, Haymarket, 1917
J. E. Harold Terry, *General Post: A Comedy in Three Acts* (London: Methuen, 1917)

Theatre Workshop and Charles Chilton, *Oh What a Lovely War* (1963)
First produced London, Theatre Royal Stratford, 1963; London, Wyndham's, 1963

Theatre Workshop and Charles Chilton, *Oh What a Lovely War* (London: Methuen, 1965)

* Thomson, David Cleghorn, *War Memorial* (1929)
First produced by Edinburgh Philosophical Institution Dramatic Society, Edinburgh, The Hall, 1929
David Cleghorn Thomson, *War Memorial: A Parochial Satire in One Act*, Scottish National Plays Series no. 4 (Glasgow: Wilson, 1930)

Thurston, Ernest Temple, *The Cost* (1914)
First produced London, Vaudeville, 1914
E. Temple Thurston, *The Cost: A Comedy in Four Acts* (London: Chapman & Hall, 1914)

Trevelyan, H. B. [Guy Bolton], *The Dark Angel* (1925)
First produced London, Everyman, 1925
H. B. Trevelyan, *The Dark Angel: A Play of Yesterday and To-day* (London: Benn, 1928)

Trevor, William, *Scenes from an Album* (1981)
First produced Dublin, Abbey, 1981
William Trevor, *Scenes from an Album*, New Irish Plays (Dublin: Co-op Books, 1981)

Van Druten, John, *The Return of the Soldier* (1928)
First produced London, Playhouse, 1928
John van Druten, *The Return of the Soldier: A Play in Three Acts* (London: Gollancz, 1928)

Van Druten, John, *Flowers of the Forest* (1934)
First produced London, Whitehall Theatre, 1934
John van Druten, *Flowers of the Forest: A Play in Three Acts*, in: *Famous Plays of 1934–5* (London: Gollancz, 1935), 463–569

Wall, Harry, *Havoc* (1923)
First produced London, Repertory Players at Regent Theatre, 1923; London, Haymarket, 1924
[novel based on the play: A. L. Muir and Harry Wall, *Havoc* (London: Readers Library Publishing Co., 1926)]

* Wentworth, Marion Craig, *War Brides* (1915)
First produced New York, B. F. Keith's Palace Theater, 1915

Marion Craig Wentworth, *War Brides: A Play in One Act* (London: Heinemann, 1915)

Whelan, Peter, *The Accrington Pals* (1981)
First produced London, Royal Shakespeare Company at The Warehouse, 1981
Peter Whelan, *The Accrington Pals: A Play* (London: Methuen, 1982)

* Williams, Edward, *One Goes Alone* (1934)
Edward Williams, *One Goes Alone*, in: Geoffrey Whitworth (ed.), *Twelve One-Act Plays* (London: Sidgwick & Jackson, 1934), 183–206

Wilson, John, *Hamp* (1964)
First produced Newcastle, Theatre Royal, and Edinburgh, Lyceum, 1964
John Wilson, *Hamp: A Play in Three Acts* (London, New York: Evans, 1966) [filmed as *For King and Country*, 1964]

* Winter, Keith, *Air Raid* (1937)
Keith Winter, *Air Raid*, in: William Armstrong (ed.), *8 New One-Act Plays of 1937* (London: Lovat Dickson, 1937), 111–34

Worrall, Lechmere, and J.E. Harold Terry, *The Man Who Stayed at Home* (1914)
First produced London, Royalty, 1914; Apollo, 1916
Lechmere Worrall and J.E. Harold Terry, *The Man Who Stayed at Home: A Play in Three Acts* (New York, London: French, 1916)

* Yeats, William Butler, *The Dreaming of the Bones* (1919)
First produced Dublin, Abbey, 1931
W. B. Yeats, *The Dreaming of the Bones*, in: *The Collected Plays of W. B. Yeats* (London: Macmillan, 1960), 431–45

Zangwill, Israel, *The War God* (1911)
First produced London, His Majesty's, 1911
Israel Zangwill, *The War God: A Tragedy in Five Acts*, in: *The Works of Israel Zangwill*, vol. 11 (London: Globe, 1925)

Zangwill, Israel, *We Moderns* (1924)
First produced New York, Gaiety, 1924; London, New Theatre and Fortune Theatre, 1925
Israel Zangwill, *We Moderns: A Post-War Comedy in Three Movements (Allegro, Andante, Adagio)* (London: Heinemann, 1926)

2
Chronological Listing

The arrangement of the plays by the year of first production and/or publication produces some interesting results. It should however be pointed out that it has not always been possible to obtain the date of the first production in the amateur theatre. Therefore some plays may actually predate, by a year or two, the year given here.

1909   Du Maurier, *An Englishman's Home*
        Jones, *The Knife*

1910   Monkhouse, *The Choice*

1911   Zangwill, *The War God*

1912   —

1913   —

1914   *Barrie, *Der Tag*
        Hicks and Knoblauch, *England Expects—*
        Jerome, *The Great Gamble*
        *Malleson, *'D' Company*
        Thurston, *The Cost*
        Worrall and Terry, *The Man Who Stayed at Home*

1915   *Barrie, *The New Word*
        Barrie, *Rosy Rapture, Pride of the Beauty Chorus*
        *Binyon, *Bombastes in the Shades*
        *Brockway, *The Devil's Business*

Cannan, *The Right to Kill*
Dryden, *The Breath of War*
*Hogg, *The Story of Corporal Bell*
Jerome, *The Three Patriots*
*Knoblauch, *A War Committee*
Knoblock, *How to Get On*
Knoblock, *Long Live England*
Knoblock, *Mouse*
Lee, *The Ballet of the Nations*
Lonsdale, *The Patriot*
Phillips, *Armageddon*
*Shaw, *O'Flaherty V.C.*
*Wentworth, *War Brides*

1916   Barrrie, *A Kiss for Cinderella*
Besier and Spottiswoode, *Kultur at Home*
Knoblock, *Home on Leave*
*Malleson, *Black 'Ell*
*Monkhouse, *Shamed Life*
*Monkhouse, *Night Watches*
Pinero, *Mr. Livermore's Dream*
*Shaw, *Augustus Does His Bit*

1917   Bairnsfather and Eliot, *The Better 'Ole*
*Barrie, *The Old Lady Shows Her Medals*
*Bulkeley, *The Scouts*
*Bulkeley, *The Hospital Hut*
*Bulkeley, *Home!*
Chambers, *The Saving Grace*
*Drinkwater, *X=0*
*Galsworthy, *Defeat*
Galsworthy, *The Foundations*
Hackett, *The Invisible Foe*
*Hankey, *A House-Warming in War-Time*
Howard, *Seven Days' Leave*
Jesse and Harwood, *Billeted*
*John, *Luck of War*
Jones, *The Pacifists*
*Manners, *God of My Faith*
*Porter and Bidder, *Patriotic Pence*
Terry, *General Post*

1918   *Barrie, *A Well-Remembered Voice*
         *Barrie, *La Politesse*
         Caine, *The Prime Minister*
         *Corkery, *Resurrection*
         Crocker, *Pawns of War*
         Dalton, *Sable and Gold*
         *Down, *Tommy-by-the-Way*
         Hackett, *The Freedom of the Seas*
         Hicks and Shirley, *Jolly Jack Tar*
         *Manners, *All Clear*
         Melville, *The Female Hun*
         Mills, *The Luck of the Navy*
         *Milne, *The Boy Comes Home*
         Owen, *Loyalty*
         Page, *By Pigeon Post*
         Pinero, *Monica's Blue Boy*

1919   Archer, *War Is War or the Germans in Belgium*
         *Hamilton, *The Child in Flanders*
         *Jennings, *Waiting for the Bus*
         *Manners, *God's Outcast*
         Maugham, *Home and Beauty*
         Shaw, *Heartbreak House*
         *Yeats, *The Dreaming of the Bones*

1920   Berkeley, *French Leave*
         Lee, *Satan the Waster*
         Maugham, *The Unknown*
         Schofield, *Men at War*

1921   Dane, *A Bill of Divorcement*
         Desmond, *My Country*
         Hoffe, *The Faithful Heart*

1922   *Brighouse, *Once a Hero*
         *Calderon, *Peace*
         *Ervine, *Progress*
         Galsworthy, *Windows*
         *Galsworthy, *The Sun*
         Munro, *The Rumour*

Pinero, *The Enchanted Cottage*
*Shaw, *The Gospel of the Brothers Barnabas*

1923   Granville-Barker, *The Secret Life*
McEvoy, *The Likes of Her*
Millar, *Thunder in the Air*
Monkhouse, *The Conquering Hero*
*Rubinstein, *Arms and the Drama*
Wall, *Havoc*

1924   Darlington, *Alf's Button*
Griffith, *Tunnel Trench*
Hamilton, *The Old Adam*
Zangwill, *We Moderns*

1925   Ackerley, *The Prisoners of War*
Berkeley, *The White Château*
Trevelyan, *The Dark Angel*

1926   O'Casey, *The Plough and the Stars*
Robinson, *The Big House*
Temple, *The Widow's Cruise*

1927   *Barrie, *Barbara's Wedding*

1928   *Brandane, *The Happy War*
Fernald, *To-Morrow*
Maugham, *The Sacred Flame*
Nichols and Browne, *Wings over Europe*
O'Casey, *The Silver Tassie*
Sherriff, *Journey's End*
*Smyth, *Entente Cordiale*
Van Druten, *The Return of the Soldier*

1929   Pilcher, *The Searcher*
*Thomson, *War Memorial*
Harvey, *The Last Enemy*

1930   Graves, *But It Still Goes On*
Hodson, *Red Night*

King-Hall, *B.J. One*
MacGill, *Suspense*
*Sylvaine, *The Road of Poplars*

1931   Coward, *Cavalcade*
Coward, *Post Mortem*
Mackenzie, *Musical Chairs*
*Pakington, *All Camouflage*

1932   Atkinson, *'Glory Hole'*
*Bell, *Symphony in Illusion*
Coward, *Words and Music*
Maugham, *For Services Rendered*

1933   *Armstrong, *Eleventh Hour*
*Brighouse, *A Bit of War*
Chetham-Strode, *Sometimes Even Now*

1934   *Atkinson, *The Chimney Corner*
*M.& S. Box, *Peace in Our Time*
*Box, *Fantastic Flight*
Daviot, *The Laughing Woman*
Gregory, *Prisoners of War*
*Hickey, *Over the Top*
*Popplewell, *The Pacifist*
*Reid-Jamieson, *Eleven A. M.*
Van Druten, *Flowers of the Forest*
*Williams, *One Goes Alone*

1935   Box, *Angels of War*
Box, *The Woman and the Walnut Tree*
*Dane, *Shivering Shocks*
*Evans, *Antic Disposition*
Hickey, *The Belly of Hell*
Popplewell, *This Bondage*
Rye, *The Three-fold Path*
*Talbot, *Set Fair*

1936   *Corrie, *And so to War*
*Grant, *The Last War*
*Winter, *Air Raid*

1937   *Box, *'Bring Me My Bow'*
        *Corrie, *Martha*
        *Gandy, *In the House of Despair*
        *Peach, *Shells*
        *Stewart, *The Home Front*

1938   Auden and Isherwood, *On the Frontier*
        *Flather, *Jonathan's Day*

1939   *Carroll, *The Coggerers*

1940   *Hickey, *Youth in Armour*

1941   —

1942   Minney and Sitwell, *Gentle Caesar*
        *O'Brien, *Thirst*

1943   —

1944   —

1945   —

1946   Rattigan, *The Winslow Boy*

1947   —

1948   —

1949   —

1950   —

1951   Fry, *A Sleep of Prisoners*

1952   —

1953   —

1954   —

1955 —

1956 —

1957 —

1958   Johnston, *The Scythe and the Sunset*
       Plunkett, *The Risen People*

1959   Gallivan, *Decision at Easter*

1960   Dowling, *The Bird in the Net*

1961 —

1962 —

1963   Theatre Workshop/Chilton, *Oh What a Lovely War*

1964   Wilson, *Hamp*

1965 —

1966   McCabe, *Pull Down a Horseman*
       MacMahon, *Seven Men: Seven Days*

1967 —

1968 —

1969 —

1970 —

1971 —

1972 —

1973   Rudkin, *Cries from Casement as His Bones Are Brought to Dublin*

1974   Stoppard, *Travesties*

1975   D'Arcy and Arden, *The Non-Stop Connolly Show*

1976   —

1977   —

1978   Kramskoy, *Good Morning – And Welcome to the Last Day of the Final Test*
       Sumner, *Jimmy Clay*

1979   McCabe, *Gale Day*

1980   Rowbotham, *Friends of Alice Wheeldon*

1981   Trevor, *Scenes from an Album*
       Whelan, *The Accrington Pals*

1982   MacDonald, *Not About Heroes*

1983   Reid, *Tea in a China Cup*

1984   —

1985   Hannan, *Elizabeth Gordon Quin*
       McGuinness, *Observe the Sons of Ulster Marching Towards the Somme*

1986   —

1987   —

1988   Reid, *'My Name, Shall I Tell You My Name'*

1989   Home, *A Christmas Truce*

1990   —

1991   Murphy, *The Patriot Game*

1992   Barry, *White Woman Street*
       Mac Mathúna, *The Winter Thief*

1993   Johnston, *How Many Miles to Babylon?*

1994   Bryden, *The Big Picnic*
        Ervine, *Somme Day Mourning*

1995   Barry, *The Steward of Christendom*
        Curtis and Elton, *Black Adder Goes Forth*

1996   Hims, *The Breakfast Soldiers*

1997   Murphy, *Absent Comrades*

1998   McCartney, *Heritage*

Notes

Introduction

1. Samuel Hynes, *A War Imagined: The First World War and English Culture* (New York: Collier, 1992), p. 469.
2. John Onions, *English Fiction and Drama of the Great War, 1918–1939* (London: Macmillan, 1990).
3. Margarete Günther, *Der englische Kriegsroman und das englische Kriegsdrama* (Berlin: Junker & Dünnhaupt, 1936).
4. Bernard Bergonzi, *Heroes' Twilight: A Study of the Literature of the Great War* (London: Macmillan, 2nd ed., 1980).
5. Paul Fussell, *The Great War and Modern Memory* (New York, London: Oxford UP, 1975).
6. Vincent Sherry (ed.), *The Cambridge Companion to the Literature of the First World War* (Cambridge: Cambridge UP, 2005).
7. John Fordham, 'Theatres of Resistance: Gender, Class and the First World War in plays by Sheila Rowbotham & Chris Hannan', in: Claire M. Tylee (ed.), *Women, The First World War and the Dramatic Imagination: International Essays (1914–1999)* (Lewiston: Mellen, 2000), pp. 191–205, p. 197.
8. L.J. Collins, *Theatre at War, 1914–18* (London: Macmillan, 1998), p. 178.
9. B. Ifor Evans, *English Literature Between the Wars* (London: Methuen, 3rd. ed. 1951), pp. 105–6.
10. J.W. Marriott (ed.), *Great Modern British Plays* (London: Harrap, 1929), p. 1016.
11. J.M. Barrie, *Echoes of the War* (London: Hodder & Stoughton, 1918).
12. See, for instance, John Galsworthy's 'Foreword' to Bosworth Crocker, *Pawns of War: A Play* (Boston, MA: Little, Brown & Co., 1918), n.p.
13. D.E. Hickey, *Rolling into Action: Memoirs of a Tank Corps Section Commander* (London: Hutchinson, 1936).
14. A.L. Muir and Harry Wall, *Havoc* (London: Readers Library, n.d.), 'Preface', p. 10.
15. W. Somerset Maugham, *Plays*, vol. VI (London: Heinemann, 1934), 'Preface', p. vi.
16. Howard Goorney, *The Theatre Workshop Story* (London: Methuen, 1981), pp. 125–31, 156–7.
17. See especially the volume *Women, The First World War and the Dramatic Imagination: International Essays (1914–1999)*, Claire M. Tylee (ed.) (Lewiston: Mellen, 2000).
18. Hall Caine, *The Drama of Three Hundred & Sixty-five Days: Scenes in the Great War* (London: Heinemann, 1915).
19. Fussell, *The Great War and Modern Memory*, pp. 191–230.

Part I Theatres of war: Aspects of subject matter

20. See I.F. Clarke, *Voices Prophesying War: Future Wars 1763–3749* (Oxford: Oxford UP, 2nd ed. 1992).
21. On *An Englishman's Home* see also Samuel Hynes, *The Edwardian Turn of Mind* (Princeton, NJ: Princeton UP, 1971), pp. 46–9.
22. Cecil Degrotte Eby, *The Road to Armageddon: The Martial Spirit in English Popular Literature, 1870–1914* (Durham and London: Duke UP, 1987), p. 9.
23. Allardyce Nicoll, *English Drama 1900–1930: The Beginnings of the Modern Period* (Cambridge: CUP, 1973), p. 43.
24. Ashley Dukes, 'The London Scene: War and Peace Plays', *Theatre Arts*, 14 (1930), 551–5, 552–3.
25. Anonymous review in *The Era* (21 Feb. 1917), 1.
26. Two unpublished 'naval' melodramas were Walter Howard's *Seven Days' Leave* at the Lyceum (1917) and Clifford Mills's *The Luck of the Navy* at the Queen's (1918). See the highly ironic reviews in *The Times*, 15 Feb. 1917, 11, and 6 Aug. 1918, 7 and the anonymous review of *Seven Days' Leave* in *The Pictorial London News* (24 Feb. 1917) which mentions 'the spectacle of searchlights being trained on the [German] U-boat and destroyers' guns battering it to pieces' (244).
27. Anonymous, 'Jolly Jack Tar at the Prince's', *Illustrated London News* (7 Dec. 1918), 768.
28. Muir and Wall, *Havoc*.
29. J.W. Marriott (ed.), *One-Act Plays of Today: Second Series* (London: Harrap, 1925), p. 238.
30. Hickey, *Rolling into Action*.
31. The play was part of various documentary and pseudo-documentary publications on alleged German atrocities in occupied Belgium; cf. Hynes, *A War Imagined*, pp. 52–6.
32. See Malcolm Brown and Shirley Seaton, *Christmas Truce: The Western Front, December 1914* (London: Macmillan, 1984, rev. ed. 1994); Stanley Weintraub, *Silent Night: The Story of the World War I Christmas Truce* (New York: Free Press, 2001).
33. James Lansdale Hodson, *Return to the Wood* (London: Gollancz, 1955), pp. 81–129.
34. As Paul Fussell has shown in *The Great War and Modern Memory*, homosexuality or what he calls 'the homoerotic' or 'a sublimated (i.e. "chaste") form of temporary homosexuality' (p. 272), was far more widespread in other areas of war literature, based, no doubt, on large-scale personal experience which could not be shown on stage. See Fussell's chapter VIII, 'Soldier Boys'. Cf. also Hynes, *A War Imagined*, pp. 223–34.
35. See *Plays and Players* (April 1993), 5.
36. One might add, as one further instance of purely comic treatment, William Aubrey Cecil Darlington's hugely popular *Alf's Button* (1924), where Private Alfred Higgins suddenly finds himself in the possession of a button that can conjure up the djinn from Aladdin's lamp, and is landed in a series of increasingly absurd situations. *Alf's Button*, initially a film, was first produced at Portsmouth, and then transferred to the Hippodrome, Golder's

Green, and to the Prince's Theatre, while a novel under the same title was equally successful.

37. A.M. Gibbs, *Heartbreak House: Preludes of Apocalypse* (New York: Twayne, 1994), p. 58.

38. Edward Knoblock, *Round the Room: An Autobiography* (London: Chapman and Hall, 1939), pp. 202, 207.

39. It should be mentioned that Bulkeley, in another school play called *The Hospital Hut* (Routledge, 1917), offers a sympathetic view of a wounded German soldier in an English hospital.

40. For a number of straightforward propaganda plays designed to boost recruitment during the early years of the War, see Collins, *Theatre at War*, pp. 178–84.

41. J. Hartley Manners, 'Foreword', *Three Plays* (New York: Doran, 1920), pp. v–vii.

42. Collins estimates the number of popular spy plays on the British stage during the war years at nearly 100 (*Theatre at War*, p. 185).

43. Anonymous, 'Five Villains at the Lyceum', *Times* (3 Oct. 1918), 5. For a plot summary, see *The Era* (9 Oct. 1918), 15.

44. Anonymous, '"All-Sketch" Matinee at the Queen's Theatre', *Times* (28 July 1915), 9.

45. *Five New Full-Length Plays for All-Women Casts* (London: Lovat Dickson & Thompson, 1935).

46. 'Rebel Networks in the First World War', in: Sheila Rowbotham, *Friends of Alice Wheeldon* (London: Pluto Press, 1986), pp. 5–107.

47. Cf. Martin Middlebrook, *The First Day on the Somme: 1 July 1916* (London: Allen, 1971; Fontana/Collins, 1975), p. 260. On the Accrington Pals, see also Richard Holmes, *Tommy: The British Soldier on the Western Front 1914–1918* (London: Harper Perennial, 2004), pp. 82–5.

48. See Stanley Weintraub, *Bernard Shaw 1914–1918: Journey to Heartbreak* (London: Routledge & Kegan Paul, 1973), pp. 177–9.

49. Gibbs, *Heartbreak House*, pp. 21–2.

50. For another such harmless play, in: Bulkeley, *Four War Plays for School Children* (London: Routledge, n.d. 1917), 95–126.

51. Noël Coward, *Autobiography* (London: Methuen, 1986), pp. 223–4, 227.

52. See H.H., 'The Dark Angel', *Observer* (8 Nov. 1925), 11.

53. W. Somerset Maugham, 'Preface', in Maugham, *Plays*, vol. VI (London: Heinemann, 1934), p. vi.

54. Peter Noble, *British Theatre* (London: British Yearbooks, 1946), p. 174.

55. Michael Billington, 'Govan's Wasteland', *Guardian Weekly* (9 Oct. 1994), 27.

56. For a detailed analysis of *The Silver Tassie* see my *O'Casey the Dramatist* (Gerrards Cross: Smythe, and Totowa, NJ: Barnes & Noble, 1985), pp. 94–113.

57. For the historical background to this chapter, see my article 'The First World War in Irish Drama', in: Wolfgang Görtschacher and Holger Klein (eds), *Modern War on Stage and Screen / Der moderne Krieg auf der Bühne* (Lewiston, NY: Mellen, 1997), pp. 33–51.

58. For a somewhat more favourable view of *Thirst*, see Anne Clissmann, *Flann O'Brien: A Critical Introduction to His Writings: The Story-Teller's Book-Web* (Dublin: Gill & Macmillan, New York: Barnes & Noble, 1975), pp. 262–3.

59. Cf. also Heinz Kosok, 'Two Irish Perspectives on World War I: Bernard Shaw and Sean O'Casey', *Journal of Bernard Shaw Studies*, 4 (1999), 1–25.

60. Even Michael Holroyd in his *Bernard Shaw* (New York: Random House, 1988–91), vol. II, p. 379, still echoes quite seriously Shaw's tongue-in-cheek description of his play from the Preface as 'a recruiting poster in disguise' (*The Complete Prefaces of Bernard Shaw*, London: Hamlyn, 1965, p. 475).

61. Declan Kiberd, *Inventing Ireland* (London: Cape, 1995), p. 241.

62. See Christopher Murray, *Twentieth-Century Irish Drama: Mirror up to Nation* (Manchester: Manchester UP, 1997), pp. 135–6.

63. This, it should be added, is not the only theme in *Tea in a China Cup*. For a comprehensive reading see Anthony Roche, *Contemporary Irish Drama: From Beckett to McGuinness* (Dublin: Gill & Macmillan, 1994), pp. 229–36.

64. Among all the plays discussed in this chapter, *Observe the Sons of Ulster* is probably the most complex and possibly the most ambiguous. For extended analyses, see Nicholas Grene, *The Politics of Irish Drama: Plays in Context from Boucicault to Friel* (Cambridge: Cambridge UP, 1999), pp. 246–51; Murray, *Twentieth-Century Irish Drama*, pp. 204–7; Roche, *Contemporary Irish Drama*, pp. 265–77 and also Eamonn Jordan, *The Feast of Famine: The Plays of Frank McGuinness* (Bern: Peter Lang, 1997), pp. 25–45.

65. Grene, *The Politics of Irish Drama*, p. 255.

66. According to Dalton's Preface, it is quoted in a translation by Justin Huntly McCarthy.

67. *The Letters of W.B. Yeats*, ed. Allan Wade (London: Rupert Hart-Davis, 1954), pp. 599–600.

68. Yeats's attitude is discussed at some length in my paper 'Ireland, Yeats, and World War I', *Yeats Studies*, no. 29 (1998), 3–19.

69. In an interview, Carroll explained: 'In the Irish language there is a verb called *cogar* which means to whisper in corners. But since no one understood the word, I changed the name of the play.' Fr. Marion Sitzmann, *Indomitable Irishry: Paul Vincent Carroll: Study and Interview* (Salzburg: Institut für Englische Sprache und Literatur, 1975), p. 176.

70. The controversial circumstances of the first production of *The Plough and the Stars* are described in detail by Christopher Murray, *Sean O'Casey: Writer at Work* (Dublin: Gill & Macmillan, 2004), pp. 171–9.

71. For a more detailed analysis of *The Plough and the Stars* see my *O'Casey the Dramatist*, pp. 69–88.

72. Denis Johnston, 'Up the Rebels!', in: Joseph Ronsley (ed.), *Selected Plays of Denis Johnston* (Gerrards Cross: Smythe; Washington: Catholic University of America Press, 1983), pp. 325–32, p. 331.

73. Ignatius Johns, 'Foreword', in G.P. Gallivan, *Decision at Easter: A Play in Three Acts* (Dublin: Progress House, 1960), n.p.

74. The quotations are from the discussion of *The Patriot Game* in Fintan O'Toole, *Tom Murphy: The Politics of Magic*, rev. ed. (Dublin: New Island Books; London: Nick Hern Books, 1994), pp. 145–53; pp. 146, 147, 151.

75. Jürgen Wehrmann, 'Revising the Nation: Globalisation and Fragmentation of Irish History in Sebastian Barry's Plays', in: Jochen Achilles et al. (eds), *Global Challenges and Regional Responses in Contemporary Drama in English: Papers Given on the Occasion of the Eleventh Annual Conference of the German Society for Contemporary Theatre and Drama in English* (Trier: WVT, 2003), pp. 203–16, p. 214.

76. Maugham, 'Preface', *Plays*, vol. VI, p. vi.

77. On *For Services Rendered* see also Onions, *English Fiction and Drama of the Great War*, pp. 95–8.
78. Miranda Seymour, *Robert Graves: Life on the Edge* (London: Doubleday, 1995), p. 195.
79. Robert Graves, *Collected Poems* (Garden City, NY: Doubleday, 1961).
80. Wilbur Dwight Dunkel, *Sir Arthur Pinero: A Critical Biography with Letters* (Chicago, IL: Chicago UP, 1941), pp. 93–4.
81. Anonymous review of *The Prime Minister, The Era* (3 April 1918), 1.
82. R.H. Ward (ed.), *Ten Peace Plays* (London: Dent, 1938). The plays from this collection that have clear references to World War I are discussed individually in this study.
83. According to a footnote in the printed version of *'Bring Me My Bow'*, p. 220.
84. Marriott (ed.), *Great Modern British Plays* , editor's note, p. 808.
85. '"Kultur at Home" – Play of German Life at Court Theatre', *Times* (13 March 1916), 11. The review in *The Athenaeum*, no. 4604 (April 1916), 207, is less critical. Although the play is seen as 'exaggerated', 'illogical on some points' and containing 'a glaring inconsistency', it is described as 'the best play with particular reference to the war yet put on the stage'.
86. Hynes, *A War Imagined*, p. 67.
87. Ibid., p. 40.
88. J.M. Barrie, 'Der Kaiser', *Süddeutsche Monatshefte* (München, 1915), pp. 220–6; Introduction by Erwin Volckmann, p. 220.
89. Quoted by Hynes, *A War Imagined*, p. 41.
90. Ibid., p. 42.
91. See the introduction by Sidney Heaven, in: Henry Arthur Jones, *The Pacifists: A Parable in a Farce*, The Garrick Playbooks (London, Glasgow: Blackie, n.d. [1955]), pp. xv–xviii.
92. Interestingly, the reviewer for *The Era* (29 Aug. 1917), 9, was not aware of the contradictions in Jones's parable.
93. Gill Plain, 'The Shape of Things to Come: The Remarkable Modernity of Vernon Lee's *Satan the Waster*', in: Claire M. Tylee (ed.), *Women, The First World War and the Dramatic Imagination: International Essays (1914–1999)* (Lewiston: Mellen, 2000), pp. 5–21, p. 18.
94. Ibid., p. 6; Vernon Lee, *The Ballet of the Nations: A Present-day Morality* (London: Chatto & Windus, 1915).
95. Editor's introduction to Robert Nichols and Maurice Browne, *Wings Over Europe: Drama in Three Acts*, in: Burns Mantle (ed.), *The Best Plays of 1928–29 and the Year Book of the Drama in America* (New York: Dodd, Mead & Co., 1929), p. 88.
96. See the author's Foreword in Velona Pilcher, *The Searcher: A War Play. Reading Version* (London: Heinemann, 1929), n.p.

Part II   Staging the war: Aspects of presentation

97. R.C. Sherriff, *No Leading Lady: An Autobiography* (London: Gollancz, 1968), p. 6; my italics.
98. Ibid., p. 5.
99. Ibid., p. 35.

100. Ibid., p. 4. The Sam Browne belt survived the early production; it was still worn by Peter Egan in the 1972 revival at the Mermaid. See Rosa Maria Bracco, *Merchants of Hope: British Middlebrow Writers and the First World War, 1919–1939* (Oxford: Berg, 1993), p. 186.

101. Miles Malleson, 'Preface', *'D' Company and Black Hell: Two Plays* (London: Hendersons, 1916), n.p.

102. A.C. Ward, *The Nineteen-Twenties: Literature and Ideas in the Post-War Decade* (London: Methuen, 1930), p. 158.

103. Bracco, *Merchants of Hope*, p. 151.

104. C.O.G. Douie, 'Two War Plays', *Nineteenth Century and After*, CV, 628 (June 1929), 838–48, 847–8.

105. Frank Fox, 'These Scandalous War Books and Plays', *National Review*, no. 568 (June 1930), 192–200, 194.

106. Douglas Jerrold, *The Lie about the War: A Note on Some Contemporary War Books* (London: Faber, 1930), p. 36.

107. Anonymous, '"By Pigeon Post": War Play at the Garrick', *Times* (1 April 1918), 7; italics added.

108. Quoted by Heinz Zaslawski, 'Die Werke Sean O'Caseys, unter besonderer Berücksichtigung seiner zweiten Periode', unpubl. diss. (Vienna, 1949), p. 81.

109. The visit to a front-line brothel (red light for privates, green light for officers).

110. J.O.T., '"The Prisoners of War" at the A.D.C.', *Cambridge Review*, 51 (15 Nov. 1929), 122.

111. William Archer, 'Preface', *War Is War or The Germans in Belgium: A Drama of 1914* (London: Duckworth, 1919), pp. v–vi.

112. Hynes, *A War Imagined*, p. 141.

113. Admirably collected by Weintraub in *Bernard Shaw 1914–1918*.

114. Anonymous review of the printed edition, *Dublin Magazine*, n.s. I, iii (1926), 64–5.

115. William Irwin Thompson, *The Imagination of an Insurrection: Dublin, Easter 1916: A Study of an Ideological Movement* (New York: Oxford UP, 1967), p. 209.

116. For a detailed discussion, see my *O'Casey the Dramatist*, pp. 69–88.

117. For a general analysis of *The Big House* see Hartmut Vormann, *The Art of Lennox Robinson: Theoretical Premises and Theatrical Practice* (Trier: WVT, 2001), pp. 177–85.

118. O'Casey took the title from a song by Burns called 'Go Fetch to Me a Pint o' Wine'; see *The Poetical Works of Robert Burns*, ed. Logie Robertson (London: Oxford UP, 1904), p. 319.

119. See Part I, ch. 10.

120. Nicoll, *English Drama 1900–1930*, p. 90.

121. Ibid.

122. Raymond Mander and Joe Mitchenson, *The Lost Theatres of London* (London: New English Library, 1968), pp. 58–9.

123. J.P. Wearing (ed.), *The London Stage 1930–1939: A Calendar of Plays and Players*, 3 vols. (Metuchen, NJ, and London: Scarecrow Press, 1990), vol. II, p. 54.

124. Letter to Kenneth Frederick Howse dated 29 Jan. 1951, quoted by Saros Cowasjee, *Sean O'Casey: The Man Behind the Plays* (Edinburgh and London: Oliver & Boyd, 1963), p. 120.

125. See Brenna Katz Clarke and Harold Ferrar, *The Dublin Drama League: 1918–1941* (Dublin: Dolmen Press, 1979).

126. Gabriel Fallon, *Sean O'Casey: The Man I Knew* (London: Routledge & Kegan Paul, 1965), pp. 46–7. For a survey of the highly divergent critical opinions on O'Casey's relationship to international expressionism, see my *O'Casey the Dramatist*, pp. 109–11, 351–3.

127. See Fussell, *The Great War and Modern Memory*, pp. 118, 131–5; and Middlebrook, *The First Day on the Somme*, pp. 54–6.

128. Fussell, *The Great War and Modern Memory*, pp. 27–8; and Middlebrook, *The First Day on the Somme*, p. 124.

129. Fussell, *The Great War and Modern Memory*, pp. 83–4.

130. Field Punishment No. 1, 'the infamous "crucifixion" in which the prisoner was tied spreadeagled to the wheel of an artillery piece', was abolished by an Act of Parliament as late as 1923 (Hynes, *A War Imagined*, p. 465).

131. Fussell lists numerous further details from 'real life' which (as Fussell did not realise) went into *The Silver Tassie*.

132. In an afterword to the printed edition, Rudkin discusses the various obstacles to staging the play and possible ways to overcome them. He also adds some (primarily critical) remarks on the first attempt, by the Royal Shakespeare Company, to put the play on the stage: David Rudkin, 'Thoughts on Staging the Play', *Cries from Casement as His Bones Are Brought to Dublin* (London: BBC, 1974), pp. 81–4.

133. For an exemplary survey see Annegret Maack, 'Das zeitgenössische Dokumentarspiel', in: Heinz Kosok (ed.), *Drama und Theater im England des 20. Jahrhunderts* (Düsseldorf: Bagel, 1980), pp. 158–69.

134. Peter Cheeseman, 'Production Casebook: The Staffordshire Rebels', *Theatre Quarterly*, I, no. 1 (1971), 86.

135. Charles Marowitz in his chapter on *Oh What a Lovely War*, in: Charles Marowitz et al. (eds), *The Encore Reader: A Chronicle of the New Drama* (London: Methuen, 1970), p. 232.

136. See especially Middlebrook, *The First Day on the Somme, passim*.

137. Ibid., p. 260.

138. 'Afterword Fact and Fiction in *Friends of Alice Wheeldon*', in: Rowbotham, *Friends of Alice Wheeldon*, p. 203.

139. Israel Zangwill, 'Poetic Drama and the War', *Poetry Review*, 7 (1916), 29–35, 32, 34, 35.

140. *The Works of Israel Zangwill*, vol. 11 (London: Globe Publ., 1925), 'Note to First Edition', pp. vii–ix.

141. For a detailed analysis of *A Sleep of Prisoners*, see the 2nd ed. of Derek Stanford, *Christopher Fry: An Appreciation* (London: Nevill, 1952), pp. 204–16. On Fry's language, cf. ibid., pp. 196–203.

142. Ward, *The Nineteen-Twenties*, p. 158.

143. Brian Murphy, as quoted by Howard Goorney, *The Theatre Workshop Story* (London: Methuen, 1981), pp. 125–6.

144. Christopher Innes, *Modern British Drama 1890–1990* (Cambridge: University Press, 1992), p. 247.

Part III   Engaging intellect or emotions: Aspects of attitude

145. *Daily Express* (23 Jan. 1929); quoted by Bracco, *Merchants of Hope*, p. 178.

146. Sherriff, *No Leading Lady*, p. 73; italics added.

147. Ibid., p. 72.

148. Ibid., p. 109.
149. Ibid., pp. 33–5.
150. Bracco, *Merchants of Hope*, pp. 152, 153.
151. Ibid., p. 152.
152. Another, much later instance where the finished product was universally accepted as an anti-war play although the existing documents of the play's genesis show that the original intention was far from it, is *Oh What a Lovely War*.
153. Some of them quoted by Holmes in *Tommy*.
154. See Part II, chap. 1.
155. An example is MacGill who declared in the Foreword to his novel *The Great Push* (1916): 'The justice of the cause which endeavours to achieve its object by the murdering and maiming of mankind is apt to be doubted by a man who has come through a bayonet charge.' Patrick MacGill, *The Great Push: An Episode of the Great War* (Edinburgh: Birlinn, 2000), p. xv.
156. Dukes, 'The London Scene: War and Peace Plays', 551–5; 551, 552.
157. A.B. Walkley, 'The Theatre and the War', *Cornhill Magazine*, ser. 3:47 (1919), 425–34, 428. Walkley apparently refers, among others, to Barrie and Galsworthy.
158. Hynes, *A War Imagined*, p. 39.
159. Ibid., p. 40. The situation is also described, with variations, in Knoblock's autobiography: Edward Knoblock, *Round the Room: An Autobiography* (London: Chapman & Hall, 1939), pp. 202–3.
160. Quoted by Hynes, *A War Imagined*, p. 218.
161. Ibid., p. 219.
162. Quoted ibid., p. 220. Hynes discusses *Loyalty* at some length; see pp. 219–23.
163. Innes, *Modern British Drama 1890–1990*, p. 95.
164. Fussell, *The Great War and Modern Memory*, p. 77.
165. Clayton Hamilton, 'The Drama and the War', *Bookman*, 47:3 (May 1918), 287–92; 287, 289.
166. See Part I, chap. 3.
167. Manners, 'Foreword', *Three Plays*, pp. v–vii.
168. J.C. Trewin, 'The Great War and the Theater, 1914–1918', *Dictionary of Literary Biography*, vol.10, II (Detroit, MI: Gale, 1982), pp. 277–84; 279.
169. Holmes, *Tommy*, p. 536. In his chapter 'Friend and Foe' (pp. 528–54), Holmes describes in some detail this relationship, including a number of instances where the treatment of prisoners and the wounded reflected a different attitude.
170. Cecil Lewis, *Sagittarius Rising* (London: Folio, 1998), p. 18 note [first published in 1936].
171. J.C. Trewin, *The Theatre since 1900* (London: Dakers, 1951), p. 111.
172. Collins, *Theatre at War*, p. 217.
173. Ibid., p. 186.
174. See, for instance, the chapter 'Myth, Ritual, and Romance' in Fussell, *The Great War and Modern Memory*, where some of the widespread legends are referred back to their origins.
175. Ibid., p. 185.
176. Anonymous review of *Seven Days' Leave*, *The Era* (21 Feb. 1917), 1.
177. Edgar White, review of *By Pigeon Post*, *The Era* (3 April 1918), 1.

178. Anonymous review of *The Luck of the Navy*, *The Era* (7 Aug. 1918), 11.
179. Collins, *Theatre at War*, p. 188.
180. Bruce Bairnsfather, *Bullets and Billets* (London: Grant Richards, 1917), pp. 66–7.
181. See above, Part I, chap. 9.
182. '"Kultur at Home" – Play of German Life at Court Theatre', *Times* (13 March 1916), 11.
183. Review of *Kultur at Home*, *The Athenaeum*, no. 4604 (April 1916), 207.
184. Holmes, *Tommy*, p. 28.
185. Viscount Bryce, *Report of the Committee on Alleged German Outrages Appointed by His Britannic Majesty's Government* (London: Eyre & Spottiswoode, 1915).
186. Hynes, *A War Imagined*, pp. 52–6.
187. John Galsworthy, 'Foreword' to Crocker, *Pawns of War*, p. v.
188. Anonymous review in *The Era* (9 Oct. 1918), 15.
189. See the brief review, signed H.H., in the *Observer* (8 Nov. 1925), 11.
190. Maurice Maeterlinck, *Le Bourgmestre de Stilmonde: Drame en trois actes* (Paris: Bibliothèque-Charpentier, 1920), p. 21.
191. Archer, in the Preface to *War Is War* (p. vi), goes to some lengths to disclaim any previous knowledge of Maeterlinck's play; doth the gentleman protest too much?
192. Collins, *Theatre at War*, p. 196.
193. Noel Annan, *Our Age: The Generation That Made Post-war Britain* (London: Fontana, 1990), p. 92.
194. See the chapter on 'Socialism and Criticism' in Collins, *Theatre at War*, pp.191–9.
195. For a detailed analysis see Heinz Kosok, '"No War Is Right": Shaw's *O'Flaherty V.C.'*, *The Shavian*, 9, no. 6 (Winter 2003–4), 3–8.
196. Collins, *Theatre at War*, p. 152.
197. Kiberd, *Inventing Ireland*, p. 241.
198. Wilfred Owen, 'Disabled', in: Lyn Macdonald (ed.), *Anthem for Doomed Youth: Poets of the Great War* (London: Folio, 2000), pp. 245–6.
199. Goorney, *The Theatre Workshop Story*, p. 126.
200. Hynes, *A War Imagined*, p. 308.
201. Ibid., pp. 377–8.
202. Ibid., p. 142. Italics added.

Part IV   Popular failures and successes: Aspects of reception

203. For a comprehensive survey of the theatre during the War, see Collins, *Theatre at War*, chaps 1 and 2; and Michael Sanderson, *From Irving to Olivier: A Social History of the Acting Profession in England 1880–1983* (London: Athlone Press; New York: St Martin's Press, 1984), chap. 8.
204. Collins, *Theatre at* War, p. 204.
205. Ibid., p. 3.
206. Figures of long runs in this chapter are based on the statistics section in *Who's Who in the Theatre*, Ian Herbert (ed.), 17th ed. (Detroit, 1981), vol. II, pp. 221–69.
207. Trewin, *The Theatre since 1900*, p. 113.

208. Collins, *Theatre at War*, p. 178.
209. Hynes, *A War Imagined*, p. 220.
210. Ibid., pp. 218, 221.
211. Collins, *Theatre at War*, p. 217.
212. Ibid., p. 185.
213. Trewin, 'The Great War and the Theater, 1914–1918', p. 281.
214. *The Invisible Foe*, although not primarily a war play, is listed in the *Revels History of Drama in English* among 'the plays with a war theme – jingoistic in tone and suitably distant from disturbing reality' (Hugh Hunt in *The Revels History of Drama in English*, ed. T.W. Craig, vol. VII, London: Methuen, 1978, p. 30).
215. Anonymous, 'Submarine Thrills at the Lyceum', *Times* (15 Feb. 1917), 11. Another reviewer testified to 'wildly enthusiastic first-night applause' (Anonymous, '"Seven Days' Leave" at the Lyceum', *Illustrated London News*, 24 Feb. 1917, 244).
216. Bruce Bairnsfather, *From Mud to Mufty: With Old Bill on All Fronts* (London: Richards, 1919), pp. 237–8.
217. J.C. Trewin, *The Gay Twenties: A Decade of the Theatre* (London, 1958), p. 42.
218. Collins, *Theatre at War*, p. 197.
219. Hynes, *A War Imagined*, pp. 80–1.
220. Ibid., pp. 148–52.
221. H.F., 'Our Theatre in War-Time', *The Athenaeum*, no. 4618 (June, 1917), 283–4.
222. P.P.H., 'The Drama and the War', *The Outlook*, 35 (27 March 1915), 405–6.
223. E. Temple Thurston, 'The Playgoer after the War: What We Will Demand of the Theatre', *The Era* (9 Oct. 1918), 15.
224. Zangwill, 'Poetic Drama and the War', 31, 30, 34.
225. Walkley, 'The Theatre and the War', 425, 426, 430.
226. Quoted by Hynes, *A War Imagined*, p. 293.
227. Marriott (ed.), *Great Modern British Plays* ; see the editor's note, p. 808.
228. See 'Stage and Screen History' in the programme to the 2002 production at the Lyric, p. 5.
229. Ted Morgan, *Maugham* (New York: Simon & Schuster, 1980), p. 247.
230. Ibid., p. 356.
231. Bracco, *Merchants of Hope*, p. 151. Bracco (pp. 145–95) describes in detail the play's genesis, its stage history and its reception.
232. Sherriff, *No Leading Lady*, p. 111. The book documents at great length Sherriff's somewhat naïve surprise at the reception of his play.
233. Ibid., p. 181.
234. Quoted by G.A. Martelli, '"Journey's End": A War Play and the Younger Generation', *Cornhill Magazine*, ser. 3:66 (1929), 740–2; 740.
235. Ibid., 742.
236. Bracco, *Merchants of Hope*, p. 154.
237. Ward, *The Nineteen-Twenties*, pp. 158–9.
238. Hynes, *A War Imagined*, p. 442.
239. Douie, 'Two War Plays', p. 847.
240. Fox, 'These Scandalous War Books and Plays', 192, 194.
241. Jerrold, *The Lie about the War*, p. 37.
242. Cf. Bracco, *Merchants of Hope*, p. 178.

243. See the programme to this production, n.p.
244. W.F. Deedes, 'Notebook', *Daily Telegraph* (26 January 2004), 18.
245. Robert Thicknesse, 'Back to the front', *Times* (17 January 2004), 25.
246. Matt Wolf, 'New start for "Journey's End"', *International Herald Tribune* (4 Feb. 2004).
247. Quoted by Jerrold, *The Lie about the War*, p. 7.
248. The affair is summarised by Robert Hogan, *The Experiments of Sean O'Casey* (New York: St Martin's Press, 1960), pp. 184–206. It is documented in full in *The Letters of Sean O'Casey*, ed. David Krause, vol. I (London: Macmillan, 1975), pp. 225–326. See also Kosok, 'Ireland, Yeats, and World War I', 3–19.
249. Sean O'Casey, *Autobiographies II* (London: Macmillan, 1963), p. 335.
250. Michael J. Lennon, 'Seán O'Casey and His Plays', *Catholic World*, 130 (1929–30), 295–301 and 452–61; 460–61.
251. Noël Coward, 'Present Indicative', *Autobiography* (London: Methuen, 1986), p. 227.
252. Goorney, *The Theatre Workshop Story*, p. 126.
253. Ibid., p. 127.
254. '*Oh What a Lovely War*', programme for the 1998 Roundhouse production, p. 10.
255. J.W. Marriott, *The Theatre* (London: Harrap, rev. ed. 1945), p. 140.
256. Rex Pogson, *Miss Horniman and The Gaiety Theatre, Manchester* (London: Rockliff, 1952), pp. 169, 170–1.
257. Basil Dean, *The Repertory Theatre: Being the Substance of a Lecture Delivered before the Members of the Liverpool Playgoers' Society on the Fifth Day of October, 1911* (Liverpool, 1911). For the complete play lists, see Grace Wyndham Goldie, *The Liverpool Repertory Theatre: 1911–1934* (Liverpool UP; London: Hodder & Stoughton, 1935).
258. For the Birmingham play lists, see Bache Matthews, *A History of the Birmingham Repertory Theatre* (London: Chatto & Windus, 1924); and T.C. Kemp, *The Birmingham Repertory Theatre* (Birmingham: Cornish Brothers, 1943).
259. Matthews, *History of the Birmingham Repertory Theatre*, pp. 205, 69–70.
260. Cecil Chisholm, *Repertory: An Outline of the Modern Theatre Movement* (London: Davies, 1934), p. 193.
261. See the play lists in Goldie, *The Liverpool Repertory Theatre*, pp. 226–70.
262. For a history of the amateur theatre (not, one should add, as comprehensive and systematic as one might wish) see George Taylor, *History of the Amateur Theatre* (Melksham: Venton, 1976). Cf. also the various occasional publications by the British Drama League.
263. Hannah Logasa and Winifred Ver Nooy, *An Index to One-Act Plays* (Boston, MA: Faxon, 1924); with 5 supplements by Logasa: *1924–1931* (1932), *1932–1940* (1941), *1941–1948* (1950), *1948–1957* (1958), *1956–1964* (1966).
264. John Hampden (ed.), *Ten Modern Plays* (London: Nelson, 1926, 25th impression 1964).
265. Taylor, *History of the Amateur Theatre*, p. 61.
266. Dan H. Laurence and Nicholas Grene (eds), *Shaw, Lady Gregory and the Abbey: A Correspondence and a Record* (Gerrards Cross: Smythe, 1993), p. 94.
267. St John Ervine, *Bernard Shaw: His Life, Work and Friends* (London: Constable, 1956), pp. 470–1.

268. Hynes, *A War Imagined*, p. 379.
269. Taylor, *History of the Amateur Theatre*, p. 146.
270. Muriel and Sydney Box, *Ladies Only: Six One-Act Plays with All-Women Casts* (London: Harrap, 1934).

Part V   'Good' versus 'bad' war plays: Aspects of evaluation

271. For surveys, see for instance Christoph Bode, 'Literary Value and Evaluation: The Case for Relational Concepts', in: Hans-Joachim Müllenbrock and Renate Noll-Wiemann (eds), *Anglistentag 1988 Göttingen: Vorträge* (Tübingen: Niemeyer, 1989), pp. 309–24; J. Strelka (ed.), *Problems of Literary Evaluation, Yearbook of Comparative Criticism*, 2 (University Park and London: Pennsylvania State UP, 1969); and R. von Heydebrand, 'Wertung, literarische', *Reallexikon der deutschen Literaturgeschichte*, vol. IV (Berlin: Walter de Gruyter, 2nd ed. 1984), pp. 828–71.
272. For a more detailed discussion of these criteria, see Heinz Kosok, 'Literary Evaluation and the Canon of English Literature in Foreign-Language Teaching', in: Bettina Missler and Uwe Multhaup (eds), *The Construction of Knowledge, Learner Autonomy and Related Issues in Foreign Language Learning: Essays in Honour of Dieter Wolff* (Tübingen: Stauffenburg, 1999), pp. 243–55. A comprehensive list of the criteria favoured by certain 'schools' of literary evaluation is provided at the end of the detailed study by M. Schrader, *Theorie und Praxis literarischer Wertung: Literaturwissenschaftliche und didaktische Theorien und Verfahren* (Berlin and New York: Walter de Gruyter, 1987).

Index